Researching Learning Difficulties

A Guide for Practitioners

Jill Porter
and
Penny Lacey

P·C·P

Paul Chapman Publishing

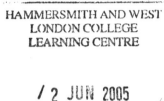

Paul Chapman Publishing
A SAGE Publications Company
1 Oliver's Yard
55 City Road
London EC1Y 1SP

SAGE Publications Inc
2455 Teller road
Thousand Oaks, California 91320

SAGE Publications India Pvt Ltd
B-42 Panchsheel Enclave
Post Box 4109, New Delhi 110 017

Library of Congress Control Number: 2004106511

A catalogue record for this book is available from the British Library

ISBN 0 7619 4850 3
ISBN 0 7619 4851 1 (pbk)

Typeset by GCS, Leighton Buzzard, Bedfordshire
Printed in Great Britain by Cromwell Press, Trowbridge, Wiltshire

CONTENTS

FOREWORD

Engaging with children and young people with learning difficulties tends to push one into the role of researcher. We find ourselves continually adducing, testing and revising hypotheses about why the child or young person is behaving in a particular way. To be a researcher is to seek systematic evidence, to reflect upon that evidence and as a result to move inductively or deductively to a deeper understanding of the world. The process can be summarised in the mathematician George Polya's problem-solving approach: understand the problem, try to use experience from related problems to plan an attack, carry out the attack and finally ask yourself whether you really believe the answer you've got (Polya, 1957).

Jill Porter and Penny Lacey bring to that process a rich depth of knowledge and experience of (in total) over 50 years of working with, and researching the lives of, children, young people and adults with learning difficulties. Both now, as well as conducting research in the field, train professionals in research methods and supervise research students investigating research questions relating to learning difficulties. They are thus uniquely well placed to open the issues to a wider audience and there is a striking synergy in this book between knowledge of learning difficulties and understanding of the research process.

In writing about the research process Jill Porter and Penny Lacey highlight issues emerging with increasing prominence over the last few years. This includes a strong emphasis on the ethical aspects of research about, and with, children and young people with learning difficulties. A decade ago it would have been rare to find a doctoral thesis or research report in which substantial material addressed ethical issues, but it would now be unusual not to find a section devoted to this, at the very least within an account of methods and methodologies. The salience of these issues is illustrated by the increasing reference to ethical codes developed by professional bodies such as (in the UK) the British Educational Research Association, the British Psychological Society and the British Sociological Association. Similar bodies internationally also provide ethical guidelines. The possible tensions surrounding ethical decisions in research are highlighted when this involves bringing together professional groups who have traditionally worked in separate spheres. One person's gatekeeper is another's co-researcher; one researcher's commitment to sustaining confidentiality is another's abdication of social responsibility.

There is a pressing need for good research evidence as a basis for decisions about policy and provision. The political culture of initiative after initiative (Sure Start, Children's Fund, Children's Trusts, Valuing People, SEN Action Programme, P scales, etc.) can leave users bewildered and focusing on surviving the latest initiative; lacking time, energy and motivation for systematically evaluating those policies. The role of universities is surely to keep addressing the hard (and perhaps unpopular) questions and one mechanism for bringing clarity to the kaleidoscope of new policies is sound research. Research will lack credibility and impact if it is conducted in a token way. Sadly, public money is being wasted on poor quality and bland 'evaluations' which act only as a sop to funders and a brief 'stroking' to those whose work has been 'evaluated'. This timely book, written in a highly accessible way, with a transparent and evident understanding of the context implicitly reflects Polya's guidance and so provides a coherent basis for users as well as practitioners, of research involving children and young people with learning difficulties.

Ann Lewis
Professor of Special Education and Educational Psychology
School of Education
University of Birmingham

Polya, G. (1957) *How to Solve It* (2nd edn). Harmondsworth: Penguin.

INTRODUCTION

In many ways this book has an ambitious agenda. It is not targeted at a single discrete audience; instead it celebrates the diversity of work that is currently undertaken in the field of learning difficulties with a concern to enable people working within different spheres of activity to share something of their work to contribute to the bigger picture. This is especially important when working within a minority field that is easily overlooked by more generic service providers. It is also consistent with services which are commonly multi-disciplinary as the focus of activity is less sharply delineated with respect to education, health and social care and where collaboration between agencies has been government policy for almost 50 years (Lacey, 2001). It would appear from our analysis of the literature that when it comes to research practices only a minority of researchers look beyond their own discipline. Indeed, they often fail to look for relevant literature outside their own field, thereby not capitalising on that which is already known.

One of our overriding drives is the desire to ensure that provision for people with learning difficulties continues to develop, and at a faster pace than in the past where the rhetoric has often not matched the reality of the daily lives of many people with learning difficulties. It is a time when the aims of provision are less easily defined in a generic way. When quality of life is recognisably less about concrete and tangible services and more about the quality of relationships. When choice and diversity of provision are argued for but we have still to develop those decision-making skills in *all* people with learning difficulties. When community placement can lead to a diminution of social networks rather than expansion. When the agenda for inclusion has not only created tensions of deciding where schooling takes place but has created a potential strait-jacket in our perceptions of the nature of the curriculum. Arguably research has never been so important in enabling us to determine the way forward.

Evidence suggests however that research in the field of learning difficulties is diminishing – at least as measured through publications. Nowhere is this so apparent as in the fields of education and health. There are many potential reasons for this including tensions that make research hard to carry out in this field, not least the difficulty of delineating the client group and validating research on small, heterogeneous populations experiencing diverse forms of provision. These issues are explored within this book from the perspective of both the user and the producer of research with the intention of aiding the reader in accessing research which is directly relevant to the field in which they work and in critically evaluating the implications for their own practice and research.

The aim is to provide a source book for teachers and other professionals working with children and adults with learning difficulties and disabilities that will enable them to:

- access selected recent and relevant research in the field of learning difficulties, drawn from a range of disciplines and groups of people
- reflect on different types of research methodologies, their relative strengths, weaknesses, constraints and possibilities in relation to learning difficulties
- undertake their own research in the field of learning difficulties.

Values and assumptions underpinning research

Typically discussion of the values underpinning research tend to polarise viewpoints, seeking to make firm distinctions and emphasise differences. The result can be a stereotyping, a caricature of people working within different paradigms. Traditionally a distinction is made between quantitative and qualitative approaches to research but as we shall argue, there is a need to go beyond simply categorising research with respect to the type of data produced and to look at the underlying philosophy. Descriptions of positivist research often conflate their approach with those adopted for the study of natural science and fail to recognise the developments and changes in thinking that have occurred in scientific methodology. What we don't often hear is an acknowledgement that post-positivists see knowledge not as absolute proof but as conjectural, seeking ways 'to establish procedures and criteria that can support commonly adjudicated truth claims that do not depend solely on those subjectively experienced or believed' (Phillips and Burbules, 2000, p37).

The value of subjective beliefs underpins the use of interpretevist and social constructionist approaches to research where the emphasis is on exploring meanings. To pursue this transforms the relationship between the researcher and the researched as dialogue and interpretation are fundamental to the process of inquiry. Thus while one approach does not deny the possibility of multiple *truths*, the other actively explores multiple *beliefs*.

The strongest contesters of both these research paradigms are those who argue for research to be emancipatory, that there needs to be a sea change in the power relationship between researcher and researched and to privilege the voice of the disabled. This concern draws our attention firmly to the political nature of research and the question of who sets the research agenda. Dyson (1998) argues for researchers 'to become reflexive in their awareness of how they are enmeshed in these processes, for them to struggle against the undue exercise of power, and for them to align their researching with the interests of the less powerful rather than he more powerful' (p3). He also draws our attention to the way in which foregrounding one voice silences others: 'for every group recognized as oppressed, another's oppression is denied or ignored' (p10). This is a potent reminder in a field where the voices of some are more easily accessed than those of others. As he continues: 'research which proceeds on the assumptions about coherent voice and clear political agenda may foreground and advantage those groups who conform most clearly to that image at the expense of those groups who do not ...' (p11).

In representing research which spans the range of approaches we aim to promote a dialogue between researchers that recognises the relative contributions to be made and the place and importance of different kinds of knowledge. More globally there is a demand for evidence-based practice, a phrase now firmly linked with positivist and post-positivist approaches to research. As we will argue, these approaches often pose particular difficulties for studying small and heterogeneous populations. However, interpretative approaches can also be problematic as the dialogue which plays a central role in their methodology places limitations on the richness of data collected from those at the heart of the service – the consumers. This in turn can shift the emphasis from research which has an explicit emancipatory function to that which is better described as participatory. In this book we examine these methodological difficulties and bring together the literature on offsetting them, drawing on expertise both within and outside the field of learning difficulties to make suggestions for the way forward.

An outline of the book

Chapter 1 takes a historical perspective on learning disabilities and on learning disability research. We felt it was important to give an overview of what had occurred over the previous century before examining in detail current research. We look back through the twentieth century at the slowly evolving change in attitudes towards people with learning disabilities, the development of provision and, of course, research, noting the twin discourse of care and control that permeates accounts at the time.

Chapter 2 is set firmly in the present and examines what shapes the agenda for research in learning disabilities and difficulties. We look for example at who carries out research, and at different types of research and their contribution to forward planning. We consider the different ways in which research is funded and at the types of research and research practice required by different funders. We highlight concern for the utility of research that shapes the view of what is worthwhile and fundable research, the emphasis on impact and on dissemination. Collaborative research is seen as central to achieving these qualities, ensuring a stakeholder influence on the research agenda. There is increasing recognition of the importance of participatory research among some funders of research, most notably voluntary bodies. Other funders may recognise the rhetoric but be slower in heeding the additional time requirements and the cost implications of this. Where time and money are limited it is likely that those who are most difficult to reach will be those whose views are sacrificed in order to meet deadlines.

In Chapter 3 we examine the trends in research, comparing publications that fall a decade apart. We do this not so much to make future predictions but to examine the continuities between the rhetoric of research and its practice. To this end we look at changes in both topics and methodologies. The outcomes of this analysis have in large part shaped the contents of this book. Our analysis of research strategies was notably hampered by the need to make interpretations of the design and methodology adopted. Others have also pointed to the lack of specific reference to design (Hogg *et al.*, 2001), as if description of research methods or tools is sufficient to justify the approach to research. This no doubt has contributed to some of the limitations in the robustness of the data noted in many reviews of the literature. Little research can be described as adhering to interpretative or constructivist designs. Although it is not uncommon for qualitative data to be collected, it is often either reduced to categories that are subsequently treated numerically or used as illustrative of views through the use of quotes with little verification or further analysis, thereby compromising the integrity of the research.

Our review highlights the high proportion of research that can be considered evaluative. This includes both large- and small-scale studies, complex studies of services and simpler investigations of interventions. We chose to make a distinction between studies that are explicitly referred to by the authors as using an evaluation design from those which might also be described as having the purpose of evaluation. We carry this through to dividing into two separate chapters the evaluation of services and those of instruction strategies or interventions. Although this reflects current practice we have done this with a number of reservations. One of the difficulties for research that looks only at instruction without reference to the wider service in which it is being used is that it makes an assumption that these factors have no impact on practice. We would argue that the culture of the service, its organisation and systems are highly likely to have an impact on the use of a particular strategy however tightly described or structured it might be. It is unlikely for example, that there are no differences between the way, say, a particular ICT programme might be used in a day-care setting, a further education college or a work setting. In order to evaluate this programme it might well be important to examine the culture, organisation, staffing and other aspects in operation as well as the expressed aims of the establishment.

In Chapter 4 we look at broad issues of evaluation, utilising the general literature to inform a more specific look at the challenges of evaluation in the context of learning disability services. Strategies for evaluating services have largely moved away from simple measures, based for example on 'on-task' behaviour, to the collection of multiple measures but notably using 'quality of life' as the prime indicator together with an economic assessment of costs. At one level the use of these tools enables comparisons across studies but they presuppose the efficacy of using globally defined standards. Their use can be criticised as reductionist unless they can successfully reflect the individual values of all service users. We also highlight the danger of cost utility measures whose primary function is to consider whether the money could be used more effectively elsewhere, a short stepping stone to placing a value on the life of a person with learning difficulties. We therefore consider the limitations of using such indices and argue for the importance of looking not simply at outcomes but also at the processes including the systems and structures that support change, thus emphasising the formative potential of evaluation research. One of the fundamental issues in evaluating services must be the inclusion of stakeholder views and arguably the service user should be central in developing the research.

In Chapter 5 we look more specifically at evaluation in the context of instruction and intervention. Our analysis suggests that researchers intent on adopting experimental and quasi-experimental designs to investigate inter-ventions need to ensure that there is compatibility with the theoretical model which underpins the theory of change or intervention. Structured systematic interventions such as those based on aspects of applied behaviour analysis are particularly well suited to these methodologies while those underpinned by other theories of learning may be better served by ethnographic methodologies. We look at recommendations for good practice in the use of these different methodologies.

Our exploration of methodologies highlights the difficulties for researchers but also reveals the potential of adopting new developmental approaches to analysis such as those described under the banner 'design experiments.' These methodologies, which aim to investigate how, when and why learning occurs, include iterative cycles of reflection but with a more overt role for theory than action research has historically done. Thus theory is used to generate the design but not as a straight-jacket to impede other explanations of change. Collabora-tion forms an important element of the work and again the link with practitioners working in the field is fundamental to ensuring an ongoing programme of evaluation. This methodology has exciting new potential in creating and exploring novel learning environments that are underpinned by a body of research data.

A recurring theme of the book is the importance of including the views of participants and in Chapter 6 we examine the continuum of involvement from collaborative research design and dissemination, through to eliciting the views of those with limited communication skills. We adopt a broad stance to promoting participatory approaches embracing those who recognise the importance of including the voice of all those with learning difficulties and those who more fundamentally seek to close the gap between the researcher and the researched. Although we would debate whether it is appropriate to specifically refer to this research as emancipatory, we would suggest that research will be most meaningful where service users have an input into establishing the research agenda. Indeed, for those who have the most difficulty expressing their views it is vital that the research questions are relevant. If we are actively to seek to gain data that has a demonstrable validity we must recognise that it is difficult to express an opinion if the question has no interest or place in your life.

Our chapter on participatory research explores a number of challenges that researchers face. We caution against setting too firmly the parameters of what is possible, drawing on innovatory studies to illustrate developments in the field. At the same time we recognise that despite these creative approaches researchers can inadvertently constrain the range of views expressed through the selection of different modes of response. The selection of symbols, methods that produce visual imagery such as the camera, ICT or simple drawing may all impact on the type of message that is conveyed. One of the recurring issues is the need to validate the views expressed through the collection of additional data using other methodologies. For us these other means are to be seen as a supporting resource rather than the main evidence. One might make the same case for the use of proxies where the starting point for discussion might be an account of the expressed views of the person whether this is based on linguistic or behavioural data, prior to systematically checking with others who know the person well.

We also raise a number of key ethical issues, taking as guidance the twin principles of the pursuit of truth and preserving the psychological well-being of the individual. These principles raise a number of tensions for the researcher and we illustrate how others attempt to address them. It becomes apparent in our analysis that the process of assent, the cornerstone of ethical practice, should not be seen as a one-off event to be gained at the start of the project, nor to be replaced by the consent of a gatekeeper.

Chapter 7 is devoted to small-scale research and the aim here is to draw together small-scale examples throughout the rest of the book and with a variety of other studies to examine the value of such research. Four aspects of small-scale studies are considered in detail: qualitative case studies, action research, ethnography and practitioner research, and part of the aim is to encourage practitioners to carry out their own research.

The final chapter is entitled 'Looking beyond the discipline' and its aim is to encourage readers and researchers to move beyond their comfort level and consider research that has been carried out in disciplines other than their own. We show how, on the whole, researchers are discipline-bound and rarely venture outside, even when citing other research that has influenced their thinking. We use the example of challenging behaviour to explore the perspectives of different disciplines and conclude with an examination of a small number of papers that are multidisciplinary in origin.

As the reader will conclude we have not taken a purist stance to research, espousing the adoption of one paradigm in favour of another, nor one particular research design. However a number of specific messages are central to our research position:

- There is a distinctive contribution to be made by different approaches to research in the field of learning difficulties.

- The veracity of research depends in part on achieving consistency between the research question, the design and methods adopted and the criteria by which we judge the authenticity of the findings.
- The use of a mixed paradigm approach therefore requires the application of different criteria to different parts of the study. Research that aims to discover the 'truth' is likely to be judged in relation to its validity and reliability. Research that aims to explore 'meanings' is likely to be judged in relation to such criteria as its credibility, transparency and confirmability. Mixed paradigm research therefore has to adopt different steps to establish its worth in different parts of the process. Moreover, there will be a shifting relationship between the researcher and the researched, as the emphasis changes from valuing objectivity to subjectivities.
- Although 'best fit' provides a useful guide in selecting the approach to research, it is not unproblematic.
- Given the heterogeneity of the population and provision, there is an important role for small-scale formative studies that are informed by theory and collaborative in nature.
- Greater attention needs to be given to stakeholder views in the development of a research agenda, and the involvement of participants in the research process.

While we would not claim to be the first in framing these views, it is timely to review their place in the field of learning difficulties. In focusing very specifically on issues of research design in this field we aim to raise the quality of research that is carried out by making the issues underlying the process of decision-making more transparent. Inevitably the result is that there is more to consider; the process becomes more complex as there is a realisation of the need to go beyond developing appropriate research tools to tackling the thorny issues of design, which appear from the literature to often get overlooked. We aim to raise the level of expertise of new professionals entering the field of research and to nudge experienced researchers into considering alternatives to their well-trodden ways. If research *is* to have a contribution to make to the development of future provision then we must ensure that it is of an appropriate quality to do so.

CHAPTER 1
Historical perspective

This first chapter focuses on

- historical perspectives on learning difficulties
- research associated with learning difficulties.

We begin with a general historical overview of learning difficulties across the past century, primarily to give a backcloth against which to view changes in research during that time. Our aim is to bring together different contexts. It is more usual to find, for example, a history of education for children (Pritchard, 1963; Cole, 1989) or of adult care (Kanner, 1964; Race, 1995) or recently, of the lives of individuals with learning difficulties (Atkinson *et al.*, 1997).

We have tried to maintain authenticity by referring to people with learning difficulties in the terminology of the day. Those writing in the first half of the twentieth century largely use the terms 'idiots', 'imbeciles' and 'feebleminded' and those in the second half use 'severely and moderately subnormal', 'mentally handicapped' or, in the case of the USA, 'mentally retarded'. It was not until the last few years of the century that people started to use 'learning difficulties' or 'learning disabilities'. Across the centuries, people with learning disabilities have been variously feared, revered, despised, pitied, tolerated, respected or largely ignored. The past century, for example has seen huge changes from the workhouse and eugenics movement, through institutionalisation and de-institutionalisation to community care and disability rights. Children with severe disabilities have moved from being viewed 'ineducable' through to being educable (but requiring segregated provision) to being eligible for education alongside their non-disabled peers in mainstream schools. People's thinking has shifted considerably, but not evenly, across the last 100 years. The inter-war years, for example, did not produce substantial change in the lives of people with learning disabilities, partly because of the Depression and the lack of funding for services but also because intelligence was thought to be fixed and any attempts to change it were futile.

In writing this chapter we are mindful that the history of learning difficulties has been a marginal activity that has led to 'errors and unsupported assumptions' (Stainton, 2001). The increasing use of life history accounts provides important insights into the lives of people with learning difficulties. In contrast professional accounts both objectify and sanitise events. There is also a noticeable gap in accounts of how national policy translated to local action. Armstrong (2003, p1), writing in the context of special education, highlights the 'competing and often contradictory discourses, policies, social interests and practices' that are also notable in our wider history of provision. It is also important to recognise that consensus on solutions can be reached despite competing viewpoints (Myers and Brown, 2003). It is difficult to investigate the past without employing the perspective of the present and that lens will inevitably reflect the values and assumptions of the writer. Having established our recognition of these limitations, we proceed with an account in which we have divided the twentieth century roughly into four sections: early part of the century; inter-war years; post-war years; latter part of the century.

Early part of the century

In this era people with learning difficulties were referred to as 'feebleminded' (or sometimes 'moron' in the USA), 'imbeciles' and 'idiots'. Definitions of these terms are quoted by Tredgold in the 1908 edition of his textbook *Mental Deficiency* (pp75–6) in the following way:

> *Feeblemindedness* (high-grade amentia). This is the mildest degree of mental defect and the feebleminded person is 'one who is capable of earning a living under favourable circumstances, but is incapable, from mental defect existing from birth, or from an early age, (a) of competing on equal terms with his normal fellows; or (b) of managing himself and his affairs with ordinary prudence'.

> *Imbecility* (medium-grade amentia). The imbecile is defined as 'one who, by reasons of mental defect existing from birth, or from an early age, is incapable of earning his own living but is capable of guarding himself against common physical dangers'.

> *Idiocy* (low-grade amentia). The idiot is defined as 'a person so deeply defective in mind from birth, or from an early age, that he is unable to guard himself against common physical dangers'.

There was a fourth category at this time:

> *Moral imbecility.* The moral imbecile is 'a person who displays from an early age, and in spite of careful upbringing, strong vicious or criminal propensities, on which punishment has little or no deterrent effect'.

This last category included people who had no intellectual impairment but who were considered to be morally defective. They were considered to be at risk to themselves or other people through a weakness that made them vulnerable to exploitation by criminals and immoral people. Unmarried mothers could become categorised as morally defective. For much of the century there was considerable confusion between mental and moral defectiveness, which led to the incarceration of many people who, in reality, were capable of independent living.

The early years of the century have been characterised by a continuation of the charitable acts carried out by Victorian philanthropists. The Industrial Revolution had brought attention to people who could not cope with new technological and commercial processes. There appeared to be a genuine concern, by some people, in the fate of the mentally deficient and a feeling that they should not be left to fend for themselves or placed in lunatic asylums. The work of Itard and later Seguin (Race, 1995) suggested that idiots and imbeciles could be trained in basic skills, and Mary Dendy, a pioneer in special education, opened her school for the feebleminded in 1902 in an era when other special schools were being founded for the blind, deaf and physically defective. The first open-air school (Borstall Wood) began in 1907 (Pritchard, 1963).

This optimism that was discernible at the beginning of the century appeared not to last long. Tizard (1958) suggests that there were two major events that precipitated the turn to pessimism. The first was the development of the science of genetics, building on Galton's work of the previous century, and the second was the development of ways of measuring intelligence. The first led to the Eugenics Movement which influenced public feelings and social policy for many years. In 1909 Tredgold published a paper on the feebleminded, illustrating beliefs at this time. He said:

> In the first place the chief evil we have to prevent is undoubtedly that of propagation. Next society must be protected against such of these person that have either definite criminal tendencies, or are of so facile a disposition that they readily commit crimes at the instigation of others. Lastly, even when these poor creatures are relatively harmless, we have to protect society from the burden due to their unproductiveness'. (pp102–3)

He recommended the development of 'suitable farm and industrial colonies' which could be self-sufficient, and contain the feebleminded and prevent their propagation. Studies of the families of the feebleminded had shown cases where several of the members were mentally deficient and there was a fear that society would be overrun with socially inadequate people. For example, in the US, Goddard, in 1912, wrote about a family called Kallikak with 480 descendants of one man who had a child with a feebleminded girl: 143 were feebleminded and 46 normal. The rest were unknown or doubtful. 36 of the 480 were reported to be illegitimate, 33 'sexually immoral', 24 confirmed alcoholics, 3 epileptics, 3 criminals and 8 kept houses of 'ill-fame'. Kanner (1964, p130) comments that: 'the story of the Kallikaks kindled a spark which soon burst into flames and drove a number of volunteer firefighters to frantic activity'.

The fear of being overrun by mentally deficient people is heard in the declaration made by Davenport in 1912 (quoted in Kanner, 1964, p134):

> Two mentally defective parents will produce only mentally defective offspring. This is the first law of inheritance of mental ability ... In view of the certainty that all of the children of two feebleminded parents will be defective, how great is the folly, yes, the crime of letting two such persons marry!

Clearly, in the many parts of the world, eugenics became an important influence on what happened to people deemed to be mentally deficient in the early part of the twentieth century. The 1913 Mental Deficiency Act did not include the clause (that was in the bill) prohibiting marriage but it did lay great stress on the proposed facilities for keeping people in institutions once they had been admitted (Race, 1995). Many people who did not have learning difficulties were certified at this time because they were perceived to fit within the definition of 'morally defective' and some remained in institutions for years when they were capable of living independent lives. The Act promoted segregation and control of social 'inefficients', including the certification of children who were unable to benefit from education, and likely to be a burden on society.

Segregating children was part of the agenda in Paris when Binet was asked to direct 'a study of measures to be taken, showing the benefits of instruction for defective children'. With Simon, Binet developed an intelligence scale, first published in 1905, from which it was possible to show to what extent an individual child conformed to or deviated from the norm of average. Intelligence quotient (IQ) and mental age (MA) could be calculated to help teachers to adapt instruction to the needs and grasp of individual children (Kanner, 1964). Although Binet and Simon were severely critical of earlier feelings of optimism for teaching feebleminded children because of their *permanent* low intelligence, they still advocated teaching them to read and write because 'illiteracy would bring shame' (Binet and Simon, 1914). In the view of Pritchard (1963), the geneticists conveniently overlooked the opinion that the feebleminded were educable and declared they required permanent care. These same people suggested that the day schools and classes set up to educate the feebleminded at the end of the nineteenth century were a waste of time and money. However, not everyone was as fearful as the eugenicists. Extreme views were questioned and other solutions to the perceived increase in feeble-mindedness were suggested, such as slum clearance, good nutrition and school health services (Cole, 1989). Some, such as Spence, advocated leaving the mentally deficient with their families if they were not a nuisance. He was mindful of human rights, saying that a harmless imbecile should not be shut up 'on the theory that he might do something wrong' (Cole, 1989).

It is, of course, hard to be sure exactly what was in the minds of the people who were responsible for legislation and social policy at any particular time in history but at the beginning of the twentieth century those responsible for the welfare of mentally deficient people were certainly influenced by negative feelings that: a) one's level of intelligence was fixed for life, and b) those with low intelligence (measured against a norm) were in need of care. Some saw that care as protective of society and others as a humanitarian act towards those with low intelligence.

Concern is evident in the research into prevalence carried out during this time. In 1908 Tredgold writes of the Royal Commission investigations of 1904 which was the first systematic attempt to obtain accurate information as to the number and condition of the mentally deficient. Tredgold stresses the importance of being accurate and describes the methods adopted by the Royal Commission to ensure this accuracy.

> The investigator was instructed to visit personally all public elementary schools, poor-law institutions, charitable establishments, training homes, reformatories, common lodging-houses, prisons, idiot asylums, hospitals, and indeed, any establishment likely to harbour the mentally abnormal. Further he was to see persons in receipt of out-door relief, to apply to the clergy, medical practitioners, the police, charity organisation societies, and similar agencies, and, in short, to make use of any and every channel which might help him to make the enumeration complete. (Tredgold and Soddy, 1963, p10)

Nine areas of England, two of Wales, four in Ireland and one of Scotland were chosen as samples, with a total population of nearly 4 million. The results show enormous differences in incidence across the country, which Tredgold suggests is likely to indicate real difference rather than just different ways of collecting the data. The lowest incidence was 1.10 per 1,000 in Cork and the highest 4.68 per 1,000 in Lincolnshire.

Tredgold was interested in the different degrees of mental deficiency and calculated that for every 100 aments (mentally deficient people), 6 will be idiots, 18 imbeciles and 76 will be feebleminded, so the incidence will be, per 1,000 population, 2 idiots, 7 imbeciles and 29 feebleminded. He also gave figures of where aments could be found: 32.7 per cent in institutions, 8 per cent receiving outdoor relief, 34.2 per cent in school and 5.6 per cent not receiving relief.

In 1924 Lewis surveyed a population of just over 600,000 within which he found 5,334 mental defectives of which for every 100, 5 were idiots, 20 imbeciles and 75 feebleminded. He concluded that the incidence was 8 per 1,000 population or a total of 314,000 (Tredgold and Soddy, 1963). Like the Royal Commission survey carried out in the same period, Lewis found a higher incidence in rural areas than in urban areas (10.4 per 1,000 and 6.7 per 1,000 respectively).

The two surveys found similar proportions of the different grades of mentally deficient people but in 1924 there were nearly twice as many people identified than in 1904. This is an enormous leap in 20 years and Tredgold and Soddy (1963) are not willing to accept that it merely represents a more complete enumeration, although the fact that all the data were collected by one person might have contributed to greater uniformity. They believe that there was indeed a huge increase and explain this as the advance of medical science, enabling mentally defective infants to survive and grow into adulthood. A change in public attitude would also have meant that a greater number of people would have been hospitalised and thus would have survived longer.

Inter-war years

Throughout the inter-war years more and more people were dealt with under the Mental Deficiency Acts of 1913 and 1927. Tredgold's figures (1952) indicate that the increase in mental defectives rose eightfold from 12,000 in 1920 to 100,000 in 1950. Institutions built to contain all those labelled 'defective' were large micro-societies. The Wood Report (Board of Education and Board of Control, 1929) describes them thus:

> In the all-grade institution ... the high grade patients are the skilled workmen of the colony, those who do all the higher processes of manufacture, those on whom there is a considerable amount of responsibility; the medium-grade patients are the labourers, who do the more simple routine work in the training shops and about the institutions; the best of the low-grade patients fetch and carry or do the very simple work (quoted in Race, 1995, p51).

Although there was an expansion in the number of people certified as mentally deficient during the inter-war years, there was little change in the way they were treated. During the 1920s the authorities were waiting for the Wood Committee (set up in 1924) to report, which it did in 1929, and during the 1930s much of the world was plunged first into depression and then war, both of which contributed to a state of inertia in the development of services. One group who concerned educationalists were those not certified feebleminded but who were failing at school (the 'dull' or 'backward'). The Wood Committee recommended abolishing certification and educating all children who were deemed 'educable' but experiencing difficulties, in either special schools or special classes set up specifically to help to prepare them for a productive life after school. Certification, however, remained until after the war, as did the continuing separation of feebleminded children from the dull or backward.

Eugenicist views were still strong in the inter-war years. They were, for example, part of Nazi beliefs and policies, leading to the extermination of many disabled people in Europe believed to be contaminating the master race. Kanner (1964) points out that civilisation was indeed in grave danger at this time, but not from mental defectives: 'The one man Hitler, who probably would not come out too badly in terms of the Binet-Simon Scale, did more damage than all the mental defectives since the beginning of history.' In the USA fears of being overrun by mental defectives were so great that enforced sterilisation was introduced. By 1926 sterilisation laws had been enacted in 23 states, although they were not stringently applied (Cole, 1989).

Despite this negative view of mental deficiency there were still some people who tried to change the position. Educationalists such as Mary Dendy and Ellen Pinsent developed methods of teaching children classed as feebleminded that were based on manual work rather than on academic achievement. Moreover, it was shown that following this sort of education a high proportion of children leaving special schools were successfully adapting themselves to life. However, the development of methods to help the dull and backward children in ordinary schools was more or less at a standstill while the world concerned itself with other more pressing demands.

Research during this period provides a mixed picture. Writing in the USA, Raymond (1933) suggests that research into mental deficiency had been hampered for many years by two factors: the overstatement of heredity as a cause and IQ testing. This had caused researchers to concentrate on mental aspects at the expense of medical research, which Raymond sees as essential for understanding and treating low-grade deficiency. He calls for studies on the brain, blood and internal organs and he cites a similar call made in 1915. Raymond is also sure that research in psychological, educational and social service fields have not been exhausted and suggests studies of former pupils of state schools and social experiments, alongside malnutrition, prevention and amelioration. Apart from offering suitable topics for study, Raymond also bemoans the lack of research laboratories and of funding for work in this area. He quotes Goddard, who in 1918 suggested that for every dollar spent in caring for the feebleminded, another dollar should be spent in studying the condition. In 1930, the White House Conference Committee on the Handicapped Child suggested research should command 10 per cent funding on top of costs. We have no specific figures throughout the century to test whether this was taken up but suspect it has not.

In 1944, Haskell, looking back over a 15-year period at research in mental deficiency at Wayne County Training School in the USA, argues that there had been plenty of medical explorations on causation and pathology in severe mental defect (led by Tredgold's work) but very little useful research on the feebleminded. He cites the 1934 Report on the Problem of Mental Disorder as evidence. He then examines studies that show the difference between feeblemindedness caused by organic deficit and by environmental factors, concluding that children with environmentally affected mental deficiency could advance through school whereas the organically affected children lagged behind. He also cited other studies being conducted by the Training School on drugs and allied therapy, speech disorders, electroencepholographic studies. He suggested future studies in personality and group relationships.

Two reviews of research at this time provide us with further indications of researchers concerns at the time (see Table 1.1).

Table 1.1 Topics from reviews of research in the years 1935–43

1935–40 Cutts (1941)	Identifcation and selection for special education, changing IQ and non-verbal tests describing provision, curriculum, teaching reading, progress, occupational placement
1940–43 Hockett (1944)	Characteristics of mentally handicapped, constancy of IQ describing special education programmes, teaching methods, reading, progress, occupational placement

Post-war years

During the post-war years terminology began to change from 'mental deficiency' to 'mental subnormality' in the UK and to 'mental retardation' in the USA. In the 1959 Mental Health Act the categories used were mild, moderate and severe subnormality. In schools children began to be referred to as remedial (backward), slow learners (dull) and educationally subnormal (feebleminded). The severely subnormal did not attend school but were cared for either in institutions or in training centres.

Immediately following the war, austerity meant that there was little change for mentally deficient people. Moreover, eugenic views were still influential as was evident even as late as 1952 when Tredgold wrote in the preface to his textbook (in its eighth edition):

> Many of these defectives are utterly helpless, repulsive in appearance and revolting in manners ... In my opinion it would be an economical and humane procedure were their existence to be painlessly terminated.

We note the reference here to the belief that euthanasia was a kindness.

By 1959 Hobbs was writing that things are 'looking good' for research in mental retardation. He lists a conference, parent support groups, excellent books, a new research journal and training for professionals. However, he goes on to say that research has been hampered by people, by whom he seems to mean psychologists, seeing mental retardation as a homogenous and uninteresting category: 'A critical look at psychological aspects of mental retardation reveals many studies that add up to very little.' For example, he cites studies that have no effect on practice and have added little to general behaviour theory, and he suggests that we need to be guided by the accumulative effects of studies. The war had interrupted research and there was little to report in the Hockett (1944) review. Research had picked up after the war when there had been an increase in interest in care and education of the mentally retarded. Parents were better organised and more voluble, which increased requests for educational provision. This increase was maintained throughout the 1950s and 1960s, stimulated by the National Institutes of Health in the USA, a conference in

London, two world seminars in 1959 and 1961 and an issue of the *American Journal of Mental Deficiency* devoted to research methodology.

Observations and inquiries into the state of mental hospitals in the 1950s showed that improvements were possible at all levels of disability. In 1949 Fuller published a seminal paper on teaching a person with profound disability a simple motor response using operant conditioning. Psychology, as a discipline, had not long been involved in mental deficiency/subnormality which, until then, had been dominated by medicine and psychiatry. Psychologists followed up the fate of some of those deemed unfit to fight in the war due to mental deficiency and found that the majority were socially and economically capable. Charles (1953, reported in Race, 1995) concluded that the prognoses for 151 people deemed mentally deficient in 1936 were unduly pessimistic when he found, 20 years later, that 83 per cent were self-supporting and 80 per cent had married and had children, few of whom were defective.

Tizard, among other psychologists, found that IQs were higher than expected in mental hospitals. In 1952 he suggested that half of the inmates in mental hospitals (about 25,000 people) should not be placed there, and that they were capable of being self-supporting. In one survey of 12 institutions, O'Connor and Tizard (1954) found an average IQ of over 75. Of their sample, 50 per cent were not in need of supervision or any special care. Tizard deplored the methods of occupational training in hospitals which were old fashioned, expensive, unmotivating and unconnected with the world outside. Other researchers demonstrated the potential for training in people considered mentally defective, illustrating how the environment and motivation were powerful factors in performance (Clarke *et al.*, 1958). In the 1950s, Tizard set up the Brooklands Experiment in which children transferred to a stimulating environment demonstrated improvements in their verbal abilities (Tizard, 1964).

Despite the findings of researchers, those in charge and staff working in mental hospitals were not changing their practices. People were still being detained who clearly should not and physical conditions in the hospitals were prison-like, overcrowded and inhuman. The Royal Commission set up in 1953 examined evidence relating to wrong detention and appalling conditions and their recommendations led to the Mental Health Act 1959. Despite suggesting 'community care', this Act did little to change the situation and people continued to be accommodated in large hospitals throughout the 1960s, although certification and the Board of Control had been abolished. According to the White Paper *Better Services for the Mentally Handicapped* in 1971, there were 52,100 people in hospitals and only 4,850 in community residential care (usually in large hostels).

During the post-war years, education was still not responsible for any children deemed 'ineducable' in the 1921 Education Act and 'unsuitable for education in schools' in the 1944 Education Act, although there was some interest in the large numbers of children who left school illiterate. The belief that IQ was immutable was gradually challenged as experience and research revealed this to be an unsafe conclusion and that dividing children into categories of educability was not helpful. Special educationalists expressed dissatisfaction with the state of education for the least able and saw an expansion of special education (schools and classes) as the only way ahead. However, teachers of the newly designated schools for the educationally subnormal (after the 1944 Act) felt isolated, undervalued or dismissed by teachers in ordinary schools despite developing approaches that enabled ESN children to develop socially and educationally.

As with the mental subnormality hospitals, there were many children in ESN schools who were misplaced if an IQ of under 70 was the criterion for entry. Many had IQs above this or were disadvantaged by their environment and could be returned to ordinary school after spending time in a special school or class boosting their attainment. Some writers felt these pupils, who had more potential than the 'organically' handicapped pupils, were taking up places properly for the more handicapped and that if teaching was better in ordinary schools there would be no need for the 'environmentally' handicapped to be in special education at all. Only limited progress was made in classrooms in the 1950s and 1960s despite the work of people such as Cleugh (1957), Tansley and Gulliford (1960), and Segal (1967).

A review that covers 1960–67 by Guskin and Spicker (1968) points to the importance of the educational research in the 1960s around pre-school education to try to avert environmentally affected mental retardation. Prior to this time, there was little interest in education for prevention because of the belief of the immutability of IQ. Guskin and Spicker also look at studies on the efficacy of special schools and special classes and note that the evidence is inconclusive. Earlier studies (1945–60) had shown poorer academic results in special classes/schools but poorer social adjustment in ordinary classes. However, these were criticised for methodological flaws, for example not comparing like with like. Further studies showed that where children had a higher IQ, their gains were greater wherever they were placed. Guskin and Spicker refer to many other studies relating to the educable mentally retarded ('moderate subnormal' in the UK at this time) but report that there is little research into trainable mentally retarded (in the UK called 'severely subnormal') despite the growth of classes for this group. The few existing studies do not show many gains for children attending school but results suggest that is because of an inadequacy of curriculum content and poor teaching rather than the inability of children with severe mental retardation to learn.

During the 1940, 1950s and 1960s, there was a series of reviews in the *Journal Review of Educational Research*. Table 1.2 contains a list of the topics covered in the reviews relevant to this point in history, giving an indication of the concerns of researchers at the time.

In 1941, interest had focused on the changeability of IQ but psychologists now moved on to investigate different aspects of learning and psychological processes, which had been neglected since earlier in the century (Dunn and Capobianco, 1959). For example, McPherson (cited by Dunn and Capobianco) found only 14 studies on learning and motivation in the period 1904–48 but

Table 1.2 Topics from reviews of research in the years 1943–69

1943–52 Kirk and Kolstoe (1953)	Definitions and classifications studies in psychometrics, sociometrics, social and vocational adjustment, effects of educational programmes, organisation, curriculum, parent education, training for severely handicapped
1952–58 Dunn and Capobianco (1959)	Prevalence studies, reading, arithmetic educational approaches, adult adjustment, speech and language development, learning and motivation, basic learning theory and classroom application, training for severely handicapped
1959–62 Cain and Levine (1963)	Terminology, population trends test development, screening procedures, learning, motivation, motor performance, educational provision, curriculum adaptations post-school adaptations, family and community relationships
1962–65 Blackman and Heintz (1966)	Structure of intelligence, classification, intelligence tests, comparisons between special schools and special classes, teaching methods, teaching machines, social factors in school adjustment, perceptual process, motor responses, learning, discrimination, operant conditioning
1965–68 Prehm and Crosson (1969)	Testing education and rehabilitation, placement, curricular adaptations, behaviour modification, psychological processes, memory, language, personality, social adjustment (too many studies for the writers to report)

recent activity in the 1950s had seen increased productivity, improved methodology and a shift in orientation towards basic learning theory and its classroom applications. In 1966, Blackman and Heintz identify three basic schools of thought in the approach to research at the time:

• neurophysiological inadequacy
• cultural deprivation and personality aberration
• behaviour deficit.

At the end of the period reviewed there is a growing interest in operant conditioning, behaviour modification and learning machines. Trends in educational research seem to fluctuate, with interest in reading giving way to more generic teaching approaches and curricular adaptations, and occupational placement giving way to post-school adjustments. There is also recognition that while some psychologists were motivated to improve conditions (Tizard, 1983), others saw people with mental handicap as 'a convenient captive population available for theoretical work of great triviality'.

From the 1950s onwards, psychology may have been the dominating influence on mental handicap research but there were also a number of sociological studies. The studies in the 1960s and 1970s led the way towards some of the work based on a social model of disability being carried out today, although they all found a very entrenched medical model in the places they observed. Goffman's (1961) *Asylums*, Edgerton's (1967) *The Cloak of Competence: Stigma in the Lives of the Mentally Retarded* and Morris's (1969) *Put Away: a Sociological Study of Institutions for the Mentally Retarded* were pioneering studies. The life for children in institutions was the subject of other studies, for example, Oswin's (1971) *The Empty Hours: A Study of the Weekend Life of Handicapped Children in Institutions*, Hales' (1978) *The Children of Skylark Ward: Teaching Severely Handicapped Children*, and Shearer's (1980) *Handicapped Children in Residential Care: A Study of Policy Failure*. Without exception all these studies painted a depressing picture of what it was like to grow up and live in a long-stay mental handicap hospital. Until this time, few researchers had looked very hard at what was going on in the hospitals and these studies, although not always intended to be rigorous research, have helped to legitimise ethnographic study in this area.

Latter part of the century

Terminology has changed several times in the past 30 years from 'mental subnormality' to 'mental handicap' to 'learning disabilities' or 'learning difficulties'. The White Paper in 1971 uses mild, moderate and severe mental handicap and the White Paper in 2001 uses people with learning disabilities. Learning difficulties is mostly used in schools, although some adults prefer to use that term to describe their difficulties.

The often appalling conditions in the mental handicap hospitals came to public notice through reports on the cruelty and neglect of patients such as those at Ely Hospital in Cardiff (The Howe Report; DoH, 1969) and research such as the survey by Morris (1969). Morris found dilapidated and decrepit buildings; dormitory conditions with no privacy; little need of nursing care; little assessment of need; poor staff-to-patient ratios; and isolation from the community. King *et al.*, (1971) and Oswin (1971) found similar conditions in child care where rigid routine, lack of individuality, depersonalised provision and social distance between staff and children dominated institutions. Despite the scandals being reported, hospitals were still being built in the 1960s, alternatives being tried and found to be enormously expensive to run (Barclay, 1999).

Although two decades of experiments with community alternatives to hospital care had passed, there was little change for the large majority of people with learning difficulties/disabilities living in institutions in the 1970s, with only 10 per cent of those people using mental handicap residential services living in community homes (DHSS, 1971). Legislation and policy documents at the beginning of the 1970s began to be more influenced by the Scandinavian principles of 'normalisation' and community care was promoted more specifically. The White Paper *Better Services for the Mentally Handicapped* (DHSS, 1971) advocated a reduction in hospital beds from 90 per cent to 40 per cent of the residential provision for the mentally handicapped, although there was little guidance on how this was might be achieved. Critics at the time accused the government of not being radical enough. For example, officially there was still a role for large-scale hospitals; the three agencies of health, education and social services were not brought together to form one unified service (Race, 1995) nor were funds provided to enable community provision to be set up quickly.

At the same time as the White Paper was being prepared, the fight for mentally handicapped children to be included in education was being won. The 1970 Education (Handicapped Children) Act transferred responsibility from health to education. Around 32,000 children, newly termed 'educationally subnormal (severe)', became entitled to special education as a result of this legislation and about 400 new schools were formed from the former junior training and hospital centres (DES, 1978). At this time, there were some 8,000 children living in hospital but they were relatively quickly moved into the community either to their family homes, to foster homes or to small children's homes. There was considerable evidence to suggest that children did not thrive in hospital environments. Very few were sick and in need of medical care and all needed the loving care of a family or family substitute (Bowlby, 1953; Tizard, 1966).

Opposition to the 'medical model' was beginning to be expressed by those influenced by normalisation principles (for example Shearer, 1980) but it was hard to make much headway in moving towards the 'social' model of disability. It was also clear that mental handicap hospitals were the 'Cinderellas' of the health service. They had been chronically underfunded and staff were viewed as being of lower calibre and lesser status than those in other services (Felce, 1996) and this did not change overnight because hospitals were expected to close.

Based on the experiments of the 1950 and 1960s, small residential hostels for 20–25 people were set up in Wessex during the 1970s and were seen as models for others. They were eventually criticised for not going far enough towards 'ordinary' homes and lives and in some cases continuing to foster the kinds of outmoded thinking prevalent in the old hospitals (King's Fund, 1980). The King's Fund *Ordinary Life* project was influential throughout the 1980s and set the pattern for the best of the current provision which enables people, with support, to live in ordinary houses in the community, use community facilities and access all the things non-disabled citizens can.

Between 1980 and 1992 hospitals discharged more than 29,000 people and by 1992 more than 40,000 people were living in the community, although this was still only 44 per cent of those in residential care. In the mid-1980s it was clear that progress was very slow and the Audit Commission in 1986 recommended transferring responsibility for the mentally handicapped from health to social services to speed up the transfer. This was eventually achieved in the 1991 NHS and Community Care Act. Local authorities became the 'gatekeepers' to and for community care with the responsibility for assessing needs and producing 'care plans'. They also purchased care from providing services in the climate of encouraging a mixed economy of care providers in both the public and private sectors.

Psychological research on development, functioning and education of the mentally handicapped expanded rapidly during the period 1960–80 (Hogg and Mittler 1980, 1983). An appreciable body of knowledge was established and new ways of conceptualising mental handicap and the needs of mentally handicapped people were developed. One of the most important topics at this time was assessment and its role in helping people to devise the right intervention for individuals with mental handicap. Briefly, the work on assessment concerned the inapplicability of global testing that gave a single score such as IQ and mental age testing at the extreme end of mental handicap; and that led to the development of tests of sensorimotor development, for example Uzgiris and Hunt (1975). The results of this work enable interveners to understand functioning in different areas of development. Observational techniques were devised to produce baselines against which to plot development (Kiernan and Jones, 1977).

Intervention was seen in a holistic way, incorporating the individual's total social and physical environment. Hogg and Mittler claim that a holistic view has had a profound effect on both services for and research on mentally handicapped people. The twin approaches of behaviourism and child development were at their height in the 1970s and 1980s. Behaviourism provided the means through which progress through developmental stages could be measured and child development provided the steps through which people with mental handicap could be led towards competence. Thus a 'scientific' approach to mental handicap was developed. It enabled researchers and interveners to demonstrate that learning based on 'normal' developmental scales was possible, however slow.

During the late 1980s and 1990s the size of homes was decreasing and the independent sector was growing (Felce, 1996). Staff who ran the small community homes struggled (and still struggle in the new millennium) to find ways of working that resulted in a good quality of life for residents. During the 1970s and 1980s, behaviourally orientated programmes were written to try to improve the daily living skills of people who had previously been living in a situation where they needed few such skills. Tasks such as making a cup of tea or putting on a coat were analysed and taught deliberately and often painstakingly. During the late 1980s and 1090s much of this work was 'consigned to the dustbin of the previous decade' (Felce, 1996) in favour of the wider conceptualisation of the 'Five Accomplishments' devised by O'Brien, which encouraged staff to work with service users to accomplish presence in the community, make meaningful choices in their lives, learn to communicate effectively, perform functional and meaningful activities and participate in a network of personal relationships.

During the 1980s the advocacy and self-advocacy movement was also growing, with the advent of 'People First' from North America and the development of consulting with service users about their wants and needs (Brechin and Swain, 1988). It is hard to say when self-advocacy, as a social movement, began. The first international People First conference was held in 1984 and this led to a group being set up in London and to the second international conference in Twickenham (Goodley, 2000). Self-advocacy, opinion and choice have become central to current policy on learning disabilities and the latest White Paper Valuing People (DoH, 2001) included people with learning difficulties on their advisory group, something not even considered for the previous White Paper in 1971.

In the same period a new journal became established called *Disability, Handicap and Society* which published research from a sociological perspective. Most of the articles related to the wider interpretation of disability but there were some that specifically considered people with mental handicap/ retardation. For example, Luckin (1986) gives an historical view on Edgerton's study of people released from hospital who tried to lose the stigma of mental retardation by passing for 'normal'; Lea's (1988) paper is a study of the writings about themselves by six people with mild mental retardation which challenges the pessimistic assumptions that are made of mental retardation; Di Terlizzi (1994) reports a study of the life history of a person with learning disabilities, revealing that she lived a very barren life. Life histories have become important over the past few years and the book by Atkinson *et al.*, (1997) not only gives graphic descriptions of life in institutions after the war but also discusses aspects of collecting personal histories through oral work, photographs and archive documents. Gray and Ridden (1999) demonstrate how to use life-maps (rather like a concept map drawn with arrows showing the direction of the person's life) to gather information about personal histories. Their book contains several examples of the memories of people with learning difficulties in the second part of the century.

In summary: across the century

Progress within services for people with learning difficulties/disabilities was notably slow over the first 70 years of the century, although the last 30 years saw important changes. The 1971 White Paper *Better Services* lay the foundations for change but it has taken 30 years to fulfil the commitment to help people with learning disabilities to live 'as normal a life' a possible by closing almost all large institutions. According to the 2001 White Paper *Valuing People*, there were almost 59,000 people living in hospitals in 1971; in 2001 there were 1,500 (although another 8,500 were in accommodation managed by the NHS, some of which were on the campuses of hospitals). There are no children reported to be living in long-stay hospitals. Those who cannot live with their families are either fostered or adopted or are in residential schools. Few live in children's homes.

It is apparent in our review that medical and psychological accounts dominate and are embedded within a number of legal documents. These accounts especially emphasise deficit and need rather than provide a social construction of disability. The twin discourse of care and control has served in effect to legitimise similar practices. One could argue that the contribution of research has been to perpetuate these views and may have contributed to the slow agenda for change. In contrast to these objectified accounts, life histories provide powerful illustrations of the effects of policy on the lives of those children and young people placed in institutional care. Di Terlizzi (1994), for example, provides a powerful description of the impact of changing environments on the abilities of a young woman with learning difficulties. It is not a lone story – it resonates with larger-scale research elsewhere in the literature (Oswin, 1971; Morris, 1969; Ryan and Thomas, 1980; Armstrong, 2003). Research of this kind provides a different account of history, one of oppression of one set of people by another; of social control of a group who threaten the comfort and sensibilities of another; of marginalisation to obviate the need to change the norms of society to accommodate difference; of the rationing of resources in favour of the powerful over the powerless.

Research has revealed some important lessons about the ways in which provision impacts both on daily life and on the opportunities available to people. Changing expectations should in turn fuel changing aspirations but as we have seen, the gap between policy and practice has been very evident and the pace of change slow. We must ask what research, has to offer in creating a better future. Although there has been a growing body of research the research community itself has criticised the lack of impact of research, as well as its underfunding. The dubious motives of some researchers has also been recognised. In Chapter 2 we look more specifically at aspects that contribute to the development of a research agenda and the ways in which that can influence policy and practice.

Research agendas

In this chapter we consider research agendas across different disciplines and different types of research. It is important to locate our own position here. Educational research is a broad church. It is an area which draws heavily on a variety of different disciplines: psychology, sociology, history, philosophy, to name a few. Indeed many educational researchers are aware of the need for their research to reflect the outlook and allegiance to their originating discipline. As Paechter (2003) notes: 'Janus-like, they [researchers] simultaneously look towards and address the worlds of education and of their disciplinary base.' (p108)

Educational research is described by one respondent in the Hillage report (Hillage *et al.*, 1998; p12) as: 'ranging from curiosity driven research, mainly of interest to the researcher, through research which is policy relevant … to highly applied research conducted for a particular sponsor. ' We would argue that this places us in a sound position to look more widely on research with learning difficulties.

In this chapter we use educational research as a base while we reflect on research from other disciplines. We ask questions about the influences on research practice and how research agendas are set. We explore the influence of funding bodies on the type and nature of research to be produced and on who undertakes it. We echo a number of questions raised by Noonan Walsh (2003) in the context of comparing research across countries. Who sets research priorities? Do they reflect local, global or national issues? Are they commissioned to appease certain groups? Who should be involved in the research process ? Who should carry out the research? With these questions in mind we establish some principles for the development of a research agenda.

Who does research?

We start the chapter by looking at who does research because this has important implications for the type of research that is produced. Logan *et al.*, (2000) identified the top researchers and their institutions in the area of developmental disabilities between 1979 and 1999. Previous research had indicated that state universities in the US accounted for a significant proportion of research. Their own research found clearly identified leaders in applied research in developmental disability, with the top three names accounting for 30 per cent of published research. Notably also the top researchers were predominantly men. (Indeed in the top 25 researchers only two were women.) This small group clearly have the potential to dictate what research is carried out, what topics are of interest and what kinds of research questions are important to ask. Logan *et al.*. found that the top researchers also overlapped with those within the field of behaviour analysis and therapy. Immediately we can recognise the very specific influence on what we know and understand in the field of learning difficulties/disabilities. Universities dominate the list, notably American universities which are not funded with federal research grants. This raises an interesting question of differences in the degree to which researchers in America have their research channelled through a national agenda compared, for example, with those in the UK. Logan *et al.* call for an increase in research productivity in service delivery settings as they state 'research conducted in the context of actual service delivery would serve to increase the contextual validity of these studies.' (p259).

We might ask whether these findings and conclusions are purely a reflection of the way in which the sample was constructed through the selection of journals. If we look at a similar study on the opposite side of the world we see some interesting similarities and differences. An Australian study (Lim *et al.*, 2003) compared trends in research productivity across two decades. The first study, carried out between 1980–1990, revealed 19 productive institutions and these were largely universities in Australia, New Zealand and the US. Their review of Australian journals found a slightly broader picture of research than Logan *et al.* because here publications represented research carried out by 17 countries in 166 different institutions, a not dissimilar picture to that a decade earlier. Unsurprisingly, given the methodology the highest proportion of articles came from Australian institutions (37 per cent) but these were followed by American institutions contributing 25 per cent of the research publications and the UK 12 per cent. Again authors were almost always affiliated to universities. Compared with a decade earlier there was a decrease in the proportion of work published by Australian researchers in these journals but an increase in the proportion of top institutions.

We might infer from these studies that American research has largely dominated, particularly that which draws on the specific framework of applied behavioural analysis. Worldwide universities contribute most of the work in the field. We must however recognise the dangers of conflating research publications with output. But the evidence suggests that globally, research that is disseminated and has the potential to impact may rest with relatively few researchers working within narrow spheres of activity.

One issue this raises is the extent to which research is driven by the interests of the researcher. Is it appropriate to conclude that this research is of an academic nature rather than linked closely to practice? This distinction has been made by those critiquing educational research in the UK (Hillage *et al.*, 1998), but, based on this largely non-educational research it would appear to be a relevant issue across the field of learning difficulty. There are many alternative ways in which to categorise different types of research. We now turn to consider these before looking at their relationship to the type of funding available.

The nature of research

There are many ways of distinguishing between different types of research. For example, we can do so with respect to their purpose, which could be descriptive, evaluative, exploratory, explanatory or even emancipatory. As we shall see later in this book the trend has been towards evaluation research although the rhetoric has been for emancipatory research. Alternatively, we can consider the place and role of theory in research. Typically a distinction is made between pure and applied research, although these categories are not altogether useful. They assume for example that applied research is not underpinned by theory. As we have seen by looking at the top researchers, it would appear that this is far from true, certainly of those who apply behaviour analysis. As we will show in later chapters, it is important that research which evaluates provision is supported by a theoretical model which steers the researchers in their selection of what to look at in terms of both the outcomes and to the processes which underpin these. We also should not expect that applied research is always about changing practice. As Paechter (2003) points out, we may specifically aim to leave practice alone. Ethnography for example is interested in studying rules and systems. In its original anthropological form the intent was not to change them. Many ethnographic studies within the field of learning difficulties have made such revelations that attention was drawn to the need for change. There is an overriding assumption that research should *ultimately* lead to some intervention, and concern if it doesn't have direct message for changes in practice.

Policy-driven research

In the UK the channelling of research is apparent in the documentation of government agencies. Comparisons are often made between educational research and medical research, with calls for evidence-based practice and greater accountability. The Department of Health for example is explicit about the type of research it will fund; that which will:

> support its work on policy development and evaluation in public health, health services and social care in order to ensure that policy is based on *reliable evidence* of needs and of *what works best* to meet those needs. (Department of Health, 2002)

We can compare this to the DfES research strategy for 2003, a key element of which is:

> Developing a better, well founded evidence base for future policy development and practice. (DfES, 2003)

and earlier statements by the then Secretary of State, which clearly articulated the need for

> social scientists to help to determine what works and why, and what types of policy initiative are likely to be most effective. (Blunkett, 2000)

While this rhetoric can be seen to underpin the policies of a number of different government agencies, it is problematic within the field of special educational needs. This is well demonstrated in the process of literature review carried out by Evans and Benefield (2001) for the Centre for the Evaluation of Health Promotion and Social Interventions, a body set up to mirror the work of Cochrane for medical research. This particular review was on classroom strategies for pupils with emotional and behavioural difficulties. A total of 265 articles, books and chapters and conference papers were identified, of which 48 fell within the criteria for review. Of these, 33 contained data for extraction but only 11 were regarded as methodologically sound. This clearly indicates the dearth of robust educational evidence on which to base policy. Within the field of learning difficulties it is even more problematic (Hogg *et al.*, 1995). While this is not the only type of systematic review (Davies, 2000), it is one in which the process of deciding which studies to include is transparent.

Budge (2002) describes a number of difficulties:

> Review groups panning for golden insights into inclusive education and gender stereotyping had little to show for their efforts. And the group who spent a year trying to work out how ICT affects literacy development admitted: 'The answer is inconclusive … because there is insufficient research of high quality.' There is also concern about the spiralling costs for Universities undertaking this work for so little output. Only one of the first four reviews producing strong findings.

One response is to ensure that research in the future is more clearly targeted. This policy has been adopted in the UK by government agencies funding research which not only specify the research area but also dictate the research question and methodology. Later in the chapter we will look more closely at the type of research funded but here it is sufficient to draw attention to the way in which it can legitimise certain forms of research activity. For example, if you visit the home page of the Department of Health and enter 'learning disability' into the search facility you are lead to aetiology-related medical research and an invitation to click on the National Programme on Forensic Mental Health Research. This research is described as being for 'people with difficult, dangerous or extremely vulnerable behaviours which present a risk to themselves as well as others'. The home page does not link you even through the search facility to the large-scale Valuing People research initiative. The discourse of care and control would appear to be foregrounded today much as it was a century ago.

Projects funded by government agencies are increasingly specific both in their articulation of the aims and purpose of the research and the research questions and methodology through which to address these. In the bigger field of special educational needs there is argument for regular systematic reviews, large-scale longitudinal datasets, and studies with more emphasis on impact and therefore also on the process of dissemination (Hillage *et al.*, 1998). One of the difficulties for researchers can be the ethical issues raised by the way in which the findings are disseminated. Commonly the findings are reduced to key messages they wish the reader to receive (Pring, 2001; Scott, 2000), scant attention is given to methodology in the report and description is largely relegated to an appendix. This prevents the reader from critically evaluating the research and judging for themselves the robustness of the findings. There can also be a danger of short-termism and neglecting the wider picture. The immediacy of the research may be lost in a climate of change where policy can be transformed more quickly than research can be funded and carried out.

Theory and research

Theory has many possible roles in research. One approach to research takes as a starting point a theoretical position and seeks to elucidate this through the collection of data. Much (but not all) of the psychological research carried out during the 1960s investigating aspects of learning and development can be seen to typify this approach. Thus research on people with learning difficulties was designed to inform theory, for example to provide insights into the modularity of development or the information processes that support learning. This kind of research is largely driven by an academic interest. While we might criticise the motivations of such researchers, the role of theory in research is important in providing a framework for analysis, contributing fundamentally to an explanation of the findings.

Both policy-related research and that which is theory driven can be seen as limited because the scope of the findings are largely predicted in advance. Thomas (1998, p56) argues against the constraining use of theory and the systematic rational approach to research in favour of chaotic advancement, 'imaginative freedom in which solution suddenly appears'.

An alternative is argued by those who see theory as emerging from the findings. Strauss and Corbin (1998) describe the way in which theory is grounded in data that is systematically collected and analysed and the theory and its elaboration evolve during the research. These two approaches are not necessarily contradictory. The iterative process of data analysis and theory refinement is not very different from those of researchers whose theory is not validated by their findings and who consequently seek alternative explanations and refinements to theory. While the process may not be as unique as suggested, notions of theory may be. Theory can be understood as the articulation of a framework of beliefs that underpin practice. For some it can simply take the form of a reference to something that is abstract or symbolic rather than actual. It may be a personal theory of explanation. For Strauss and Corbin (1998), 'Theory consists of plausible relationships among concepts and sets of concepts.' There are clearly differences in the extent to which theory may have been elaborated and the degree of complexity and sophistication in which it is articulated.

However formal the theorising, there is a shared problem of the restrictions it potentially places on the research. As Thomas (1998, p98) suggests, 'There is a danger that in compacting, trimming, and generally forcing the world with which we work into theoretical molds we distort and misconceive those worlds.'

Researchers run the risk of ignoring aspects that are not consistent with a theoretical account and as Thomas continues: 'Theory systematises and tidies cognitive leaps and doesn't act as a vehicle for creativity … agrees on the merit of reflection but what we need is some adhocery and less structured problem-solving.'

There can be no doubt that theoretical research has its critics and may contribute directly to the lack of impact or perceived relevance it has for those working more directly in the field. As Pring (2000, p76) states:

> We need to ask how far research should employ the more theoretical language of specialist disciplines, thereby distancing itself from everyday discourse of the teacher, and how far it may remain within that discourse with all its imprecision and practices.

To look for more creative research we have to consider two further and contrasting positions, 'blue sky' research and practitioner research. Hargreaves (2001), despite his position within a government agency (that responsible for teacher training), makes a convincing case for the place of blue sky research, although such research is less likely to receive central funding. This research is not clearly defined but typically application is seen as secondary to its contribution to knowledge. It follows the radical new ideas of the researcher and utilises innovative methodologies and/or developments in theoretical under-standing and connections with other fields. What in Hargreaves' view would educational research look like? It might link with other fields such as the neurosciences, fostering creativity in the combination and recombination of different areas of expertise. It would draw on concepts of social capital, which he describes in the following way: 'Social capital is mainly about the nature of trust in human relationships and the social networks of communities' (p7) to be distinguished from economic or cultural capital. Blue sky research would be essentially innovative in its combination of different theoretical frameworks.

So far we have looked at research that is carried out in academic contexts, but there is also a strong case to be made for practitioner research which is developmental, where the outcome may be unclear when the research is started. Many practical innovations within the field of learning difficulties arise from professionals working creatively, but little is subject to systematic research and publication. Where practitioners do carry out such research, it is likely to be the result of an award-bearing INSET programme. The research is most likely carried out for its inherent worth either to that professional or the organisation for which they work.

Advocates of action research see it as bridging the divide between research and practice, serving to answer the question 'How can I improve my practice?'. Action research is an educational tool based on reflective enquiry with iterative cycles of planning, action, observation and reflection. It is well suited to professionals working in a variety of different settings. More recently new models of developmental research have been outlined as a way of incorporating action with research. While there may be concerns about the robustness of this kind of research which is vulnerable to bias, this may be offset by increased validity and, through its collaborative nature, it is open to scrutiny. The utility of action research contrasts with the more limited impact of much research within the field of psychology and sociology. It could be said to contribute directly to practitioner knowledge. The establishment of research communities serves to ensure that knowledge is not isolated, but builds on the findings of others.

Research agendas are therefore framed by the nature of research being carried out. Here we have shown both the strengths and the limitations of narrowly conceived research, whether it is driven by policy or by theoretical position, or indeed by both. These types of research contribute to establishing a foundation of knowledge on which to draw in the shaping of future provision. But there is an important role for the creativity both of blue sky research and of practitioner research, in breaking down barriers in traditional thinking together with expectations of what is and is not possible. If we consider who carries out research we can see that professionals working directly within the field are relatively unsupported in contributing to the research agenda.

The place and contribution of different types of research are illustrated by the Medical Research Council (2000) who have suggested a stepwise approach to research in recognition of the difficulties of evaluating complex health interventions in which there are many different components. In this four-phase approach the relative contribution of different methodologies are reflected. Prior to the phase 1, there is an exploration of theory to identify those which will inform the intervention and analysis and this is followed by a modelling phase that may include qualitative data collection using focus groups, case studies or small observational studies. Phase 2 involves an exploratory trial using alternative forms of intervention. The outcome of this is then subject to a randomised control trial to provide large-scale valid and reliable data. Finally, phase 4 is a longitudinal study looking at the intervention in more naturalistic or uncontrolled settings. This framework recognises the relative strengths of different models of research and has much to inform those working within the social sciences.

Funding

Different types of research call for different types of funding. The availability of access to funds can encourage or constrain particular sorts of research and research agendas. Identifying funding for research can be a particularly complex procedure for the new researcher and specific guides have been written both in the UK and in the US (Locke *et al.*, 2000) facilitating the targeting process. Funding for educational research is lower in the UK than for other European countries (Hillage *et al.*, 1998). There are a range of potential sources including government agencies, voluntary and philanthropic organisations and centrally funded research bodies. These will have an impact on the scale of the project, its time-scale, and the conception of worthwhile research.

We have seen that much American research, as represented by publication in journals, is driven by researcher interests and theoretical positions. There is a clear steer within UK funding sources to achieve a more collaborative and co-ordinated process. For example, the Department of Health provides specific statements of the ways in which their research agenda is linked with other funding bodies: those that fund research in higher education; the European 6th Framework programme; and with social care research funded by local authorities and charities and the national research councils such as the Economic and Social Research Council (ESRC). It is worth looking at the ESRC in more detail as it was once the leading funder of blue sky research.

The ESRC describes itself as the UK's leading research funding and training agency addressing economic and social concerns. Their aim is to provide high-quality research on issues of importance to business, the public sector and government. These issues include economic competitiveness, the effectiveness of public services and policy, and quality of life. A series of thematic priorities have been established based on the views of a range of people and sectors in response to the Science White Paper *Realising Our Potential*. The White Paper set out to tackle the problem that while world-class research was undertaken in the UK, it was not fully exploited either commercially or in the public interest. All the research councils were required to address this problem by working more closely with users of research and introducing the criterion of 'relevance' more clearly and strongly into their funding decisions.

Riddell *et al.*, (2001) provide an example of the type of research funded by the ESRC in the field of learning disability. This takes the concept of the 'learning society', and investigates its meaning for people with learning difficulties. It is not a piece of research designed to answer a simple evaluative question; instead it examines the premises of human capital and the policy implications with respect to lifelong learning. It 'explores the ways in which people with LD experience the Learning Society'. It was funded through the ESRC research programme The Learning Society: Knowledge and Skills for Employment which aims to understand the diverse constructions of a learning society. The research consists of two phases, a survey of provision and case studies of 30 adults in two local authorities in Scotland and illustrates in some detail the restrictions in life chances experienced by people with learning difficulties.

Increasingly funders are concerned to ensure that research has an impact. An important criterion against which research bids are judged is in relation to the proposed processes of dissemination. This is important because in the past the first (and often only) call on researchers was to put in a report to the funding body. The short time-scale of much contract researching still make this a likely outcome. However, impact has become a key word in judgements of research worth.

Research funders, in their concern for impact, also recognise the value of collaborative research. This is evident in centrally funded research and also in that provided by voluntary organisations. For example, the National Lottery Commission funds service providers for research, thus ensuring its relevance and impact on practice, and does so with organisations linked to universities. The government department for education has had a Small Programmes Fund which is only accessible to voluntary agencies who are working with or seeking to support pupils with SEN. These two examples, which span the scale of funding, provide an indication of the move away from direct funding of research to universities and by implication the perceived value of previous 'academic' research.

Research in the immediate future

A significant proportion of the immediate future research in the UK will be related to the agenda set by the White Paper *Valuing People* (DoH, 2001). The government promised £2m to support the programme of research and development called 'People with Learning Disabilities, Services, Inclusion and Partnership'. Grant and Ramcharan (2002) see research priorities to be related to services, especially the views and experiences of people with learning disabilities in the evaluations of innovations. Other topics such as life-span work, transitions and ethnicity are seen as important, as is ensuring that this short-term research strategy is genuinely knowledge-building while making good use of participatory research with people with learning disabilities. The strategy began in 2000 with the commissioning process, in which academics and people with learning disabilities were involved, which drew 144 outline proposals for studies. 124 of these proposals fell within the Department of Health's brief and were considered for funding. By March 2002, 10 projects had been commissioned on the themes of 'choice and control', 'health', 'social inclusion', 'service quality' and 'making change happen'. All the projects are of three years in duration. From the website (accessed in July 2003), it appears that two further studies are to be commissioned. The first is on the use and outcomes of mainstream health care and the second on establishing a baseline against which to judge the outcomes of 'Valuing People'.

This approach has a number of distinctive features which are unusual in federally funded research in this area. The most important of these is the engagement of self-advocates across all phases of the research *including* the commissioning process. As a four-year programme it provides a more sustained approach to research that is transparent in its link to policy. While a number of other funding organisations have actively promoted collaborative research with people with learning difficulties, the scale and publicity of this activity are probably unprecedented.

Grant and Ramcharan (2002) refer to the government agenda as 'a relatively modest initiative' in financial terms but are hopeful that 'the knowledge–action–policy loop' will be closed so that stronger working partnerships can be made between all those with stakes in the research. It is an optimistic view but realistic in terms of how long learning disabilities will remain high on the government's agenda.

Some research into learning difficulties in educational settings is likely to be supported by the DfES in the future, as it has been in the past. Of the 1,154 studies commissioned between 1997 and 2003, 40 related specifically to special educational needs, though not all those would have been directly related to learning difficulties. Of the 188 projects commissioned in the years 2000–3 through the SEN Small Programmes Fund (accessible by voluntary organisations) 13 seem to be directly related to learning difficulties (either because the category appears in the title or the project is being carried out by a voluntary organisation specifically related to learning difficulties).

Voluntary and philanthropic organisations have an important role to play in shaping the future research agenda. For example, the Foundation for People with Learning Disabilities has commissioned four studies within the 'Count Us In' research programme on meeting the needs of young people with learning disabilities and mental health problems. They cover aspects of ethnic minorities, anxiety and depression, changes in emotional well-being for young people with profound and multiple learning difficulties and evaluating a project in Somerset. The Joseph Rowntree Foundation does not have a specific theme for learning disabilities but among the priorities for 2003 were 'Poverty and disadvantage' and 'Support for those outside paid work', both of which could include people with learning disabilities. The Nuffield Foundation similarly has themes that embrace people with learning disabilities, such as 'Access to justice' and 'Educational provision and children's needs' but with all these general themes, the needs of people with learning disabilities are not usually considered a priority for funding, so it is debatable how much research will emanate from charitable foundations such as these.

There has been increasing recognition of the dangers of atomising research and the need for coordination to ensure that there is not needless or unplanned duplication in research. As a consequence a number of research centres specifically for learning disabilities/difficulties around the UK play an important role in contributing to the shape of future research. All of these centres have current research projects on aspects of service evaluation, and three have in common challenging behaviour and ageing or life-span topics. One is also working on aspects of sexuality and abuse; another specialises in children's services, accessible information, aspects of sexuality, mental health and transition; a third on mental health and child and family; and the fourth on primary care, quality of life, transition, transitions and epilepsy. It is clear that these centres, and others, will be affected by government policy as much as anything else. It is proving increasingly difficult to obtain research funding for projects that are not promoted by the Departments of Health, Education and Social Services.

Conclusions

Our review of research agendas has taken a broad stance to considering the variety of research that is undertaken in the field of learning difficulties and has discussed their relative contribution. We have argued for research that is framed by both policy and theory but also made a case for the existence of more creative, inspirational research ideally carried out by both practitioners and academics. There is much to be gained through collaboration, both across working contexts and across disciplinary areas. Studies suggest that the field of learning difficulties has been dominated in the past by a relatively narrow group of people. We can see that funding policy in the UK seeks to promote collaboration and importantly to include stakeholders in shaping the research agendas. At the same time, however, the dominance in the UK of central funding that is tied to policy initiatives may have a constraining effect on the shaping of the future unless at the same time innovatory research is actively supported.

While we recognise the importance of blue skies research and would argue for the importance of building knowledge, we would also stress the importance of impact. Important questions for researchers to ask are 'what influence will my research have?' 'What contribution will it make to the lives of people with learning difficulties?' These questions are vital if the research agenda is, in the words of Paechter (2003), to have utility. Of equal importance is a commitment to the integrity of the research process, that it should be rigorous in every aspect, the way it is planned, carried out and reported. We would echo Paechter's claims for research to be transparent in its methods and open with respect to 'sympathies and biases', justifiable ethically in an explicit way. It is with these characteristics in mind that we have selected to focus not on the content of research in learning difficulties but on developments in methodology. Our next chapter focuses specifically on the direction research has taken. We look in more detail at the trends in learning difficulty research, which, in turn has shaped the focus of subsequent chapters of the book.

CHAPTER 3
Trends in research

We can approach an analysis of trends in research in learning difficulties in a number of different ways. We could explore the changes in topic areas that are considered to be of interest, as we have started to do in previous chapters, or we might look for changes in the groups of individuals who are the focus of the research – this might be the professionals or service providers, the consumers and/or their families. Another significant aspect of study is to explore changes in research methodologies, particularly in the light of the criticisms of research and the current demands for evidence-based practice in a complex social field. We can take the enquiry wider to reflect on shifts in the nature of research and in the way both research and the researcher are viewed. It could be argued that this type of investigation enables the reader of research to examine the broader links between the way people view research and the type of research questions that are considered important. This again has implications for the kinds of topics that are more likely to be studied and the methods or research tools that enable them to do this. To provide an example of this, we can look at an argument that Söder (1989) makes for a move away from an investigation of attitudes towards people with learning difficulties in which the investigator collects questionnaire ratings of responses to statements and which assumes that there are right and wrong attitudes. This type of research typically seeks to answer questions about whether a particular group are prejudiced towards people with disability. Instead Söder proposes taking an anthropological approach to research, explor-ing *how* people make sense of their everyday world including notions of disability. This would lead to different research questions being posed around the meaning of disability, how it is created and changed. Clearly this calls for a very different set of research tools.

In this chapter we look at all three aspects of learning difficulty research: topics, methods and methodologies. We begin by looking at what others are claiming to be shifts in our thinking, and to make a series of inferences about implied trends. We then turn to examine the extent to which these changes can actually be identified in the empirical literature and discuss the methodological difficulties a seemingly simple task of review can create.

An appropriate place to begin is perhaps to echo the caution made back in 1990 by Clarke and Evans (1990, p177):

Prediction of future research trends is hazardous; some initial discoveries may be serendipitous yet lead to major revolutions in knowledge. Yet others exploit existing findings and advance logically step-by-step; in these cases future trends are more easily anticipated.

This might equally be true of identifying any emerging trends, where simple numerical comparison of research using particular methodologies or in particular topic areas is a seductive analysis but provides only a partial picture. The extent to which this reflects a changing profile should most usefully be plotted longitudinally *and* be contextualised, including comparing research practice with the discourse of research at that time.

Shifting research paradigms?

Traditionally the distinction has been made between qualitiative and quanti-tative research. The limitations of this approach have been widely recognised, including the false nature of this dichotomy when quantitative data are often reported in part in descriptive terms and qualitative data are often coded and categorised and given numerical values (Hammersley, 1992). Such arguments also obscure some of the more fundamental differences between research, for example the starting place for the research, the role and nature of theory, the philosophical values and assumptions that underpin different forms of research.

Scott (2000) argues strongly for the need for the informed reader to learn not only about the decision-making that underpins the selection of methodology but also to be clear about the epistemological and ontological assumptions of the researcher. Only if we know how the researcher views the nature of knowledge (their epistemological beliefs), whether for example their view is that research is about finding out about facts, about universal truths that operate irrespective of the beliefs of the individuals, or conversely whether they adopt the view that there is a need to investigate the way individuals construct their world, the meaning they ascribe to events, can we use appropriate criteria to make judgements about the 'worth' of the findings. This is not necessarily a straight forward task. Scott (2000) makes the criticism that researchers tend to present their research as unproblematic and seek 'to conceal from the reader the constructed nature of the account which has been produced' (p68).

Making a distinction between researchers on the basis of the philosophical underpinning of the research is also not without criticisms (e.g. Pring, 2000) as it presents (as we have done) a view that there are clear boundaries between paradigms. One look at research texts illustrates that this categorical approach to differentiating between paradigms is uncertain. Mertens (1998) for example distinguishes between positivist/post-positivist (research that seeks to discover one reality within the confines of probability, and where objectivity is key), interpretive/constructivist (reality is socially constructed, consequently there are multiple realities and therefore research is about subjective experiences) and emancipatory approaches (where those multiple realities are influenced by issues of power and equity). Denzin and Lincoln (1998) refer to a continuum of positivist, post-positivist, constructionist and critical paradigms; Pring (2000) makes a distinction between the scientific paradigm and the constructivist paradigm; and Scott (1999) and Smith and Hodgkinson (2002) draw attention to the current debates between the neo-realists and the relativist views of research and of the nature of reality. This diversity in categorisation no doubt reflects differences in the standpoints of the writers but can be confusing to the reader, especially where their own training has not invited them to question the place of different kinds of research.

Despite the complexity a recognition of some of the key differences, as Scott (2000) has suggested, has important implications for how we judge research. Different paradigms have different ways of identifying sources of bias and the use of criteria based on one set of premises is arguably inappropriate for research grounded in a different set (Oakley, 2000). This has important implications for those researchers who advocate the use of mixed methodologies, and the taking of a purely pragmatic approach to research design as it requires them to recognise and use distinctively ways of ensuring the worthiness of their research. For example, in research that seeks objective measures reliability is a key characteristic, what one researcher finds another should also. If, however, we believe that research is about exploring meanings and we want to understand the subjective views of an individual we will probably recognise that in making that exploration we as researchers are having an impact on that meaning. Meaning becomes co-constructed between the researcher and the researched. Reliability is therefore not the issue; rather we might seek to demonstrate the credibility of the findings, that we have indeed used active listening, been reflexive in our analysis and that our findings are the result of substantial engagement in the field.

Traditional approaches to research

Historically, positivist research designs have dominated the field of learning difficulties as they have most of the field of special education (Skritic, 1991, 1996), reflecting the heavy influence of psychiatry and psychology. Researchers have striven to gain an objective explanation, investigating learning difficulties in much the same way as a complex phenomenon in the natural world. The debates have centred on technical methodological issues rather than philosophical ones and have been firmly linked to questions of how we might best understand 'the condition'. Three broad issues permeated research. Firstly, the description of groups of individuals and the nature of their difficulties; secondly, research into aetiologies (notably Down syndrome) to obtain a more precise analysis of the psychological characteristics of particular groups; and thirdly, that of amelioration or intervention to lessen the effects of the condition. The first two issues can be seen to dominate such early writing as Penrose (1949) and Tredgold and Soddy (1963) but also later writings such as those of Clarke and Clarke (1975), Evans and Clarke (1990) and Hoddapp and Dykens (2001).

Two particular debates are worthy of discussion here as they had particular implications for the development of appropriate research methodologies. In the post-war period two views characterised psychological approaches to studying the nature of learning difficulties (Detterman, 1987) and were portrayed as diametrically opposing views. Each supported the use of different methodological designs. In short, the defect theory adopted particularly by Ellis and colleagues (Ellis 1969, 1970; Ellis and Cavalier, 1982) strove to investigate how people of different IQs performed on learning tasks with the result that many specific deficits were proposed, in attention and discrimination, in memory and in generalisation. These investigators tried to discover the differences that are the result of the learning disability. The methodology proposed by Ellis (1969) was based on matching individuals on the basis of chronological age (CA), although others adopting this approach have used groups matched on both chronological and mental age (MA), (e.g. McDade and Adler, 1980) or just inferred MA (Mackenzie and Hulme, 1987).

The contrasting approach, the developmental position, expressed by Zigler (1969, 1982), held that the 'mentally retarded' passed through the same stages of development as non-retarded children, but with a slower rate of progression and a lower ceiling. This approach was originally limited to studying those individuals without organic damage and used an experimental design which matched children according to mental age in order to reveal that they performed equally on developmental tasks. Over time the developmentalists have become increasingly differentiated as a group and the theories have widened along with the individuals investigated. Some researchers have adopted a 'similar structure' approach, arguing that not only do individuals pass through the same sequence but they reveal similar reasoning at each stage (Weisz et al., 1982).

Concerns about the technological efficacy of these designs were already being raised in the 1960s, for example by Baumeister (1967), and in the 1970s by Clarke and Clarke (1975). These authors consider in detail the myriad of difficulties of comparing 'subnormals and normals' matched either on CA or MA and the solution at least for some in focusing their interest on the unique laws of the behaviour rather than trying to find out the similarities.

> A few investigators have argued against attempts to match experimentally on either an MA or CA basis, on the grounds that it is not always a valid assumption that either of these is the most relevant variable that could be used, and may lead to the introduction of systematic differences between groups on variables other than these. (Clarke and Clarke, 1975, p26)

They also go on to point out that experimental matching leads one to leave out individuals who cannot be matched or who alter the means on the matching variable. Few studies used random allocation from a specified population.

Additionally they raised questions about the meaning of development, and the validity of MA scores. Equal MA scores can be achieved by different routes; moreover, the score is a result of how the individual performs with test material, their motivation and previous experience as well as possibly some true ability. The design is also based on the premise that individuals are matched on an independent variable but there is a danger that the performance rests on some aspect that has been measured as part of the MA test. Averaging group data is also problematic given that it disguises greater variability in performance in special populations.

The extent of their caution is reflected in the following:

> these problems have been outlined at some length because, although they permit no easy solution, it seems essential that research workers should be aware of them, since the conditions derived from much of the early experimental work on mental retardation must be regarded as equivocal, due to a failure on the part of the investigators fully to understand the many pitfalls. (Clarke and Clarke, 1975, p28)

Twenty years later, concern is still evident about the use of these approaches, as Turnure (1990, p187) reveals in his criticism of the way that psychologists approach the evaluation of intervention: 'finding 10 subjects … who can be treated exactly enough alike in some experimental condition to produce statistically significant differences compared to some other group.' He raises a particular concern about their focus on groups to provide summative rather than formative measures and their lack of attention to individual differences and its implications for research in effective interventions, an issue we will return to later.

These and other aspects are explored more fully in Chapter 5 but here they enable us to make a cautious inference that given these difficulties the use of such research designs might be in limited use in current practice.

Howie (1999) also draws links between research approaches and the way in which needs are conceptualised. She makes a distinction between defect and developmental theories, arguing that the defect theory, in contrast to developmental theory, provides little sense of individual difference nor the continuum of special educational need. Her analysis of developmental research approach focuses particularly on Vygotsky (rather than Piagetian influences) and consequently the importance of understanding changes in time within the child's social and cultural context. This promotes an increased recognition of the child's unique characteristics and their interaction with the learning environment. Her analysis leads her to argue for a growing shift away from a model of special educational needs involving the use of categorical labels to recognising a continuum reflecting different levels of assistance needed to perform a task. From this we would predict that intervention studies should increasingly utilise dynamic methods of assessment and focus on formative outcome measures. It should be recognised that within the continuum of learning difficulties there are those for whom there is a very small difference in supported performance to unsupported attainments and for whom a micro-level of analysis is required.

The third of the four paradigms that Howie (1999) identifies is an ecological one drawing naturally on Bronfenbrenner's theory of human development. Others previously have also pointed to the importance of this shift in thinking. Hogg and Mittler (1980, p15) pointed out that:

> remarkably little research has been published on the interactions of severely and profoundly mentally handicapped individuals in natural settings. Undoubtedly this state of affairs is changing, and a number of significant studies already provide a basis from which to develop further research.

Clarke and Evans (1990), in an edited book which focuses on describing different etiologies and the implications for intervention, call for future investigations on the impact of 'powerful and prolonged ecological change' thus shifting from a study simply of individual variables to include systemic ones.

One might predict from this that, despite a rather slow start, there would continue to be an increase in the ecological validity of studies and exploration of their implications for service delivery. Howie (1999) adds an important element to her ecological analysis. She suggests that one is not only looking at the environment to determine aspects which promote or hinder development but also at the way the individual perceives that environment and the affordances it offers (Gibson, 1979). This hints at a more fundamental change in research paradigm to acknowledge the importance of exploring meaning. This change is at the core of Howie's final model, the discursive model which, in contrast to the objectivism of behaviourism and experimentalists, focuses on the subjectivities, the meanings people construct and the relationship these have to the interactions between a person and a context. At the heart of the methodology is the study of discourse and this provides the framework for the research. She argues that the strength of this approach lies in addressing power relations.

Certainly elsewhere in the literature there is a call for a paradigm shift towards a more participatory and emancipatory form of research, where the researched become the researchers (Goodley and Moore, 2000; Chappell, 2000). Emancipatory research focuses on changing the social relations of research production, thus changing the power relations between the researcher and the researched and providing a meaningful influence on policy (Oliver, 1992). Participation and reciprocity are fundamental characteristics of the method-ology. While many of the proponents of this approach to research see it as an integral development of adopting a social model of disability in general, this has not always been extended in the literature to a recognition of social explanations of learning difficulty (Chappell *et al.*, 2001). Consequently much of the research may best be described as interpretative or ethnographic rather than emancipat-ory, with a focus on understanding the social lives and experiences of people and presenting these to the outside world. Additionally, research that is participatory is not necessarily conducted by people holding a social model of disability (see Kiernan, 1999). Chappell (2000) provides a useful definition of the characteristics of emancipatory research including that:

- it should be used as a means of improving the lives of disabled people
- there should be more opportunities for the people with learning difficulties to be the researchers
- it should be commissioned by organisations that are democratic and accountable to disabled people.

She draws attention to the fact that in participatory research the origins of the research agenda may not lie with disabled people although there should be collaboration with them at every stage of the research process including the collection and analysis of data.

Perhaps one of the most influential aspects of the shift is a recognition of the importance of collecting the views of people with learning difficulties and the challenges that poses for research with those who have limited language skills (Porter and Lewis, 2001). Ramcharan and Grant (2001) provide a useful summary describing research on the views and experiences of people with intellectual disability. The literature they review falls into three categories: user movement media, where documents are produced in different formats notably as part of self-advocacy movements; 'testaments of life' using narrative life history accounts (e.g. Atkinson and Walmsley, 1999); and research-based studies using structured and unstructured approaches to interview on the experiences and lifestyles of different age groups often as part of a larger study (e.g. Cambridge et al., 2002; Emerson et al., 2000). An overwhelming theme of these approaches to research is concern about how to elicit the most valid data from all those involved. Gradually as researchers become more committed to the importance of eliciting views, they become less prone to collecting data from samples that might best be described as convenient and the methodological tools become increasingly debated and refined. There does, however, remain an issue of the extent to which such data can be meaningfully collected in a single instance in the way that interview data is usually conceived and the role of practitioners in supporting this (Porter, 2003).

This research strategy is more easily developed as a small-scale collection of qualitative data, not least because individual responses and how they were elicited can be reported in depth. One of the challenges posed by Ramcharan and Grant (2001) is how this can be extended to larger-scale research in a way that makes a sizeable and routine contribution to the way that services are evaluated. We return to the issue of evaluation research later in the chapter.

There are a number of key issues which still have to be grappled with by those adopting emancipatory and participatory approaches (Walmsley, 2001). These include how one makes research findings accessible, the domination of topics that are most amenable to qualitative research, the contribution of theory to research and the role of the academic (Goodley and Moore, 2000; Walmsley, 2001). The approach also raises a number of important ethical issues, not least the nature and means of gaining informed consent (Clegg, 2000; Freedman, 2001; Lindsay, 2000; Masson, 2000). While the literature demonstrates the development of tools for gaining better understanding of the views of those with limited language (Grove *et al.*, 1999; Murphy and Cameron, 2002) relatively less attention has been paid to the means for explaining the implications of agreeing to be involved in a research project. These issues will be explored more fully in Chapter 6.

Topic changes

The development of new paradigms within research in learning difficulties provides for a sea change in the way that topics are identified for research. We therefore turn briefly to consider what trends may be apparent in topic areas. Some have previously argued that there will be more applied research and less pure research (Clarke and Evans, 1990) and one might anticipate that changes in policy would be a major impetus for research. Certainly in education there has been criticism that research has been too retrospective, tied to investigating the impact of such changes rather than helping to determine future policy (Blunkett, 2000). With respect to adult provision Walmsley (2001, p205) argues that normalisation or social role valorisation 'set the agenda for learning disability research for two or more decades'. This research seeks to evaluate the quality and outcomes of services, including the development of quality-of-life measures. The parallel for education would be around inclusive schooling, and the development and evaluation of inclusive practices. Both the normalisation and inclusion movements, it might be predicted, would be increasingly important topics for research that have been given further emphasis in the Department of Health (2001) White Paper *Valuing People* and in the DfEE (1998) *Programme of Action*.

As we have noted, however, research on aetiological aspects of learning difficulties continues to be an area for publication. Dykens and Hodapp (2001) in a major review of research in 'mental retardation' between 1980 and 1999 characterise research as falling within three themes: psychopathology, families and developmental approaches, each of which demonstrates a growing body of knowledge in relation to specific genetic syndromes. Dykens (2001) refers to this as 'a ground swell of syndromic research' and predicts that the goal is to 'examine links between genes, brain and behavior, or to make genotype-phenotype correlations', while also noting 'the vexing comparison group issue'. While the conclusions of their review no doubt reflect a search strategy in which psychology research texts dominate, few would disagree that issues to do with behaviour and with mental illness are an important topic of current research and reflect concerns of all service providers and families and a recognition that:

one of the most robust research findings to date is that, relative to the general population, persons with mental retardation are at *increased* risk for psychiatric illness, and severe behavioral or emotional dysfunction. (Dykens and Hodapp, 2001, p50)

Summary

While clear attempts to categorise research within philosophies or paradigms may be problematic, they are useful for teasing out some predictions for trends in research. The overview so far has demonstrated a growing pluralism in approach to research, with:

- an acknowledgement of the problematic nature of experimental designs including the use of comparison groups
- concern that too little attention is paid to individual differences
- recognition of the need for more 'ecological' research that is meaningful and relevant to the lives of people with a learning difficulty and considers the interaction between the person and their environment including systemic factors
- recognition of the need to develop new technologies for evaluation including the voice of the service user
- an expectation that people with learning difficulties will contribute to setting the research agenda.

With respect to research topics we note an expectation of the influence of the normalisation movement in provision for adults and inclusion in mainstream schooling for children to dominate the research agenda. Given also the drive for more participatory forms of research we might also expect issues of choice, advocacy and developing communication to inform the research agenda. In contrast to policy-driven research we might anticipate ongoing research around particular aetiologies and characteristics of specific groups.

In the following section we put some of these conclusions to the test. Given the theme of this book, attention will not purely centre on outcomes of the research but also reflect on the influence of the methodology. We start with an exploration of our decision-making in searching and analysing the literature to highlight the problematic nature of this process and help to inform the novice researcher and the user of research about some of the pitfalls and often unacknowledged tensions that exist.

Review methodology

There are many alternative ways of putting together a literature review; however, the starting place must be to establish clear goals for the review. In many respects this review is not conventional. C. Hart (2000, p13) for example defines a literature review as:

> The selection of available documents (both published and unpublished) on the topic, which contain information, ideas, data and evidence written from a particular standpoint to fulfil certain aims or express certain views on the nature of the topic and how it is to be investigated, and the effective evaluation of these documents in relation to the research being proposed.

Our goal was to make an overview of the nature of empirical research that is being undertaken in the field of learning difficulties with the aim of identifying trends. Our standpoint as educationalists influenced the process in two different ways. Firstly, it was viewed as essential that the methodology facilitated the identification of educational research in addition to that carried out in other disciplines. Secondly, the keywords adopted must be inclusive of those used in educational (as well as other) settings. The 'topic' was broad and given the constraints the researchers did not attempt to be evaluative of the relative contribution of the research outcomes. Rather we set out to establish what people say they are doing and how they describe that research.

There are a number of different approaches taken to identifying the literature, each of which influences the outcome. Many use a combination of systems, particularly where the body of literature is small and hard to identify (e.g. Hogg *et al.*, 2001). For example, one can use online database sources on a keyword basis although computerised systems can be limiting (Locke *et al.*, 2000). One can look in the key journals in the field whilst recognising that each has a pre-disposition to publish some material in favour of others, with a continuing dominance of psychology and psychiatry. The requirement to investigate research published over time also influenced the methodology as new journals appear, some of which are only available online. A decision was made to look at research published in the last decade as a likely minimum period in which to identify possible changes. Because of the decision to try to include as wide a variety of kinds of research as possible and in particular to ensure good representation of educational research, *Special Needs Abstracts* was used as the starting point to identify relevant research. It has the advantage of including world-wide publications from diverse sources, and although available online there was a perceived advantage in having access to a concrete text. This quickly became apparent in checking for under- and over-identification of relevant research. The adoption of descriptors is always problematic particularly when the publication field is international and the time-scale not sharply focused.

An initial approach was made using the index and identifying keywords where we would be reasonably confident of finding research in learning difficulties. Reliability checks were made in two ways. Firstly, cross-checking that those identified words did refer to work in the relevant area. Secondly, a second person was asked to adopt the same process. Where there was disagreement a generous decision was made to include those keywords as well and further cross-checking took place. The system proved not to be foolproof. In looking through those identified papers, others were discovered that had not been included. The more laborious approach was therefore adopted to check each of the abstracts individually, whereupon the difficulties of key word approaches became even more apparent. Some abstracts appeared without keyword descriptors and presumably had been indexed on the basis of the title; others had identified keywords that related to the topic such as 'bullying' or 'gender', but made no reference to the sample. Each article was then checked to ensure it included the empirical collection of data or analysis of secondary data, or was a systematic approach to literature review

Findings

A final total of 88 empirical articles were identified in 1990–91 and 59 in 2000–01. A first immediate concern can therefore be raised that there is less research published in this area than ten years ago. The total number of SEN abstracts for the two years is roughly similar (491 versus 485). However, if one looks at the proportion of the identified literature that has an empirical basis it appears that although there are fewer studies, writers are more likely to include empirical data in articles that do reach publication. One reason for this may be the pressures in higher education settings to increase the output of publications based on research. Others have also pointed to diminishing levels of research publications (Gersten *et al.*, 2000).

Issues of terminology

The ten-year overview highlighted the shifts in terminology that are used to refer to research in this area (see Table 3.1). References to mental retardation and mental handicap have almost disappeared. Taking first the term, 'mental retardation', this was used as a descriptor in 15 per cent of articles in 1990/1 compared with only one of the 59 articles in 2000/1. The shift is even more dramatic if we take the term 'mental handicap' where 22 per cent of articles used this term in 1990/1 but none in the most recent year. Both terms have been heavily criticised, not least by people with learning difficulties themselves (Goode, 2002).

Table 3.1 Changes in terminology

Descriptor Category	1990/1 (%)	2000/1 (%)
Difficulty	7	14
Handicap	22	0
Retardation	15	2
Disability	27	51
Aetiology	24	29
Other	6	5

However important, this does not imply a growing consensus in the use of terminology. One of the largest American associations, the American Association on Mental Retardation, has only recently debated changing its name and the implications for its identity (Taylor, 2002). This debate demonstrates the continuing wide expanse of views on the subject of terminology from those voicing concern about 'prattling practitioners of political correctness' (Walsh, 2002) and 'the assumptions, assertions, and dynamics that one encounters mostly from the politically correct' (Wolfensberger, 2002) to those who argue for the right of people to decide on their own social label (Goode, 2002) and who recognise that 'a paradigm shift in mental retardation is likely to have profound implications for the education, care and treatment of millions of human beings' (Smith, 2002).

Our review suggested that the most frequent descriptors in more recent research appear to be based on notions of disability. These account for over half the articles. The keywords include reference to degree of disability but the most widely used terms are 'intellectual disability' and 'developmental disability', the former being used in research with adults, the latter with children. Interestingly the term 'learning difficulty' is relatively seldom used, either in 1990/1 (7 per cent of articles) or 2000/1 (14 per cent of articles). One likely explanation is that this term is one largely adopted by educationalists in the UK; indeed when the same individuals move to adult provision, services are referred to as those for people with learning or intellectual disabilities. This suggests that relatively little published research is currently being carried out by educationalists in the UK with a focus on learning difficulty.

Topics

Research on aetiology

The previous review by Dykens and Hoddapp (2001) proposed a resurgence of interest in aetiology-based research. Table 3.2 indicates that this suggestion is partially supported by our search. A particular interest is indicated in the area of autism, although only one of these articles could be described as directly investigating syndrome characteristics. The others investigate services, intervention and the curriculum. This possibly reflects concern more widely in the media for the growing numbers of children identified with autism and the implications for educational provision (Berney, 2000). In contrast, 1990 publications on autism included papers on brain dysfunction, genetics and an experimental single case intervention study. If we take Down syndrome research in 1990, this was likewise largely concerned with aetiological characteristics including incidence, morbidity and survival, handness and speech dysfunction, academic attainments and cognitive development, dementia, thyroid disorder, cerebral specialisation, spinal degeneration, epilepsy and developmental aspects such as pointing behaviour and imitation and acquisition of grammar. In 2000–01 there were far fewer publications although these too could often be described as aetiology-specific studies, including a longitudinal study of

Table 3.2 Proportion of research on aetiology

Aetiology	1990/1 N = 88	2000/1 N = 59
Autism	3%	15%
Down syndrome	15%	10%
Fragile X	1%	3%
Rett syndrome		2%
Prader Willi	1%	
Angelman	1%	
Tourette's	1%	
Total*	22%	30%

*(A few studies included more than one group)

progress and attainment, comparison of attainments in memory and language according to educational placement, comparison of test scores across time, attentional control in forced choice reaction times as well as a study of parents telling their children about Down syndrome.

Aspects of children's development have previously been the focus of research with generic groups of pupils with learning difficulties. It would appear from these data, however, that there has been an interesting shift. Of the 20 per cent of studies which concerned developmental issues in 1990/1, almost two-thirds were carried out with broad non-aetiological groups of learners. There was a slightly lower proportion overall of developmental studies in 2000/1, making up some 14 per cent of studies but *all* were aetiology specific. The only use of a generic group was as a control group for one study. Does this imply that we are no longer asking questions about how children with learning difficulties develop particular skills? Does it reflect difficulties in identifying a representative population given that they are not clearly defined by provision? One possible influence in the UK may be the effect of introducing a National Curriculum, which is subject based into all schools including those that would previously have had a developmental curriculum. Thus while developmental issues continue to be important for psychologists, not least because of what they may tell us about development *per se*, they are less fundamental in informing educationalists what to teach.

Research on instruction

A second identified theme within the overview was research that relates to the development and use of instructional methods. This comprised some 17 per cent of research in 1990/1 and 22 per cent in 2000/1. Just under half the studies in 1990/1 considered aspects related to intervention and challenging behaviour or emotional difficulties. These included studies of such measures as the use of contingency contracts, group counselling, self-recording, time out, gentle teaching and visual screening, use of interspersed requests and teaching of play skills, thus suggesting that no one instructional strategy dominates the literature. The majority of studies are examples of individualised approaches with small sample sizes of one or two. In 2000/1 publications under a third of instructional studies are concerned with challenging behaviour. These more contemporary studies concern the use of physical restraint, anger management through cognitive-behavioural training and the identification of emotion with less focus on the use of individualised methods and more on small group instruction.

The remaining instructional literature for both years is diverse. Issues such as group versus individual instruction, the quality of individual education plans, individual learning opportunities and interaction were topics of investigation in 1990/1 as well as those of developing contexts that would promote assessment through teaching. Partially due to the smaller scale of the literature in 2000/1 it is harder to group approaches. Research topics included intensive interaction, co-operative learning and the use of peer tutoring.

Research that could be described as having a curriculum-related topic formed only a tiny proportion of the research. It constituted 5 per cent of the research in 1990/1 and 3 per cent in 2000/1. This perceived lack of interest in research in what to teach is perhaps unsurprising where there is centrally prescribed curriculum content.

Research on service delivery

Research that was not categorised according to development, instruction or curriculum was categorised according to its relevance to the delivery and development of particular services; whether for example the research directly informed educational services, social services, health services, or a combination.

If we consider more broadly the topics of research, there appears to have been a shift from research with direct implications for the provision of health-related services, e.g. drug intervention, eye abnormalities, obstetrics, to that of social services which in 1990/1 accounted for 14 per cent of the literature and in 2000/1 for just 3 per cent. In contrast, research with relevance to the provision of social services doubled, rising from 10 per cent to 22 per cent. Research with implications that cross service providers appears to have remained constant but low (under 10 per cent). Research in and around education services also remains broadly the same, comprising around 10–15 per cent of research.

Walmsley (2001) argued that normalisation set the research agenda in learning difficulties. Research in and around issues of normalisation or social role valorisation has remained remarkably consistent at around 16 per cent of articles. Interestingly the same is not true of inclusion where little research now appears to be carried out that explicitly concerns pupils with learning difficulties as there has been a fall from 10% to 3% of articles on this topic.

Despite adopting a review methodology that favoured the identification of educational research, we have to agree with Dykens and Hodapp that this remains a neglected area for empirical research – at least with respect to pupils with learning difficulties. Dykens and Hodapp (2001, p64) concluded with reference to inclusion that: 'For better or worse, advocacy seems to have replaced empiricism in the formulation of social policy.'

One particular aspect of research that transcends topic areas is the concern for what works and what works most efficiently and effectively, even though it may not be linked to inclusive practices. Looking across all research categories in 1990/1, 34 per cent of studies could be described as evaluative and this figure has risen to 42 per cent in 2000/1.

Methodologies

If we turn to consider the methodologies in use and ask about the types of approach used in our two samples over a ten-year period, we run into immediate difficulties in deciding how the studies should be categorised. Indeed it would be easier to describe the sort of research tools used than to provide a picture of methodologies as few researchers attempted to clearly categorise their research design, a finding echoed by others (Hogg *et al.*, 2001). Robson (2002) describes methodology under a number of headings: experimental, comparative, relational, longitudinal, case study, ethnographic, grounded theory, action research and evaluation studies, to name a few, making a distinction between fixed and flexible designs and those for particular purposes.

The way in which authors depict research methodologies reveals their own underlying assumptions about research. Stake (1998), for example, argues that case study is not a methodology as it does not define how we study the case. Indeed this raises the question of whether 'methodology' is an appropriate term to use. It is noticeable that qualitative researchers use the word 'strategy'. Janesick (1998) refers to a long list of such strategies including ethnography, life history, naturalistic study and ecological descriptive study. To impose a system of categorisation on the literature is therefore potentially limiting, but if few authors describe their design then it is left to the reader to infer and categorise. Moreover, categories are not mutually exclusive or clearly bounded, resulting in a best-fit descriptor approach. It is, therefore, with these arguments and limitations in mind that the Table 3.3 has been constructed.

Firstly it is apparent that few authors adopt anything other than positivist or post-positivist approaches to research. In 1990/1, two authors describe their studies as ethnographic and one as phenomenological, with the figures hardly changing for 2000/1, where authors of one study were explicit about the use of grounded theory and another referred to their case study as ethnographic. If we (rather generously) add these together with other studies that make specific reference to the collection of qualitative data, then some 13 per cent of studies in both 1990/1 and in 2000/1 fall into this category. This leads us to the conclusion that despite the development of new paradigms there has been little discernible change in the way research is seen in the field of learning difficulties.

The largest descriptor of methodology is survey design, followed by studies using experimental and quasi-experimental research strategies. Over a quarter

Table 3.3

Research strategy	1990/1 N = 88	2000/1 N = 59
Survey	28%	22%
Experimental/quasi-experimental	23%	21%
Literature review	10%	3%
Relational	9%	21%
Comparative	8%	10%
Evaluation	6%	9%
Case study	6%	3%
Longitudinal	6%	5%
Cross-sectional	–	2%
Ethnographic	1%	2%
Phenomenological	2%	–
Grounded theory	–	2%

of research in 1990/1 was based on survey design, dropping to just over one-fifth in 2000/1. Surveys provide descriptive data of given populations at a given point in time and many of these studies are based largely on questionnaire data. Sadly, few studies are longitudinal and provide us with a picture of change over time. Surveys are often favoured in small- and large-scale research for the perceived ease with which sizable amounts of data can be collected but they have been subject to a number of criticisms (Robson, 2002). Defining and locating the sample including the person most likely to be keeper of the desired knowledge can be particularly difficult in the field of learning difficulties where there may be a fluidity in the relationship between provision and service-user. No longer, for example, can we presume that if we want to investigate the lives of children with severe learning difficulties, they will all be placed in special schools.

While surveys add to our body of knowledge they don't on their own provide new understandings and insights – although authors may use them to try and deduce patterns or associations. Studies that have been designed specifically to investigate associations such as the relationship between two variables, we have classed as *relational* studies and those which have been designed to compare patterns or performance between groups as *comparative*. Interestingly the figures for relational studies suggest that this type of research is increasing, but contrary to our predictions the proportion of comparative studies appears largely static.

The second largest category in 1990/1 and joint second in 2000/1 was experimental/quasi-experimental designs, making up just over a fifth of studies in both sample years. Two-thirds of the studies in both years could be described as small scale, often single case studies with only one-third having a sample base of more than five. Only one study, appearing in the 2000/1 cohort, referred to the sample being randomly assigned to conditions and few used designs that would lead one to draw firm conclusions that changes were due to the manipulation of variables.

The development of evidence-based practice is often associated with a demand for random control groups and gives rise to issues of its applicability for evaluating provision for people with learning difficulties. These concerns include low levels of referrals and thus small sample size; the fact that outcome changes are typically likely to be smaller and require a more prolonged period of intervention; concern about the use of scarce resources; denying forms of treatment; lack of definitions of intervention; health concerns where for example it may disrupt a relationship between the participant and their carer; and the difficulties of gaining informed consent, to name but a few (Oliver *et al.*, 2002).

Gersten *et al.*, (2000) make a strong case for the importance of experimental and (with a number of reservations) quasi-experimental studies that use group sizes larger than 20. Their greater concern lies with improving the decision-making in researchers, use of these approaches and consequently the quality of the data. The difficulty of constituting a sufficiently homogeneous group of people with profound and multiple learning difficulties, of pre-specifying the detail of the methodology of intervention and the importance of micro levels of analysis of outcomes especially with respect to progress, militate against the use of larger-scale studies. This is not to suggest that there can be no collection of quantitative data but rather that it provides a broader landscape, a macro level of analysis against which to evaluate effective provision. This could well take the form of a set of principles with alternative research methods used for illustrating the details of their application and demonstrating their effectiveness.

In the literature there are examples of newer technologies being refined. Gersten *et al.*, (2000) argue for the use of design experiments for new and developing interventions. Kelly and Lesh (2002) provide us with a definition: 'the term is applied, typically, when describing iterative refinement of some innovation … in teaching and learning environments.'

As Gersten, *et al.*, (2000) point out, this methodology has previously been referred to as formative experiments (Newman, 1990), or developmental studies (Gersten, 1996). They conclude that: 'We believe that design experiments can and should be a critical tool in refining innovative instructional practices in real classroom environments and formally documenting their effects' (p9).

The use of iterative research methodology is also compatible with the methodologies suggested by Siegler and colleagues (Siegler, 1995; Siegler and Chen, 1998; Rittle-Johnson and Siegler, 1998) for a microgenetic trial-by-trial analysis of children's responses, enabling us to start to identify mechanisms for change as well as noting individual variations in pace and pathway.

The work in the UK of the ESRC-funded Research Building Capacity centre is looking to explicate the methodology and ask a series of questions, recognising the breadth of design environments including how they can be made more powerful, and what tools and methods best allow the rich learning data to be collected. These approaches are discussed further in Chapter 5. The question remains about the extent to which these methodologies should replace larger-scale group designs.

Whereas evaluations of instructional strategies are largely carried out through experimental and quasi-experimental designs, research evaluating aspects of service provision is less likely to use these methodologies (15 per cent in 1990/1 and 29 per cent in 2000/1), although we do see more use in the recent sample. This may well reflect the political drive to identify what works in service provision, placing an emphasis on research that looks at outcomes rather than process. Quality-of-life indicators and cost-benefit measures of effectiveness feature increasingly as the instrumentation used.

A distinction can be made between evaluation that can be considered formative, where feedback is provided directly to the service providers, and that which is summative and which is designed to determine the overall effectiveness. Pertinently there are no examples of action research within this reviewed literature which is one strategy for formative evaluation, and only one example of self-evaluation in the 2000/1 literature. One explanation for this is the professional division between researchers and practitioners, despite the call for more collaborative research. Chapter 8 explores these issues more fully. The use of both internal and external evaluators offsets some of the limitations of depending on single agency evaluators and may well strengthen the empowering nature of such research (Clarke and Dawson, 1999).

Conclusion

In this chapter we have used a broader literature to infer a number of directions to research with respect to research paradigms, methodologies and topic areas. An overview of research taken at two points in the last decade raised a number of questions about those inferences. In summary our findings suggested the following:

- There has been a change towards using the term 'disability' as a part descriptor of research samples, developmental, intellectual and learning forming co-descriptors. This demonstrates the compromised position of adopting a social model.
- Aetiology-based studies continue to be a topic of research, although there has been a shift to favouring research in autism.
- Developmental research continues to ask questions about the characteristics of particular groups although this formed a smaller percentage of research in 2000/1. In contrast to 1990/1, all recent studies were aetiology based, rather than looking generically at the nature of learning difficulties.
- Contrary to our expectations, a smaller percentage of instructional research concerns intervention for challenging behaviour in 2000/1 than 1990/1 despite the fact that overall there is a slightly higher proportion of instructional studies in 2000/1.

- Whilst research that impacts on the development of social services is growing, that for education is small and appears to be decreasing.
- Unsurprisingly therefore, there continues to be little research into inclusion or inclusive practices and little on the curriculum.
- Research on issues of normalisation remains strong and this is reflected in the evaluation of services.

With respect to research strategies:

- relatively little research is qualitative across either time periods and very few studies refer explicitly to non-positivist paradigms
- the dominant methodology is survey design followed by experimental/ quasi-experimental research for both year samples
- experimental designs are used for the majority of instructional studies in both cohorts
- service evaluation studies utilise a variety of methodologies with increasing reference both to quality-of-life indicators and to cost analysis.

The call to new research paradigms is not clearly evidenced in the practice of learning disability research. Despite the changing terminology to favour 'disability' as a descriptor, it would appear that this does not indicate the adoption of a social model. On the one hand this may well reflect the uncertain place of the social model as an account of more severe or profound learning difficulties. Almost a third of research can be described as syndromic, suggesting that a good proportion of research focuses on issues of deficit. At the same time there is recognition of the need to know what are effective practices. It can be argued that while studies typically are weak in adopting designs that prove what works, less structure can lead to studies that are more ecologically valid, reflecting the real-world conditions in which interventions occur. It is likely that for a proportion of the population large-scale research using randomised control trials will be problematic. There is however a need to capitalise on the development of new technologies that enable us to evaluate our practices with respect to individuals and small groups. In particular there is an argument for investigating the process by which change occurs rather than simple outcome measures. There are suggestions in the broader educational literature of what these designs might look like. Just as it is important to look at processes of change, so it would appear important to collect outcome measures that are formative, requiring a closer collaboration between the researcher and the researched. Moreover, if research is to be empowering, part of this process must include the views of service users including those with the most limited language. Key questions that these raise for the authors of this book are:

- How can evaluation studies reflect the complexity of service delivery?
- How can we develop methodologies for evaluating instruction?

- How do we elicit the views of all people with learning disability?
- How do we promote collaborative (and small scale research)?

These questions have shaped the focus of the following chapters.

CHAPTER 4
Evaluation research

Introduction

The potential scope of this chapter is broad given that evaluation can be seen in the context of investigating the effects or effectiveness of service, an intervention programme, strategy or an innovation. It can be seen in the context of changing policy, practice, ideology or theory and the scope can be national, regional, local or specific to an individual. It is perhaps most properly referred to as research when it embodies a systematic, principled approach (Newburn, 2001). Robson (2002) provides a useful starting point by posing the likely questions that evaluation research may seek to address, thereby demonstrating the potential breadth of the field:

- Are the clients' needs being met?
- How can the programme/service be improved?
- How is the programme/service operating?
- How efficient is the programme/service?
- Why is the programme/service not working?

One of the most notable characteristics of evaluation research is that it is carried out within the context of its purpose – it is, by its very nature, designed to be used. In the previous chapter we suggested from the review of two points spanning a decade of research in the field of learning difficulties that with respect to evaluation:

- almost half the research published in 2000/1 could be described as evaluative
- evaluation of instructional strategies consistently adopted experimental or quasi-experimental designs
- conversely, evaluation of the curriculum constituted a very small proportion of research
- there is a growing body of research that informs the provision of social services (unlike that of education, which remains rather low and static)
- evaluation of services notably used quality-of-life indicators and increasingly economic measures
- very little published evaluation can be described as using methodologies leading to formative evaluation that are presented as collaborative or participatory

- social policy appears to be guided more by advocacy/ideology than evidence.

Our review has suggested that much of the research within the field of learning difficulties is narrowly focused on outcomes rather than processes, and driven by positivist approaches to research. Much of this research evaluates instructional practices and is the focus of Chapter 5. In this chapter we concentrate on broader issues of service evaluation. Little evaluation is reported in educational settings (other than those carried out by government bodies; in the UK the Office for Standards in Education). There are however some important developments within the field of social care that could usefully inform that of evaluation within education. There has been a developing shift away from thinking about evaluation purely in terms of single measures (often based around the use of questionnaires) to multiple measures that take into account the interactional effect of different variables. Robson (2002) comments: 'give a person a tool and it changes the way they see the world'. As Pawson and Tilly (1997) argue, everything can in effect be evaluated.

We start this chapter by placing our review findings in a wider context, drawing on the mainstream literature on the nature of evaluation, and chart the changing views of the kinds of questions that this research should seek to answer. This of course cannot be discussed without looking at some of the hotly contested debates on evaluation methodology, including the pragmatic view of adopting a 'fit for purpose' approach and mixing methodologies. The purpose of evaluation research is multifold and in the course of the chapter we raise the question of the ways in which it can and should inform policy and practice. The potential use and misuse of evaluation research brings to the fore a number of ethical issues in the conduct of research which we explore before turning our attention directly to the field of learning difficulties.

Changing views within evaluation research

Strong debates are evident in the literature on the nature of evaluation research, that have parallelled paradigm wars about the place of quantitative and qualitative research. While historically much evaluation research adopted an experimental design, there has been recognition that this was not well placed to inform the development of services (Ghate, 2001; Greene et al., 2001) although there is still some who regard it as the gold standard in evaluation research (Newburn, 2001). Most specifically concerns have been expressed that it does not reflect the complexity and messiness of the real world but is based on an expectation of a controlled context in which consistent and repeatable strategies are employed. While there has been a revival in the quest for the collection of quantitative data through randomised control trails there is a growing but still hotly debated argument for adopting mixed approaches. Even the Medical Research Council (2000) proposes a staged approach to evaluating interventions which includes the collection of qualitative and quantitative data at particular phases of the framework. If one accepts a notion of methodologies that are 'fit for purpose', there is an assumption that combining methods provides an easy answer (Oakley, 2000). Oakley calls for a careful examination of the research question, stressing the importance of whether it has been answered before, and whether it makes sense to the people who are the stakeholders. In this way one does not reach simplistic solutions about the place of experimental designs nor the need to equate these only with quantitative data.

Greene *et al.* (2001) explore these issues further in putting forward four frameworks through which to view the mixing of methods. The first of these, the pragmatic approach, argues that there has been an overemphasis on the dualism between different paradigms portraying extreme viewpoints that don't characterise much decision-making within research. The pragmatic approach starts instead by examining the context of the research to inform design. The second position, the dialectical view, both recognises and values the differences between paradigms but argues for a 'conversation' between researchers that will lead to better understanding and insight yet also logical analysis. Substantive theory is the third approach, where decision-making is fuelled by the substantive issues that underpin the evaluation leading to a recognition of meaning as well as effect. The fourth view is that of alternative paradigm, noting that newer paradigms such as critical theory recognise the value of providing both subjective and objective accounts. The identification of these four frameworks suggests that although investigators may adopt mixed methodo-logies their reasoning may lie with different accounts of the research process.

Kushner (2002) maintains the importance of recognising the different value systems that underpin different methodologies that militate against their combination. Different methodologies are underpinned by different assump-tions about the research – whether, for example, there is value placed on individual or aggregated data, whether the purpose is to understand a particular case or to look more widely at provision. These decisions affect the way a particular method is developed and employed. Kushner portrays the difficulty of those on the receiving end if the messages about what is important are mixed, and she describes the disruptive effect it can have on research that is based on developing a relationship that promotes the sharing of experiences. These arguments rest more broadly with the issue of power differentials and the values placed on the plurality of voices.

Interestingly, one of the arguments that Greene *et al.* (2001) make is for the openness of views and a recognition of the 'diverse ways of knowing', for greater reflexivity and responsiveness, and yet almost inevitably some elements of data will be given greater weight than others. Grocott *et al.* (2002) provide a vivid account of the complexities and difficulties of adopting mixed methodo-logies in their evaluation of patient care. Although there are rational debates about enhanced validity and credibility, greater insight resulting from discrepancies between findings with the possibility of promoting public debate through including different theoretical stances, one must also recognise the political nature of much evaluation research and the potential impact on minority groups.

One of the criticisms directed at educational research has been a lack of link with practice, a failure to build on the research of others and to be able to answer such fundamental questions as 'what works' (Hillage *et al.*, 1998; Blunkett, 2000). There is an argument to be made that at least in part, this is the wrong question to seek to answer. Nowhere is this more true than within the field of learning disability where the heterogeneity of the population arguably make single solutions highly unlikely. We need instead to be asking how or why a particular intervention or service has its effect (Pawson and Tilley, 1997; Weiss, 1998), thus shifting research from simple outcome measures to look more closely at the processes involved. There is a second and related issue. If we seek to shift evaluation research so that it is formative rather than summative in its evaluation of a service or intervention, then it needs to be accompanied by an investigation of the change process. It is not sufficient to carry out evaluative research that seeks to inform the development of practice if there isn't an attendant understanding of the conditions that support change. This adds a third rather clumsy question of 'by what means' these processes can be best developed. The focus thus moves from a simple spotlight on a single aspect of an intervention or service to a multiple gaze that looks more widely at the processes, systems and organisational structures that support these outcomes.

The evaluation literature places emphasis on the need for a clear causal model (Ghate, 2001); a theory of change (Peterson, 2002); or the identification of causal mechanisms (Pawson and Tilley, 1997) that guide the process of research and frames the evaluation. There needs therefore to be reasonably clear expectations of what changes the service or programme is designed to bring about. Some would even argue for measurable objectives: 'if services cannot specify what changes they expect to see for 'successful' users, evaluators certainly cannot measure them' (Ghate, 2001, p25).

Others might suggest the inclusion of stakeholders' views of the anticipated benefits of a given programme or service. This may be quite widely conceived. Cole *et al.* (1998), for example, in the context of provision for pupils with emotional and behavioural difficulties suggest that the stakeholders include pupils, parents, the placing agency, others in the community as well as government agencies. This reflects the complexity of 'measures' against which effective provision might be evaluated. It will be argued during the course of this chapter that there is a strength in developing a collaborative approach to evaluation research: insight into the processes requires a sharing of the experiences of those involved, not simply a cataloguing of the systems in operation. Moreover, given diverse views about the anticipated purpose of a service or programme, evaluations of the outcomes are usefully constructed through stakeholder involvement rather than an assumption of a shared understanding of a single outcome agenda.

Services that do not have clear expectations of what users stand to gain nor routinely have stakeholder involvement, place users in a vulnerable position. Such services do not readily lend themselves to evaluation and neither the internal or external scrutiny that accompanies it.

Relationship between policy, practice and research

Given the direct links between evaluation and decision-making it is perhaps unsurprising that there are political tensions in much evaluation research. One of the issues for provision that is state provided is that the higher the quality, the greater the demand. In education this has been referred to as the bottomless pit of need. It can be witnessed in the context of respite care or the highly specialist services of special schools. In fulfilling a need, the need does not disappear. Thus political tensions are most clearly evident when evaluation concerns costs and effectiveness. The purpose of such evaluation is to make decisions about where to place economic resources. Research in this field therefore also poses a number of ethical dilemmas. It is unlikely that all stakeholders will have the same interests and concerns about the outcome. This is a particular issue where the consumer has limited economic power and choice, where their views are harder to elicit and verify and take longer to collect. These implications will be explored more fully in the course of the chapter.

It is perhaps worth briefly reminding ourselves about the dangers of adopting a simplistic view of the relationship between research, policy and practice. Evans and Benefield (2001) review the work of others in describing different ways in which policy-makers use research evidence:

- Political model – research is used as ammunition to support a pre-determined position.
- Tactical model – research is used as a delaying tactic to avoid responsibility for an unpopular policy outcomes.
- Interactive model – researchers are one set of contributors to policy formation amongst many.
- Knowledge driven – knowledge and research findings drive policy.
- Problem-solving – there is a direct application of results of a specific study to inform a pending decision.

An easy assumption cannot therefore be made with respect to the quality of evaluation research and the impact it has on policy. Additionally, rarely are the ideological assumptions made evident to the reader of a policy document and thus the reader is often prohibited from deconstructing the process of knowledge development and dissemination. They are consequently placed in a poor position to make judgements and resist powerful messages. As Scott (2000, p28) argues:

> Policy texts seek to persuade the readership of the truthfulness and credibility of the arguments which they are deploying. The principal way they do this is by suggesting that there is only one way of representing the world and this way resonates with commonsense views of representation.

If the relationship between research and policy is cloaked in mystery then the link between research and practice might at best be described as tentative. As Stephenson (2002, p74) suggests, 'faddish practices without a research base are often vigorously and confidently promoted … many teachers are unaware of the knowledge base of effective practice in special education emerging from research.'

The often widespread adoption and use of particular teaching approaches does not appear to depend on empirical evidence of their impact. Indeed the evidence for the effectiveness of specialist pedagogies is limited (Lewis and Norwich, 1999). The review of the impact of multisensory rooms by Hogg *et al.* (2001) provides a seminal case of the ways in which a particular approach may widely permeate the curriculum at a national level, with considerable potential cost implications for the organisation, without evidence of its effectiveness. Notably for this chapter, the message is less that the approaches are ineffective but that, despite the number of studies, few are sufficiently robust in their design to draw useful conclusions. Of relevance to would-be evaluators are the suggested conditions for adopting innovations in practice summarised by Stephenson (2002) as accessibility of information, the importance for educators of methods that build relationships with their students, including those that are suggested to lead to emotional well-being and improved communication. Indeed this may explain why some methods are not adopted despite a strong evidence base. Research will therefore benefit from looking at the impact of an innovation on the behaviour of teachers, and the belief systems that underpin their practices as well as the impact on students.

Ethical issues

As we have already indicated, different stakeholders will have different interests and concerns about the outcomes of a service. They will also therefore have different agendas on the purpose of evaluation and their contribution to it. Thus while all may share a wish to use evaluation to improve a service, their expectations of the likely recommendations will vary considerably. It is important that all view the work as a piece of research, and recognise the systematic nature of data collection and perhaps more significantly the reporting of that data. It is equally essential that all are aware that the process may highlight issues that are uncomfortable or unpalatable for some. There can be ethical dilemmas for external researchers in gaining consent of the contributors when the research has been commissioned by management/service providers, as they may have an automatic expectation that all members of staff will be involved or conversely that only certain members of staff have opinions worth collecting. This predetermining view can extend to service users. Researchers are called upon to negotiate what parts of the data collection process can legitimately be seen as part of their job and what are additional and unreasonable in terms of the time they take. France (2001) highlights the need for researchers to provide some 'value added' activity that serves to demonstrate their recognition of the time and commitment of those contributing to the evaluation. Staff may also have particular concerns about the way in which the data collection or presence of researchers will impinge on the activities offered by the service. Evaluation research may therefore call for sensitive collaboration and negotiation between researchers and researched.

Kushner (2002) illustrates the ethical dilemmas for researchers where funding agencies, based around customer–contractor relationships, specify the use (and usefulness) of particular methodologies, especially where these are felt to privilege the views of the more powerful. They may call for the researchers to present themselves in what feels to them to be a prejudicial way. France (2001) points to the dangers of middle-class academics finding it hard not to champion the cause of the dispossessed or to adopt an unbiased view within the research collection process. He cites the advantage of being part of an independent organisation that cannot be accused of having a vested interest in the research.

Summary

The general literature on evaluation research has drawn our attention to a number of key issues. Evaluation should seek to investigate:

- the impact of the service drawing on stakeholder views and expectations
- the processes which effect that impact
- the systems and structures that best support these processes.

Evaluation needs to take place in the context of a causal model or theory that will direct the investigation to the relevant aspects of the provision. While there is an argument for using a mixed methodological approach, this is not unproblematic. We also cannot ignore the vested interests within evaluation research which create a number of ethical dilemmas for the researcher. In carrying out this research we need to take cognisance of the fact that it will not automatically have a wider impact on policy and practice where other factors determine the way research is utilised.

Having looked broadly at issues raised by the evaluation literature, we now turn more specifically to evaluation research in the field of learning difficulties.

Criteria for evaluation

Central to the debate in evaluation research is the difficulty of reaching internal or external agreement about the nature of the criteria against which a service should be judged, or put more simply, what indicates quality. This statement acknowledges that what is generally sought is a positivist view of one truth or world view, a single objective perspective of the service rather than multiple views of the reality of receiving that service – or indeed what the meaning of that service is for those who receive or provide it – the stakeholders. While methodologies have largely moved away from traditional experimental or quasi-experimental designs, our review suggested that a positivist view of research still dominated. One will see the essence of these tensions in the debates around the relative validity of subjective and objective measures of quality of life later in this chapter.

It is interesting to look historically at the changes in the way we have evaluated services for people with learning difficulties. Ager (2002) demonstrates through reflections on his own work the predominant view of the 1970s that an important outcome measure for services was the extent to which they resulted in the achievement of greater self-help skills. This was mirrored in the type of scales used at that time, e.g. the Vineland Social Maturity Scale (Doll, 1965), The Adaptive Behavior Scale (Nihira *et al.*, 1975). There was, and indeed continues to be, a growing recognition that these measures need to reflect cultural variations – a discourse still taking place in schools to some extent. In Ager's view the normalisation movement with its particular emphasis on social role shifted the framework of evaluation to measures of task engagement as well as social interaction, but still largely with the evaluation made by others – staff, care-givers or researchers – not by the service users themselves (Cummins, 1997). The 1990s according to Ager's account saw a rise in evaluation based on choice and opportunity reflecting a wider social discourse not simply that of service providers:

> individual personal and social competence can be seen to broadly reflect the functional concerns of society through the 1970s and early 1980s, which opportunity and choice reflected the increasing social liberalism of the late 1980s and 1990s … the current ascendance of QoL approaches now reflects further shifts in the discourse, a turn-of-the-century sensitivity to such issues as pluralism and postmodernity. (Ager, 2002, pp370–1)

There is, however, a debate about the extent to which this analysis reflects shifts in philosophy about services for people with learning difficulties or a mirroring of the 'corporatisation' of services generally with its discourse of products and packages of services that need to be managed (Rapley and Ridgway, 1998). Pfeffer and Coote (1991) make a distinction between a managerial approach to quality in SEN services with a focus on customer satisfaction and a contractual culture, but where the consumer may still be powerless, with that of a consumerist approach which sees an active role for the consumer and enforceable individual rights. This level of empowerment is not evident in the debates on quality within the field of learning disability.

In the context of early childhood provision Dahlberg *et al.* (2000) propose the replacement of quality with a discourse of meaning. They argue that the concept of quality has been inherently viewed as a single standard against which to measure a service because of its history in the growth of consumerism where quality in the global market had basically two meanings. Firstly, quality was seen in relation to satisfying stated or implied needs and, secondly, that quality implied that it was free from deficiencies. Both meanings centre on notions of customer satisfaction:

The concept of quality is primarily about defining, through specification of criteria, a generalizable standard against which a product can be judged with certainty. The process of specification of criteria, and their systematical and methodical applications, is intended to enable us to know whether or not something – be it a manufactured or service product – achieves the standard. (Dahlberg *et al.*, 2000, p93)

Methods of measurement are seen as the priority; they dominate the selection of criteria and the process receives little attention, as what is looked for is conformity to that standard. There is therefore no place for a negotiated process achieved through dialogue with all interested parties. They identify three types of criteria: structural criteria that are to do with resources and their organisation; process criteria – what actually happens, what activities occur, who does what; and outcome criteria. In summary:

the discourse of quality ... has been constituted as a search for objective, rational and universal standards, defined by experts on the basis of indisputable knowledge ... Method has been emphasized at the expense of philosophy, the how rather than the why prioritized. (Dahlberg *et al.*, 2000, p99)

One of problems with existing measures in the field of learning difficulties is that the search has often ended with a universal standard that ignores the cultural differences that exist either with respect to the outcome of educational services or those of social or health-related services. Once one allows for diversity one cannot have a universal and objective norm and therefore the very notion of quality as a concept is questioned. This is apparent in the quality-of-life debates to which we now turn, despite the growing view that the concept should rest with the individual, their perspective and their values (Schalock *et al.*, 2002).

Quality-of-life measures

Certainly quality-of-life measurements are one of the most widely used in the evaluation of services for people with intellectual disability. The use of the term implies some kind of agreed understanding about definitions of quality of life and how this might be operationalised as an evaluation measure. Felce and Perry (1995; p60) define quality of life as:

an overall general well-being that comprises objective descriptors and subjective evaluations of physical, material, social and emotional well-being together with the extent of personal development and purposeful activity, all weighted by a personal set of values.

This definition indicates that, as a minimum, measures must take into account individual views of relative importance and that subjective measures must be taken alongside objective measures and *one used to inform the other*. A review of 13 measures by Cummins (1997) suggests that this uniformity of agreement is far from true.

Critiques of the use of these measures highlight differences in the espoused purpose of research. Ager (2002) proposes three potential purposes to such measures which expose the tautology between the concept and its application.

1. The scales are used as a measure of global service effectiveness – that is, a composite picture of the impact of the service on the users' quality of life, but at this level cannot easily reflect individual differences in the relative importance of different aspects of the service.
2. The measure is used as a means for comparing different services – a potential gold standard that will provide a measure of relative service efficiency.
3. The third purpose is a measure of individual service receivers' satisfaction that reflects their subjective experiences and values.

It is evident that these three purposes are not wholly compatible and critiques need to be seen within the context of different espoused purposes. It is worth looking in greater detail at some of the underlying tensions as they illustrate a number of issues for evaluation research in general as they question:

- the content of the measures
- how the measures are determined
- the methods used to collect the data
- the reliability, validity and accessibility of these methods for those with more significant learning disabilities.

Starting with issues of content, a key question for those researchers adopting this approach must be 'what are the indicators of quality and who determines these?' At one level this concerns the validity of the instruments used but at another it reflects the ideology, the purpose of the evaluation and the aims of the service. One approach to developing content has been to use a normative approach, thus creating measures that can be used by any segment of the population (assuming of course there are shared cultural values), and Cummins' (1997) review includes two examples of commercial packages. This consensual approach constrains either community or individual value systems from informing evaluations but meets the purpose of enabling comparisons between services.

The alternative approach to this is illustrated by research by Maes *et al.* (2000), who provide a rather different model where the criteria are developed jointly with reference to the aims and processes of the service provision. Their definition of quality lies in the discrepancy between the intended and actual care and support: thus the smaller the gap, the higher the quality. They are guided by a number of principles of inclusion: self-determination and empowerment; education and development; planned and methodological action; and a notion of support that makes reference both to duration and intensity and maintaining and developing social networks. They use a Delphi method and questionnaire to reach agreement on quality criteria. Additional focus groups are held with a number of clients. The resulting 13 criteria are described with reference to the care service. The use of principles to inform evaluation of services will be returned to later in the chapter.

Whilst some researchers focus their attentions on adopting criteria that are derived specifically from service users, others are starkly dubious about the usefulness of subjective measures of satisfaction. Again one returns to issues of validity. Do they truly elicit a person's opinion or do the responses reflect a general personality trait? Are they an artefact of being asked a question? What is their relationship to objective measures? A recent study by Hensell *et al.* (2002) supports the growing body of evidence that suggests that almost uniformly across groups satisfaction with aspects of life is generally high, governed by what the authors (and previously Cummins, 1997) refer to as a homeostatic mechanism that maintains an average and stable level. Satisfaction does not necessarily correlate with objective, independent measures; there is for example only a weak relationship with material well-being. Hensell *et al.* (as others) argue for taking into account *importance* as a 'mediating variable in understanding satisfaction'. One can only understand satisfaction by reference to what that individual views as important. In their own study, however, they failed to find a relationship between measures of satisfaction and rated importance. Hensell *et al.* (2002) also argue that response to these items reflect the person's own disposition rather than a response to life circumstances, and moreover these are typically high often in the face of poor living conditions. The usefulness of these measures is also questioned by Hatton and Ager (2002), who suggest that there is some evidence that attitudes are only constructed in the face of being asked to make an attitudinal response; i.e. 'quality of life is defined as what quality of life tools measure' (p258). They also raise questions about the distinctiveness of individual quality-of-life domains and about the utility of combining separate measures into a single construct.

Cummins (2002), in defence of subjective measures, suggests that they have strong and reliable correlations to other measures such as self-esteem, optimism and feelings of control and moreover that there is great predictability across studies as to what areas of life are important (relationships with family and friends) and what aren't, and that the ratings reflect this. He goes on to argue that one should not mock indicators that are highly predictable. He refers to those used in medicine such as temperature and blood pressure as very good indicators when all is not well. He also cites the difficulty of judging an aversive environment by any other means than first-hand accounts.

The last but arguably the most important issue is the degree to which such measures are effective in gaining the views of the total population. Hatton and Ager (2002), on the basis of results from the pre-test, argue that only the top 30 per cent of respondants are able to respond to more than three-quarters of the questions with sufficiently low levels of response bias. They contend that the majority of people with intellectual disabilities are unable to be interviewed in this way. This research is consistent with the findings of Perry and Felce (2002), who found the average scores of those who did not show evidence of response bias translate to a receptive language of more than 9 years. Cummins (1997) himself argues that it is important to use a Likert scale preferably using five points but not less than three if it is to reveal underlying variations between items. It is therefore perhaps unsurprising that researchers typically report that 'wherever possible' user views are collected, but experience a significant drop in the sample size at that point of data collection.

Typically the response of researchers is to collect the views of users by proxy. It is debatable about the meaningfulness of collecting subjective data not directly from the subject (Schalock *et al.*, 2002). There has also been considerable debate about the extent to which others do provide good indicators of satisfaction. As Hatton and Ager (2002) point out, studies with people with mild learning difficulties raise questions about the validity of responses from proxies because of the lack of agreement between them and their proxy on subjective measures. A study by Schwartz and Rabinovitz (2003) of verbal residents suggests that if it is necessary to use a third party, then parental views may be more accurate than those of staff. Staff in their study tended to give the highest ratings of satisfaction, thus adding to the body of literature questioning the usefulness of these measures. One of the issues it also raises is the method for selecting staff to give proxy views, few studies detailing the length of time that staff have worked with particular individuals. It should be noted that studies questioning the use of proxies typically make comparisons with verbal participants rather than look more closely for any bias in reporting the levels of satisfaction of those who are non-verbal.

There is a continuing concern about how the views of those with profound and multiple learning difficulties are gathered (Neilson *et al.*, 2000). Few studies set out with a commitment to develop innovative methods that will attempt to meet some of the difficulties, and Cambridge *et al.* (2002) are probably exceptional in this context, despite the growing body of literature describing alternative methods such as those of talking mats (Murphy and Cameron, 2002), sociometry (Male, 2002) together with means of validating communication (Grove *et al.*, 2000; Porter *et al.*, 2001). These are discussed more fully in Chapter 6.

Petry *et al.* (2001) argue that the prime issue is that there is no model for people with profound and multiple learning difficulties for the effects of care on quality of life; or, put another way, no model that will inform the selection of quality-of-life indicators. Petry *et al.* (2001) describe the setting up of a four-year European project designed to conceptualise and operationalise this concept, drawing on the literature to develop a theoretical model with three aspects: 'aspects of quality of care as a pre-requisite for good quality of life, dimensions and aspects of quality of life, and expressions of individual well-being' (p46).

Key informants will provide the content of these including parents, professional care-givers, teachers and therapists, and academics. One of the challenges of this task that can be envisaged is trying to capture the cultural nature of care that is usually firmly rooted in family dynamics. As a model, however, it could be used to create individual evaluation criteria thereby personalising the care received by the user.

The literature on quality of life has therefore raised vital issues within the field of evaluating services for people with intellectual disability about the nature of the criteria used, whether there should be broad notions of quality indicators, the extent to which it is feasible to elicit the views of all service users and how far indicators should be individualised in their application to reflect personal values and particular service aims.

Evaluation measures and education services

It is interesting to contrast these methodological debates with those within other services such as education. Here indicators generally are firmly tied to notions of outcome in the form of pupil progress and the processes that are seen to promote these which are rooted in research on school effectiveness. The issue for those working with pupils with learning difficulties is that standard measures provide a largely insensitive tool for measuring learning (Lewis *et al.*; 2003; Porter *et al.*, 2002). Research designed to evaluate special or inclusive schooling has largely looked at diverse single measures, often around issues of self-esteem, friendship, interaction loneliness and depression (Cunningham *et al.*, 1998; Heiman and Margalits 1998; Heiman, 2000a, 2000b; Kennedy *et al.*, 1997; Peetsma *et al.*, 2001; Wenz-Gross and Siperstein, 1997). There is more limited investigation of other aspects which include exam performance (Thomas, 1997a), language and memory development (Laws *et al.*, 2000), cognitive gains (Cunningham *et al.*, 1998; Mills *et al.*, 1998; Peetsma *et al.*, 2001; Pijl and Pijl, 1998) employment and access to further education and quality-of-life measures (Hornby and Kidd, 2001). A few studies have gained the views of stakeholders, parents, pupils and teachers (Jenkinson 1998; Palmer *et al.*, 2001; Norwich and Kelly, 2004; Allan and Brown, 2001) but few have achieved the complexities found in evaluation of other services where multiple variables and their interaction have been studied both in the short and longer term. There have been only limited attempts to evaluate services explicitly against the specific purposes of provision.

In the UK one of the main sources of educational evaluation is that carried out by the government agency for inspection, Ofsted. Clarke and Dawson (1999), drawing on the research of others, consider the extent to which Ofsted conforms of the following standards for evaluation:

- Utility: does it serve the needs of the intended users for useful practical information?

- Propriety: is it carried out ethically and fairly with concern for the welfare of all those involved?
- Feasibility: is it realistic, frugal, diplomatic and prudent?
- Accuracy: does it use valid and reliable methods?

Clarke and Dawson's review suggests that this main method of evaluating schools was found lacking in each respect. For example, to be useful it needs to be planned and carried out with the involvement of the stakeholders, and yet LEAs, one of the prime stakeholders, are notably excluded from involvement until after the inspection has taken place and all evaluation data has been collected. In this context of utility there can be a perceived lack of credibility, especially with respect to experience in special schools. Training for inspectors has been focused more on knowing the framework than on the process of evaluation. Further criticisms about utility arise from the size of the evidence base when conclusions are based on a snapshot of classroom practice. Given this criticism, inspections are less likely to be seen to be fair and the controversy surrounding their impact on the emotional well-being of staff raises issues about the extent to which they fulfil standards of propriety, or indeed those of accuracy: 'Much of what is judged by inspectors to be evidence of learning is, in fact, observation of the conditions for learning' (Clarke and Dawson, 1999, p171).

As the context for Clarke and Dawson's comments is undoubtedly research on mainstream provision, this raises further issues when making judgements about effective provision for pupils with learning difficulties. Where Ofsted evaluations best meet the standards is in the arena of feasibility; these concern 'due regard to practical, political, and economic concerns'. The development of the format of these inspections demonstrates the widespread concern of these issues (Ofsted, 2003).

There is a growing body of research and resulting policy guidance that integrates service development with evaluation. This takes as a starting point the principles of the service and then looks to audit provision against indicators that are directly referenced to those principles. In contrast to the approach used by some educational agencies where the ideology is cloaked, the philosophy that underpins provision is made overt. There are an increasing number of centrally driven evaluation measures that clearly articulate the principles that form the central focus to evaluations of quality. The Enhancing Quality of Life project concerns facilitating transitions for people with profound and complex learning difficulties and is an inter-agency project arising from concerns of the stakeholders, namely practitioners and parents about the quality of provision for young people with profound and multiple learning difficulties (Dee *et al.*, 2002). It translates five key quality-of-life principles: respect, choices, change, feelings and relationships into a set of indicators and exemplars. A similar approach can be seen to underpin research on the curriculum for students with learning difficulties aged 16–24, where principles were explored with service providers and service users across the range of settings (school, colleges, work-based trainers) to investigate their meaning and the ways in which they impact on practice (Dee *et al.*, 2003). Policy guidance provides explicit guidance for the development and evaluation of services built around principles of respect, self-determination, inclusion and fostering relationships. Principles were interpreted through a collaborative research process involving collecting the views of the varied stakeholders. These principles are described as providing a series of benchmarks that not only inform *what* to teach but *how* to teach and also provide an audit tool against which an organisation can evaluate its provision (see http://www.qca.org.uk/ca/inclusion/p16_ld/index.asp).

Cost analysis in evaluation research

One of the directions that evaluation studies have taken is to make comparisons between forms of provision against the indices of cost. At one level this approach has the capability to inform policy in a way that is markedly absent from research on educational provision, which is still largely ideologically driven. At the same time such scientific approaches can mask the essentially political nature of the task, and owe much to notions of 'best value' that underpin the purchasing of services (Cambridge, 2000).

There are a number of different forms of analysis that can be carried out, with distinctions made between cost–benefit, cost effectiveness and cost utility. Robson (2002, p214) defines these:

> Cost-benefit analysis attempts to compare the costs (the various inputs to a programme, such as staff, facilities, equipment etc) with the benefits accruing, with both measured in monetary terms … If the benefit to costs ratio exceeds one, this provides support for continuation or expansion of the programme.

Cost–benefit analysis depends on accurate measurement of all attendant costs as well as the identification of all the benefits. 'Cost-effectiveness analysis is similar, but here the benefits are expressed in non-monetary terms' (Robson, 2002, p214).

Essentially this can be seen as an analysis of how much it costs to produce this outcome and it has been suggested that it is only used when there are clearly identifiable and measurable outcomes (Clarke and Dawson, 1999).

Cost utility can be described in relation to the decision-making about the costs against the relative benefits of different services. As Ager (2002) points out, the analysis seeks to inform decisions about how limited resources can be allocated.

Despite the hugely sensitive nature of these debates, evaluation studies can provide important information on the interactional effect of different variables on the satisfaction of the service user. Emerson *et al.* (2000) provide a detailed analysis on the quality and costs of residential supports, comparing village communities, community-based provision and residential campuses, taking 30

62

people at random from each of the identified services. The study illustrates the use of objective and subjective measures that go beyond simple quality-of-life measures and involves all stakeholders in the process. They used questionnaires to organisers, care staff and relatives, ratings by researchers on site visits, non-participant observations and interviews with care staff and users. Comparison costs took into account differences in provision in relation to service user age, ability and level of challenging behaviour by providing an adjusted cost and through the use of matched sub-samples. The collection of data on multiple variables with a large population enabled them to look at what variables were related to higher levels of user satisfaction. These include increased day activities where there are more scheduled activities for more hours on more days of the week, spending less time in adult day centres; where there are more people with learning difficulties in their social network and fewer mental health problems; where senior members of staff had a nursing qualification. In this way the study suggests the characteristics of provision that are associated with higher levels of user satisfaction as well of course as the relative costs of provision. While this may in the short term have limited impact on national policy (Mansell, 2000) it does have implications at a local level, not least in focusing attention on the failure of all forms of residential provision to adequately provide quality in relation to employment opportunities, choice of co-residents and staff, social networks and physical health.

These large-scale studies have also provided longitudinal data. Cambridge *et al.* (2002) describe a comprehensive study examining the outcomes and costs for a large cohort of people with learning difficulties who left long-stay provision 12 years ago. In addition to the view of service users, collected through the use of focus groups, they investigated skills and behaviour, social networks together with costs of community care, care management, taking into account capital, staffing, costs of accommodation, day centres and other activities, and cost of community-based professionals including GPs. Interestingly, although the service users were described as being moderately satisfied this was less so than when previously interviewed. Costs of service had also decreased over time and users had little involvement in decisions on resource allocation.

Calculation of costs is, as we have indicated, a complex issue if it is to provide a near-accurate picture. A small-scale study by Shearn *et al.* (2000) looked at the cost effectiveness of supported employment compared to day centre support for those described as having severe intellectual disability and high support needs. The study illustrates the difficulty of small-scale research drawing on a limited sample to make an analysis of cost effectiveness (as opposed to cost benefit). They therefore had to have both a cross-group comparison where not all variables of age, gender and level of challenging behaviour could be perfectly matched, and a within-subject comparison. Items that were factored into the analysis included income from employment, day service staff wages and on-costs, managerial and administrative staff wages and on-costs, transport to and from the day centre, transport and travel expenses during the day, service users' wage and clothing allowances, training, insurance and equipment, consumables and building rental. In addition to observations of activities sampling personal development, arts and crafts, sport and other, they kept a record of staff-to-service user ratios and staff identities, enabling them to calculate staffing costs accordingly and hourly costs for infrastructure. Interestingly the study found social interaction and contact lower in employment than in the day centre, making the former more cost effective. If, on the other hand, one takes engagement in activity as a measure, no difference in cost effectiveness ratios was found between support settings.

We turn now from cost effectiveness studies to an example of a cost–benefit study. Neilson *et al.* (2000), in their evaluation of the impact of orthotic and surgical intervention on the quality-of-life, use among other measures a time trade-off measure – one that is more widely used in the general population to indicate 'how many years of life with the condition would be exchanged for remaining years in full health'. They examine the relative cost benefits of different medical or healthcare interventions in terms of the subjective gain to the individual. The implication is that a shorter, healthier life is better than a longer, unhealthy one – dangerous ground for people with a chronic condition. The measure was included as part of a questionnaire on quality of life. Additionally objective measures of functional improvement were also gathered. The study provided data that could be used to calculate cost-utility ratios, to make decisions about the allocation of scarce resources to particular healthcare activities.

Evaluation studies such as these shed a window of light on how rhetoric or ideology is evidenced in practice, how twin measures of quality and economics are increasingly used in the field of learning difficulties. Given the scale of activity and its own relative cost it raises important issues about the value of the activity to the individual service provider, how research impacts on the lives of the researched. Quality of life as a concept can be used to make decisions about life and death and the specific allocation of resources including medical treatments (Lefort and Fraser, 2002). It can too easily be equated with the value of life.

Wider views of evaluation

Strong calls have been made for evaluation of services to look at the lived experience of people with learning difficulties. Dahlberg *et al.* (2000) suggest that rather than seeking new criteria or quality indicators, we should be looking to understand and construct meanings concerning the different ways in which the services are understood. The multiple realities within that process of discourse and interaction, the participants as well as researchers are encouraged to become reflective and thereby evaluative in their judgement making. They ask the question, 'Can quality be reconceptualised to accommodate diversity, subjectivity, multiple perspectives and temporal and spatial context?' and argue that it cannot. Instead the evaluation should be about 'constructing and deepening meaning' about actual human experiences and not about abstract notions of quality. Such research however does not make easy reading for service providers, as evidenced by the title of a paper by Goble (1999): 'Like the secret service isn't it' reporting on participants' perceptions of staff and the implied purpose of provision.

Reinders (2002) indirectly contributes to the debate on meaning by contending that the nature of community living is about the 'experience of sharing one's life with people' rather than about location. As he asks, 'do we also include them in our lives as human beings?' We need, he maintains, to see people with learning difficulties as individuals, refer to them by name and include them in our informal relationships: 'we should expect them to *want us* not only as bearers of institutional roles, but as friends and companions who have *chosen them* to be part of their lives.' (p4/7). He emphasises the importance of being able to share experiences and be appreciated by others not because it is expected but as a matter of choice. He calls for a 'moral culture' in which to 'flourish'. This firmly moves the debate away from material concerns and tangible outcomes to focusing on the processes and interactions between people.

Research that focuses on the experiences of people with learning difficulties places particular emphasis on their relationships with others and also the ways in which these in turn impact on their lives and aspirations. Typically the methodology of this research has been dialectical and yet where a significant proportion of the population are known to have restricted use of language this may not always provide the best sole medium through which to fully understand these relationships. The collection of qualitative data through observations was notably missing in our review of the literature and of course runs contrary to a form of analysis based on cost effectiveness where the emphasis lies on measurable outcomes. Research which seeks to evaluate individual services against their espoused ethos or aims or indeed, as we have seen, their stated principles must also look closely at the systems and structures which support these principles. One of the challenges for researchers is to achieve this where the usual medium of dialogue provides a narrow window through which to view the world.

Conclusion

In our introduction we suggested that evaluation researchers would benefit from looking at multiple measures and the interaction between these and that these measures should be constructed to take into account the views of stakeholders. This approach is notably lacking in educational research with people with learning difficulties where, in parallel to the mainstream, single outcome measures have dominated. This has however been evidenced in research in other forms of service provision. Examples of the larger scale studies include that of Emerson *et al.* (2000) while smaller studies include those of Shearn *et al* (2000).

We have also made a case for looking at the processes as well as the systems and structures that support a change process. The development of measures that are based on generalised principles of provision are closest to this. We have noted these in both educational and non-educational settings (Maes *et al.*, 2000; Dee *et al.*, 2002, 2003) where clearly articulated principles have formed the starting point for evaluating provision. If we look at the type of principles that are commonly stated it becomes clear that the focus lies less with the outcome of provision and more with the evaluation of the practices and processes. This is most apparent in the work of Maes *et al.* (2000), where in addition to self-determination and empowerment; education and development; and maintaining and developing social networks, they cite the processes of planned and methodological action and support that makes reference both to duration and intensity against which to evaluate provision. This strategy is highly consistent with an individualised approach to service delivery and an approach within education that strives to move provision away from notions of delivering a specified curriculum or programme with predetermined outcomes to a learner-centred approach that plans provision in relation to individual aspirations. It could be argued, however, that there is a danger in completely divorcing processes from outcomes in the evaluation of provision.

Pawson and Tilley (1997) and others suggest that evaluation needs to be conceptualised within a causal model that is the starting point for explaining and investigating how that process works and account for what works for whom and in what context or circumstances. This shifts evaluation from having an essentially summative focus to play a more formative role in the development of services. More fundamentally it calls on evaluators to have a model of causation that will enable them to track the mechanisms that bring these developments about. Arguably such a model should be underpinned by an ethos of empowerment if evaluation is to bring about real change in the lives of people with learning difficulty.

In the next chapter we look at evaluation in a different context, that of promoting the development of instructional practices which characteristically has been theoretically driven.

CHAPTER 5
Researching intervention

Our review of trends in research suggested that while there had been a slight growth in the *proportion* of the research literature related to the development and use of instructional methods, in real terms the number of articles published is falling. Of concern to potential researchers must be how to develop robust systems for evaluating different approaches to instruction and teaching. Given the individualised nature of much instruction, with different targets set and often the use of tailor-made resources, it is perhaps unsurprising that much current research is small scale. Characteristically, evaluation of instruction has focused on measuring outcomes, notably through adopting a quasi-experimental approach. In this chapter we will take an historical view of these approaches and the limitations they pose for use in real-life settings. In Chapter 4 we suggested that evaluation needed to move away from simply considering single or even multiple outcome measures towards looking at the process by which change occurred. One of the essential questions must concern the teacher/staff behaviours which promote new learning. As we noted previously, stakeholder views make an important contribution to understanding the process, and wherever possible this must include the learners themselves.

A key element must be to design the evaluation in a way that is directly informed by the theoretical account which underpins the learning process. As we shall see, intervention approaches draw on a range of different theoretical models and explanations including those based on information-processing approaches to intervention, behavioural and cognitive behavioural accounts, mother–child interaction developmental accounts and social constructionist explanation of the learning process, to name a few. Of necessity therefore the focus and nature of the evaluation research are likely to present rather differently, but we will argue that they should match the theory of change which underpins the account of learning. In this chapter we will look at a range of different intervention processes and the ways in which they have been evaluated, not with a view to identifying what works and what doesn't work, or indeed as we have previously argued, how they are effective; instead the premise of this chapter is that staff need a repertoire of teaching approaches on which to draw (Norwich and Lewis, 2000; Heward, 2003). We start by looking at traditional approaches to evaluating methodology.

Experimental and quasi-experimental designs

Traditional approaches to the evaluation of instruction have adopted experimental or quasi-experimental designs. True experimental designs are based on the random allocation of participants to either a control or to an experimental group with the assumption that the two groups do not differ on average from one another prior to the intervention and that any subsequent differences are a direct result of their treatment (see Table 5.1.).

Gersten *et al.* (2000), with reference to special education, make a distinction between random allocation and random selection. They state the importance of matching individuals *before* they are randomly assigned, thus ensuring their equivalence, or alternatively of stratifying samples on salient variables and then randomly assigning. The classic method is to measure both groups before and after the intervention period, drawing a conclusion that the difference in scores post test rest with the effect of the intervention (see Table 5.2.). (In weaker studies only post-test measures are collected.)

Although this is usually hailed as the gold standard of designs it is not without problems. Typically ethical issues are cited as the major issue for personnel who are uncomfortable at withholding treatment despite the fact that it has, prior to the research study, unproven benefit. Clarke and Dawson (1999) list other issues including the effects of attrition as participants may not be lost equitably from the study, with more from one group than another leaving, thus threatening the representativeness of the sample. A less likely possibility, given the group of learners and time-scale of most evaluation studies, is that maturation could threaten the internal validity of the study, with changes resulting from natural development rather than from intervention. There is also an assumption that learners will not be affected by the knowledge of inequitable

Table 5.1 Designs in experimental research

Group designs
Experimental design – incorporates a control group and learners are randomly allocated to intervention and non-intervention groups

Quasi-experimental designs occur where there is no random allocation of participants to an intervention group but a comparison or matched group may be identified

Single subject
Repeated measures design, participants serve as their own control, researchers often comparing responses during intervention to responses before and after intervention

Table 5.2 Group design in experimental research

Experimental	Pretest	Intervention	Post test
Control	Pretest		Post test

treatment. Staff may try to compensate the control group in some manner or distribute resources in a way that reduces differences in the treatment of groups. Equally the participants themselves may respond to their difference in status perhaps with rivalry or demoralisation.

Given the heterogeneity of the population and the difficulty of accessing large numbers of participants (Schindele, 1985), a more frequent approach in learning difficulties is to use quasi-experimental designs. Indeed our review suggested that this was the most likely form of design currently used for evaluating instructional methods. A number of alternative approaches within quasi-experimental design can be identified and these differ in the extent to which they can be regarded as providing robust data. Rather than random allocation of participants, one alternative is to have a control or comparative group who are matched in some way to the intervention group. These may be matched individually or as a group aggregate on key variables, thus producing groups comprised either of matched pairs or equivalent on the overall distribution of a number of relevant variables. Among of the central issues for researchers are identifying the variables for matching individuals (see Chapter 3), what reliability can be placed in global measures of mental age or IQ or whether sub-scales relevant to the intervention should be chosen. Gersten *et al.* (2000) highlight the problem of quasi-experimental designs where the match is made after assignment to a group and where the range of scores within a group is large. This is a particular problem for many groups with learning difficultties where individuals may well have widely differing scores on key variables.

An alternative design is to compare the experimental group with generic controls who provide a benchmark against which to view attainment. This again is problematic in the area of learning difficulties, for while theoretically such measures as 'performance indicator' scales could be used (QCA/DfEE, 2001) for children, the benchmark needs to be sensitive enough to register change. Two further quasi-experimental group designs can be identified: those which use a pre- and post-test with a single sample and those in which observations are only made following the intervention (a one-shot case study). Clearly the data from these last two are relatively unconvincing in demonstrating that change is a direct result of the impact of an intervention and may best be described as descriptive or exploratory research rather than evaluative. Robson (2002) provides a useful summary of the constraints of different types of experimental design. Here we focus on issues particular to research in the field of learning difficulties.

Our analysis of current research suggested that the majority of studies were small-scale or single case studies with no control group. This methodology reflects in part the smaller numbers of learners and their heterogeneity but also the importance in special education of individualising the way in which children receive instruction. One of the difficulties, however, is the threat to external validity. Small samples need ideally to represent the range of the entire population that they are drawn from. Instead it is more likely that their inclusion in the study is accidental or convenient or that the target population is

Table 5.3 Single subject designs

ABABA	ABACACABA
Baseline	Baseline
Intervention	Intervention1
Baseline	Baseline
Intervention	Intervention 2
Baseline	Baseline
	Intervention 2
	Baseline
	Intervention 1
	Baseline

unspecified (Robson, 1985). Samples also have to act as their own control group, with traditional studies following a design of baseline, intervention, baseline, intervention referred to as ABAB designs, or ABACACABA type where A is baseline and B and C two forms of intervention (Table 5.3).

Kiernan (1985) discusses the range of profiles of baselines with a recommended minimum of three readings for each baseline based on sessions equivalent in length and timing to the intervention. One of the difficulties in the field of learning difficulties occurs where these readings produce an unstable profile with considerable variation between measures, thus requiring a greater magnitude of effect from the intervention. Indeed, Kiernan argues that a very unstable baseline suggests the need for a functional analysis to determine the factors occurring in the baseline condition. The use of a return to baseline position can be problematic for many intervention studies. The designs reflect the behavioural orientation of much of the literature. Other theoretical accounts do not necessarily assume that if you withdraw the intervention, the response of the student will return to its original position. A commonly used approach is a multiple or staggered baseline where the intervention is introduced in a staggered way across learners to demonstrate that change is due to the intervention rather than to other factors occurring in the classroom.

Already we can see that experimental and quasi-experimental design causes particular difficulties for research concerning populations which have a low incidence and are characterised by diversity on a number of key aspects that are pertinent to research on learning. So far we have raised issues concerning:

- establishing an equivalent control group
- matching on key variables with standard deviations for the group of less than 0.5
- ethical issues of withholding intervention without compensatory responses from staff
- unstable profiles of performance, including baseline measures.

Additionally it has been noted that some designs assume that a return to baseline leads to a cessation of previous responses displayed during intervention if indeed the instruction has been effective. These assumptions are incompatible with many models of learning and therefore unsuitable for evaluating instructional methods underpinned by non-behavioural theories. Even here it might be argued that their use interferes with the learning process.

Good practice in the use of quasi-experimental designs

Gersten *et al.* (2000) put forward a number of recommendations to improve the quality of research on intervention and recognise some of the delicate balances that have to be weighed in the decision-making of research conducted in the real world. The authors argue for the use of 'design experiments' for new and developing interventions which will be considered separately later in this chapter. They also recognise the importance of experimental and (with a number of reservations) quasi-experimental studies that use group sizes larger than 20. They recognise the problematic nature of this, the:

> extraordinary challenge of identifying populations that are sufficiently homogeneous to constitute a group and yet large enough to provide adequate power for group comparisons ... rarely will sample sizes of 12 to 15 be adequate unless the anticipated effects are extraordinarily strong ... minimally different treatments require larger sample sizes to uncover effective interventions. (Gersten *et al.*, 2000, p9)

If one increases the homogeneity of the group, there is a risk of reducing the extent to which findings are generalisable. Given these issues it is important that full information is provided on the sample, including descriptions of age, gender, race or ethnicity, level of English Language, socio-economic status, achievement levels on standardised tests and intellectual status with a more thorough description where studies have fewer than ten participants.

Gersten *et al.* (2000) suggest more explicit attention and provision of detail on the sample and also with respect to the instructional strategies. They cite the importance of making clear to the reader how the instructional methods will actually operate and confirm that they are indeed special. Researchers therefore need to make a valid assessment of their implementation and provide information about the nature and extent of training people receive, the length of lessons and a check that aspects of the intervention are in fact being implemented and how often. They recommend the use of 'fidelity checklists' for cruder aspects and qualitative observations for more subtle details. They argue that a minimum level is to check for fidelity at three points: at the beginning, a few weeks later to verify the occurrence of any suggested corrections and then mid to late intervention to ensure there has been no slippage. These authors also make a case for making checks in control classrooms in order to draw accurate conclusions about the exact nature of the special properties of the intervention. They recognise the danger of conflating the effects of the intervention with characteristics of the teacher. These are not automatically removed by using the same teacher across different conditions as there can be the confounding variable of teacher enthusiasm.

Their recommendations include careful analysis of the transcripts of lessons to understand which factors contribute to which outcomes and to ensure that the results are not purely due to a generic factor such as use and type of feedback and praise (unless this is the instructional device). The authors also suggest a calculation of correlations between pre- and post-test condition so that researchers can start to identify which student characteristics are most likely to predict success on a given intervention. They argue for the use of general and specific measures on pre and post tests i.e., multiple measures, and to include ones that have documented reliability and validity. They remind the reader that the shorter the study, the easier it is to be clear about attributing causation to changes in pupil performance, but that we need to know that the results will be maintained over time.

Gersten *et al.* (2000) highlight the way in which even researchers adopting conventional approaches to evaluation are recognising the need for supportive analysis of the process of the intervention. Although the authors recognise that this type of research, despite its complexity, is more likely to be collaborative it is still essentially summative in the type of data produced. This creates a number of tensions in producing data that is rooted in the real world of the classroom and yet conforms to checks of internal and external validity.

Using qualitative approaches

Increasingly researchers are looking to other methodologies which will support a more developmental approach to instructional design. Qualitative research designs based on interpretative or social constructivist approaches to research are still relatively infrequently published on instructional or intervention methods in the field of learning difficulties. In part this may well reflect the greater reliance on interview data that is characteristic of these approaches, and which often constrains their use with less articulate participants. Projects of this kind do not of course strive in quite the same way as experimental and quasi-experimental studies do to establish a causal relationship between intervention and outcome. They are however more likely to explore the relationship to gain an understanding of the ways in which teacher behaviour impacts on the learner and vice versa. Often they do this through establishing the meaning of that context for each of the participants. The focus is therefore as likely to be on the subjective experience and the interactions that take place. These of course may well be of interest to those adopting other positivist approaches to research but there the interest is on coding and quantifying rather than a more iterative analysis of the qualitative data for identifying emerging themes. Ferguson and Ferguson (2000) raise the question of the extent to which guidelines for good practice in qualitative research should strive to produce a set of definitive standards that guide editors to do more than simply apply the kind of criteria that are used to judge quantitative research in selecting manuscripts for publication. Drawing on this and other generalist writers, we can remind ourselves of some of the characteristics that shape the design of this research.

Good practice in the use of qualitative designs

While there is much consensus about good practice in experimental and quasi-experimental designs, those which set out more flexibly to collect qualitative data draw on varied traditions or in some cases across traditions. Robson (2002) compares three traditions – grounded theory, ethnography and case study – but also provides a list of general characteristics of what is viewed as good design. These include the importance of using a rigorous approach to data collection where the methods used are transparent, even though there may be an element of evolution. Multiple data collection methods are typically used. Ferguson and Ferguson (2000) suggest these to be observation, interview and document analysis. The data are collected and noted in detail in a systematic way, and analysed at different levels of abstraction. Thus themes are derived and combined to a meta-level of conceptualisation. Theory plays an important role, whether it is used to generate research questions or whether it emerges from the data, or indeed if there is an iterative relationship throughout the process of data collection and analysis. Checking and re-checking of interpretations against the data is an important aspect of the process with attention given to contradictory evidence. Ferguson and Ferguson highlight the way in which the researcher is clear to participants about the focus and process of the study, data is collected over a long time in the field, using different methods – document analysis, observation, interview, and through talking with participants about what the researcher is learning so that contradictory information can be provided. This approach results in thick descriptions, peer debriefing, and triangulation. Relationships with the participants form an important element of the design.

The following sections look at how these and other methodologies have been applied to research in classrooms before we look at new and developing technologies.

Instructional strategies

The literature on the use of instructional approaches in the field of learning difficulties continues to be divided. As we have noted, a number of different theoretical influences are apparent in the general literature and are linked to the way in which people have sought to understand the nature of learning and of learning difficulties. For example, Piagetian approaches have influenced the way we understand the functioning of people with the most profound learning difficulties through providing a developmental context and emphasing the importance of readiness and the development of the senses. Information-processing models of learning have influenced instructional approaches to developing methods to improve attention and memory; behavioural methods have been drawn on most specifically to provide a framework for intervening in challenging behaviour but also to provide a structured framework for teaching functional skills. Distinctions can also be made between approaches on the degree to which they influence control over pupils' interactions with the environment with a continuum posited by some researchers (Wolery and Schuster, 1997; Faupel, 1986). For the purposes of looking at the way in which intervention strategies can be evaluated, we have chosen to look selectively at interventions that focus on communication and interaction, an area of particular difficulty for many individuals with learning difficulties.

Reichle (1997), in a review of communication strategies, provides a useful overview that serves to contextualise the studies chosen here. He draws attention to the differences between individuals who have limited interest in social exchanges (possibly because they are not alert to others, see social contact as aversive or have no expectations of the value of contact) and those who have a limited repertoire of behaviours, including those described as challenging, but who use those behaviours for a range of communicative purposes. Both groups of individuals highlight the importance for interventionalists of not only teaching behaviours that promote ongoing communication but also of teaching a range of functions, those that are described as *protoimperative* – behaviours that access events, objects or services – and *protodeclarative* – behaviours that access attention and interaction. Firstly we examine a paper that is designed to teach a request function that can be viewed as being at one end of the continuum of structure; that is, it is designed to produce a specific behaviour. Then we turn to evaluation of an approach designed to encourage pupil engagement with their social environment without a precise specification of what those behaviours might be.

Structured approaches

Behavioural approaches are typically characterised as controlled, structured approaches that involve the manipulation of antecedent events and setting conditions and/or consequences to change behaviour. Important developments and refinements in approaches have led to the refinement of intervention strategies that while still predetermined, more closely mirror naturalistic contexts for teaching. Three particular procedures have been extensively researched that are used in combination in natural opportunities and routines to promote communication. These are mand-model, time delay, incidental teaching, and now the latest addition, behaviour chain interruption strategy (Carter and Grunsell, 2001). The essential features include the use of routines or established chains of behaviour during which an interruption occurs, often blocking the next response in the chain, a pause of several seconds before prompting by presenting a model of a communicative act – most usually a request. Presentations of prompts are increasingly delayed. The underlying explanations for this approach are varied. Carter and Grunsell (2001) review them and propose that the interruption provides a temporary removal of the reinforcement that the next action brings, thereby enhancing its value and providing the motivation to communicate. The use of a literature review to evaluate a method has considerable advantages over the use of a single study, as we will see. The description of a recent study will illustrate the use of this latest technique and our critique will illustrate some of the difficulties researchers face.

Grunsell and Carter (2002) describe the aim of the study to investigate the maintenance of requesting skills taught through the use of a behaviour chain interruption strategy (BCIS) and the generalisation to out-of-routine contexts. Four students ages 7–8 years described as having moderate to severe disabilities participated in the study. Brief details are provided about their disabilities, e.g. autistic behaviours, attention deficit hyperactivity and some description of their communicative behaviours, and other skills. The level of information largely meets the suggestions made by Gersten *et al.* (2000) as although standardised test information is not included (the authors note that none of the students scored on psychometric tests) they provide individual sub-scale scores on the Adaptive Behaviour Inventory. Routines were selected that occurred daily, had three or more steps (the considered minimum), and individuals were able to perform at least some of these independently. Symbols were selected through which students would make a response by touching them. The design was a multiple baseline across subjects taken using three measures (according to Kiernan, 1985, the minimum) during one activity, music, the targeted session for routines. Interruption occurred at the point at which the child would receive an instrument, in order to elicit a request by the child touching the symbol of the desired object. An increasing time delay for prompts was introduced so that on the first day after a three-second delay the child was prompted to touch a symbol of their known preferred instrument, on day two a five-second delay and additional ten-second delays for each subsequent day. Intervention stopped when the child reached the target performance on three consecutive days. When this had been achieved a generalisation phase was introduced with interruptions introduced to two other classroom routines prior to moving on to a maintenance and out-of-context generalisation phase. Maintenance probes were carried out, initially daily, and then at weekly intervals for 18 weeks across settings.

In design terms the study met many of the concerns of the original review that studies had failed to look at generalisation both to other routine situations and also out-of-routine contexts. One of the difficulties for the authors, however, is in establishing that the presence of symbols in the classroom did not in itself constitute a prompt. Can we have confidence in the validity of the study? The authors have used a staggered baseline and systematic probes to evidence responses. Fidelity checks were made of over a third of sessions to check for procedural reliability, which confirmed 100 per cent adherence. Inter-observer agreement checks were also made of all discrete trails achieving 100 per cent on all measures, which the authors ascribe to the extensive training provided and the very overt nature of the children's responses.

Such studies lend themselves reasonably well to quasi-experimental designs. The structured systematic nature of the intervention coupled with the explicit behavioural outcomes required of the child make for the collection of comparable data. Evaluative reviews which look across studies can help to compensate for the small-scale nature of much work. In this way we can learn about the diversity of individuals for whom such approaches have been used, together with the varied contexts in which research has been carried out. However, the studies don't substantially serve to illuminate the process or indeed inform the reader of the importance of different elements of the process. If we turn to look at the literature on less structured intervention methods, illustrated here by reference to interactive approaches, we can see that researchers face a number of difficulties but such methods do serve to investigate more explicitly the ways in which teacher and student behaviours lead to learning.

Interactive approaches

The 1980s saw an upsweep of interest in interactive approaches (Smith, 1988): a broad collection of approaches where the focus lay with the process rather than product of learning. In part cognitive approaches to learning underpinned the thinking, drawing on developmental psychology to inform the selection of learning activities that were linked to the child's mental representations of the world (Smith, 1990). Unlike behavioural approaches these approaches don't strive to produce a definitive system to follow as this is characteristically teacher dominated, and one of the hallmarks of interactive approaches is that the teacher follows the child's lead (McConkey, 1988) and strives to create contexts for learning that are meaningful for the child. Some of the tensions that arise in evaluating less prescriptive methodologies are evident when one considers research on interactive approaches (Hogg, 2002). In this section we examine the evaluation methods employed by researchers to investigate the effectiveness of these approaches, firstly as they have been developed for learners with profound and multiple disabilities and then for those with more moderate learning difficulties.

Intensive interaction

Intensive interaction is a term used to described an approach to teaching that is:

> characterised by regular, frequent interactions between the practitioner ... and individual with learning disabilities, in which there is no task or outcome focus, but in which the primary concern is the quality of the interaction itself. (Hewett and Nind, 1998, p2)

This method developed in part as a reaction from those concerned with what they saw as a reductionist view of learning by those using structured prescriptive teaching approaches. It is an approach to working with children and adults based on care-giver interaction which focuses on developing social and communicative development in those individuals who are pre-verbal (Nind and Hewitt 1994; Hewett and Nind, 1998). A number of core features can be identified, with the adult following the lead of the child, 'joining in with, imitating and weaving interactive games around their ... behaviours', introducing other alternative behaviours in a playful burst–pause pattern, imitating the behaviour of care-givers with young infants. Immediately we can anticipate some of the difficulties of evaluating an approach that is not targeted at producing fixed behaviours to a systematic presentation of adult behaviours. Here not only are adult responses dependent on the learner but the nature of those responses rests with the creativity of the adult. This does of course also raise interesting questions about the implications of basing an approach on mothers and neurologically unimpaired children to working with professional practitioners and children and adults who will be taking in and processing information rather differently (Hogg, 2002).

Nind (1996) and Nind and Kellett (2002) describe the evaluation design as 'quasi-experimental [using] ... a multiple-baseline interrupted time series', collecting video recordings over a 12–18 month period, taking 5 minute samples in both interactive and everyday sessions. The central features are described as

- mutual pleasure and interactive games
- change in teacher behaviours to 'become engaging and meaningful'
- teacher aiming for optimum level of attention through careful adjustments in pace, pauses, repetition and rhythms
- responding to behaviours as if they were intentionally communicative
- following the lead of the learner and responding contingently.

Nind's (1996) research reports six cases on which she used staggered multiple baseline using an interrupted time series design typically used in dyadic interaction (Bakeman and Gottman, 1997). This enables a mathematical model to be constructed of the cycles of activity and thereby to identify significant patterns of interaction. While the learners serve as their own controls, as in Grunsell and Carter's study, the design promotes an understanding of the process of change in that interactional data is collected. Rather than gathering and reporting teacher behaviour, the studies by Nind *et al.* required the collection of data that demonstrates the relationship between the acts. There is, however, a gap when it comes to reporting the data; for while graph data is presented to the reader, the results of the data analysis including descriptive statistics, the detail of the trend analysis is not presented to the reader. This study reflects the tension for researchers in adopting methodologies that are typically used to provide summative data on outcomes rather than to provide an analysis of the process. We therefore learn the outcomes, that all the subjects made advances on the scales for communication and sociability, but with 'great variation in the magnitude of the new developments' (p61). We don't learn from the interactive data how this new learning emerged.

If we look not just at this but other studies, a number of issues for researchers can be identified. The first of these concerns the extent to which specific intervention behaviours can be identified and isolated. For example, Nind (1996, p62) comments that the 'nebulous nature of the teaching approach under investigation were not sufficient to ensure a clear-cut start of intervention'. Watson and Fisher (1997, p87) note in their two studies that 'interactive styles varied greatly and were unique to each pupil'. Given this, we highlight the importance, if quasi-experimental designs are to be used, of baseline measures being subject to the checks raised by Gersten *et al.* (2000) to ascertain in what is essentially the control situation the extent to which it contained elements of intensive interaction. There also appears to be uncertainty about the extent to which new behaviours are evident in other settings. Elgie and Maquire (2001) looked at the ten-minute period immediately following intensive interaction. Watson and Fisher (1997) imply that there will be no impact on other settings as their evaluation was based on comparing responses to specific intensive interaction sessions to those made in a music lesson with a contrasting teacher-directed approach.

Studies have also varied, perhaps unsurprisingly, as to what behavioural measures are collected, and the place of standardised assessment in this. Elgie and Macquire (2001), for example, look at hand movements, vocalisations as well as self-injurious behaviour; Watson and Fisher (1997) provide detailed qualitative descriptions; Kellett (2000) identifies key behaviours as attending to facial gaze, social physical contact, joint focus or activity, eye contact, contingent vocalisations, engaged social interactions. While Kellett's study moves to greater specificity, it is unclear the extent to which these might be distinct behaviours or about the underlying hierarchy.

Elsewhere the authors of these studies discuss the ethical dilemmas of asking teachers to adopt practices that are consistent with this methodology (Kellett and Nind, 2001). Teachers, having been taught an approach and having used it to good effect with one child, are frustrated by having to withhold it for subsequent children for the duration of their staggered baselines. Moreover, the authors note the confusion for the child when adults are intensively responsive to them one moment and passive at another. As they note, 'the potential distress to pupils was too high a price to pay ...' (p54). It is worth noting in this context that it is a method that has been specifically introduced for those individuals described by Elgie and Maguire (2001) as 'effectively cut off from the world' and for whom other approaches have proved unsuccessful.

Although Samuel (2001) argues that it is appropriate to use quasi-experimental designs (providing they are validated in a wide variety of settings and with comparison to other methods), these issues present a strong argument that this design places inappropriate constraints and expectations on the approach for the purposes of evaluation. Indeed, as others have argued, perhaps what is required is a move away from conventional approaches to evaluation (Hogg, 2002).

We turn now to take a look at a study with a very different type of design, one that was aimed at examining the relationship between teacher and pupil behaviour and which espoused the measurement of behavioural indicators of learning.

Interaction and reflection

One of the key elements in interactive approaches is dialogue. Watson (1996) identifies a teaching style that promotes reflection in pupils with moderate learning difficulties based on research in classrooms. Few studies cited so far have adopted a predominantly qualitative approach to the collection of data. This study also reflects the way in which evaluative research can be used to elucidate a process rather than to verify one. The theoretical underpinning to this work draws in part on meta-cognitive theories of learning and also on social constructivist approaches. Thus it draws on research that suggests that children with learning difficulties fail to use cognitive strategies that aid learning (for example, they may not use rehearsal strategies to aid memory) and research that suggests that learning occurs in a setting where it is mediated through interaction with one who is more expert. This qualitative research is based on observations made in four classes for 10–11 year olds in four special schools, with the teacher selecting two target children in each class as being fairly clear speakers and without behavioural difficulties. Teachers are told that the researchers are interested in children's thinking and wanted to observe normal classroom practices. Interesting ethical issues are raised by studies of this kind because ultimately teachers will be compared with one another, thereby raising questions about the nature of informed consent.

Fifty hours of classroom data were recorded across the variety of curricular experiences, using radio-microphones and making a running observational record. The first classroom recording was not included in the detailed analysis as it was viewed as part of the familiarisation process. The strength of this combined use of methods is demonstrated as it enables the researchers to be sure when children are in fact talking to themselves but also includes access to non-verbal responses such as sighs. In keeping with the research paradigm, the meanings of the activities were sought from the researched. Teachers were interviewed about their plans for that session and their expectations for the target pupils and as a follow-up to ask how they felt it had gone. Target pupils were also informally interviewed after each session about what they had been doing, what were the difficult and easy things, what they liked and disliked. The researchers returned one year after the data collection to talk with the teachers about their long-standing beliefs of how children learn.

A grounded theory approach was taken to the data analysis, looking for patterns in the teachers' interaction based around identified episodes. These events were ones in which the pupil was intellectually challenged and showed reflective talk – in reasoning, expressing doubt, qualifications and where they referred to their own thinking, the errors or difficulties they had. Episodes were longer than 30 seconds and were occasions when pupils 'expressed puzzlement, gave an explanation, justification or correction, spontaneously commented on difficulty or used strategies like checking their work' (Watson, 1996, p88).

The researcher eschewed the use of behavioural indications that pupils were thinking hard, not least because these were often shown by the absence of behaviour – stillness and silence. Instead the author set broader criteria that were indicative of cognitive involvement. Episodes were taken only from sessions that were seen by the teacher to be representative of the way she organised pupil groupings and not ones that she had judged to be unsatisfactory. The episodes were deemed by the author to be critical learning opportunities, often accompanied by emotional expressions, whether of frustration, elation or anger. This resulted in the identification of six categories of teacher talk. Interestingly teachers were consistent across sessions in the proportion of talk that fell into each category. The author meets potential criticism of the limited nature and size of the data base by reference to other influential research but also argues that: 'Evidence of generalization is often best shown by the recognition felt by experienced practitioners' (Watson, 1996, p69). She therefore has extensive use of direct quotes to contribute to the authenticity of the research. She also uses a range of converging sources of data through observation and interview and the non-verbal properties of the audio recordings.

The report of her findings centre in large part on talk that was described as actively encouraging reflection, through for example asking pupils for justification, explanation, asking hypothetical questions, pointing out contradictions and inconsistencies and suggesting learning strategies. Perhaps unsurprisingly, this talk was more characteristic of some teachers than others where conversations were longer on average, indicating that this style did not inhibit children's dialogue but encouraged sustained participation, involving longer utterances. Reflective periods occurred in both individual and small group settings. Classrooms in which reflective episodes were rare were ones where teachers responded without reference to pupils' interests, with broad general encouragement and a focus on predetermined goals so that pupils ideas were not developed or capitalised on. In contrast where reflective episodes were high the teachers referred explicitly to pupils strategies and talked of planning, monitoring and checking but also asked pupils for their ideas and explanations. They asked whether things 'made sense' and made reference to other interpretations or possible misunderstandings and used their own experiences as examples. Finally, the researcher looks at the ethos of the different classrooms, especially focusing on those in which there were higher levels of reflective thinking. Using excerpts of dialogue, the classrooms are portrayed as showing a positive ethos characterised by exchanges that demonstrate respect between the teacher and pupils, high expectations and where pupils' thinking is valued, hence raising their self-esteem.

This example of a grounded theory approach is very different from the ways in which instructional strategies have traditionally been evaluated. As we have seen, judgements are made using qualitative criteria – authenticity, thick description, recurrent patterning and confirmability. The result is that the study as published provides evidence of the interactional effects of teacher and student behaviour in a way that quasi-experimental studies largely do not do. It is not our intention here to praise one design or study in preference to another but to emphasise the importance of using a design that is fit for purpose. More specifically we hope to illustrate through this highly selective look at the literature the importance of adopting a design that is consistent with the theoretical underpinning of the subject which one sets out to investigate.

In the final section of this chapter we look at the development of a methodological approach that in part spans the divide between prescriptive quasi-experimental approaches and more qualitative grounded approaches to provide a formative method of evaluation.

Design experiments

Those adopting this approach often cite the work of Ann Brown as an inspiration for the development of these methods (Kelly and Lesch 2002; Gersten *et al.* 2000). She in turn drew on work in engineering with the idea of developing a prototype that was field tested (in the classroom) and studied in the laboratory. For the purposes of this chapter Cobb *et al.* (2003) provide a useful starting point in presenting what they describe as 'crosscutting' features that make design experiments different to other methodologies.

Purpose

Cobb *et al.* (2003) specify that the purpose of design experiments is to develop theories of the processes of learning and the ways in which these processes are supported. The Design Based Research Collective (2003, p5) place an emphasis on the *application* of the theory: 'an emerging paradigm for the study of learning in context through the systematic design and study of instructional strategies and tools.' Not only are they therefore concerned with what works, but they aim to investigate how, when and why learning occurs. In order to achieve this it is necessary to look at the ecologies in which learning takes place, not solely at the level of child and teacher but at the school or even the regional level.

Test-bed

The pivotal aspect of the method is to provide a test-bed for innovations. Cobb *et al.* (2003) use the metaphor of 'crucibles for the generation and testing of theories'. This cannot be achieved purely through naturalistic methodologies as it is necessary to have some control over the setting. Lobato (2003, p19) in contrast stresses the natural context in which the research takes place:

Rather than systematically vary the conditions of learning a single variable at a time in the laboratory, a design experimenter examines multiple dependent variables in order to develop a qualitative profile linking different instructional conditions with corresponding effects on learning within a complex social milieu.

Previous research is used to establish the key elements, to distinguish these predictable influential from incidental factors. However, at the same time there is an acknowledgement of the need to be able to recognise subtle changes even though they may be unanticipated. Sloane and Gorard (2003) suggest that, drawing on the engineering model, an integral part of the process is a recognition of failure, as errors form an important source of information. They place design experiments within a context of modelling drawn from statistics, thus framing for the reader the need to distinguish between 'what is known with near certainty ... what is reasonable to assume ... and what is unknown.' (p30).

Iterative cycles of reflection

Design experiments are described by Cobb *et al.* (2003) as iterative, featuring 'cycles of intervention and revision' with systematic collection and reflection on evidence. A likely feature of such cycles is the 'parallel development of measures sensitive to the changing ecology of learning' (p10). An integral process is to establish collaborative forums in which reflection can take place, keeping logs or audio recordings of these exchanges and thus interpreting past events but planning for new revisions that will test out these reflections.

Role of theory

Theory plays an important role in generating the design but also is tested through the evaluation of the design in both a prospective and reflective way. In this way the research does not serve purely to confirm a hypothesis but also to enable other explanations to emerge. Cobb *et al.* (2003) refer to the development of 'humble theories' – those which are sufficiently detailed to inform design in a precise way and thus inform practice in the classroom but are not so narrow that they are tied rigidly to a context nor so broad that the theory does not specify the circumstances in which changes in learning occur.

Collaboration

An important element of this methodology is that researchers and practitioners work together, thus helping to ensure meaningful contexts of study where local interpretation is seen to add to the salience of the findings rather than distorting the methodology. Thus how and why an intervention works across settings over time generates important knowledge (Design Based Research Collective, 2003). One way to facilitate reflection and the development of theory is to gather together a design team where diverse opinions are likely to be a feature of discussions, thus drawing on different experiences and sources of expertise.

These central ideas are developed in diverse ways and although Kelly and Lesch (2002) report on project work to explicate a design experiment method-ology, the writing in the field suggests that at this stage at least the words 'design' and 'experiment' naturally lead to slightly different configurations depending on where the emphasis lies. While researchers recognise that they meet some of the challenges posed by experimental and quasi-experimental design of controlling variables and producing unnatural contexts, for many they remain true to a paradigm that focuses on the systematic testing of hypotheses. Therefore, although researchers are adopting a common term to describe a methodology that in many senses bridges the gap between theoretical research and educational practice (Design Based Research Collective, 2003), it can be seen that there are differences in the way these are conceptualised.

Design Based Research Collective (2003) point to the different ways in which validity, objectivity and reliability are construed to be more like qualitative designs in that they use thick description with systematic analysis of data that is consensus building around interpretation of data. Triangulation takes place in that typically multiple sources and kinds of data are collected with attention given both to intended and unintended outcomes with cycles of enactment and repetition of data analyses. However, they also acknowledge the tension in achieving objectivity and the need to question the researchers' assumptions, especially where the research, as often happens, is carried out in a single setting over a long period of time therefore requires a reflective partnership that can be sustained. 'We stress that design-based research should not become a euphemism for "anything goes" research or oversimplified interventions' (p 7). This concern reveals the tension underlying an approach which attempts to bridge a divide between traditionally structured approaches and those more commonly associated with action research methodology.

Conclusion

Whatever one's research philosophy, traditional approaches to evaluation, as we have seen, are pragmatically difficult in the field of learning difficulties, and this no doubt has contributed to the dearth of published research (Gersten *et al.* 2000) despite the development of innovative instructional practices in the field (DfEE, 2000). In this chapter we have examined a small selection of research in the field of communication and interaction to explore the tensions that exist for researchers in adopting a methodology that is not consistent with the theory underpinning the intervention. More specifically, there are hazards in adopting approaches that place a natural emphasis on evaluating specified outcomes when the focus of learning is the interactive processes. Design experiments would appear to offer an alternative way of conceptualising and designing collaborative classroom research.

The Design Based Research Collective (2003) put forward a number of potential general uses that have application to the field of learning difficulties:

- creating and exploring novel teaching and learning environments
- developing theories of learning that are rich accounts through recognising contextually based elements and their effects
- advancing and consolidating knowledge of design of instruction through recognition of principles and patterns in design
- promoting the capacity for innovation through cultivating partnerships and collaborative ways of working and through promoting the capacity of people to use a different lens to understand aspects of classroom practice.

These are valuable outcomes in moving forward our understanding of instructional strategies for pupils and young people with learning difficulties.

CHAPTER 6

Participatory research

Introduction

Internationally there has been a long history of recognising the importance of hearing the voice of the child in matters that relate to them. This is well illustrated in the United Nations Convention on the Rights of the Child (1989), although the difficulties of achieving this with *all* children have been more slowly acknowledged. More recently in the UK, there has been renewed emphasis in both adult and child services, on the voice of the service user in the decision-making processes, and this is well reflected in a range of government guidance. It is probably best evidenced in the active if not central involvement of people with learning disability in the development of the new Learning Disability Strategy, *Valuing People* (DoH, 2001; Holman, 2001). This has been described as a landmark document (Grant and Ramcharan, 2002), not least for the scale of inclusion of people with learning difficulties in its development and production. The title of an accompanying report, *Nothing About Us Without Us* (People First *et al.*, 2000), provides an appropriate indication of the way in which policy, practice and research should be developed. A further proposal to set up and train a new group of legal professionals as 'intermediaries' also reflects the seriousness of accessing the views of people with learning difficulties. These principles are also evident if we turn specifically to consider education. The Special Educational Needs Code of Practice (DfEE, 2000a) is underpinned by a fundamental belief that 'the views of the child should be sought and taken into account' (para 1.5) in decision-making about provision to meet their educational needs. In contrast to the earlier code, it is accompanied by detailed discussion of the ways in which this might be achieved. Equally the Disability Right Code of Practice (2002), based on the importance of not treating disabled pupils less favourably, gives children themselves the right to appeal. Given these drives it would seem remarkable for researchers to fail to recognise the importance of eliciting the views of this group of people.

Although our review of trends suggested that the proportion of empirical research that adhered to qualitative paradigms was still relatively slight despite the well recognised concerns about positivist methodologies, there is an important body of literature reflecting on what might all-embracingly be referred to as inclusive research (Walmsley, 2001). A broad distinction can be made between 'research on' and 'research with' people with learning difficulties

(Kiernan, 1999). In this chapter we will reflect on the full range of approaches to 'research with' people with learning difficulties, identifying differences in both the ideological and paradigmatic approaches. The aim is to explore some of the inherent difficulties but also to set out the developments, for while many have been cautious about the extent of involvement it is important to look across disciplines at what might be described as research that is both innovative and radical (Goodley and Moore, 2000). We will argue that while it is important to recognise the many challenges, it is probably pre-emptive to set the boundaries too firmly in relation to what is and is not possible.

Identifying different standpoints

Traditionally a distinction has been made between emancipatory and participatory approaches to research (Chappell, 2000; Kiernan, 1999; Walmsley, 2001; Barnes, 2002), with attempts to identify some fundamental differences. However, we start the process of understanding the viewpoints of different researchers, as we have throughout the book, by looking at the philosophical and theoretical underpinning. For example, many researchers will recognise that without exploring the perspectives of all involved, research will reveal an incomplete or partial picture (Porter and Lewis, 2001; Lewis and Porter, submitted for publication). This concern does not only arise through a rights agenda but reflects a model of psychology adopted. If we want to understand what is happening in a particular environment then we need to see it through the varied perspectives of those who are part of it. This approach is particularly characteristic of psychologists working within a humanistic psychology paradigm who are influenced by phenomenology (that reality lies in the perception of an event rather than the event itself). The emphasis lies with the subjective experience. Others, however, who would not describe themselves as psychologists, might also adopt an interpretive or hermeneutic approach to research where knowledge is concerned with illumination and meaning and who might well adopt an interactive mode of data collection where questions and methods evolve in the course of the study.

Within other research traditions, the driving force is that research should be empowering, that there should be reciprocity and gain and it should encourage self-reflection (Oliver, 1992). This approach is more overtly underpinned by a social model that seeks to explain disability in relation to the barriers that society erects and the consequent oppression experienced. Thus a fundamental role for research is to bring about change in policy and practices through revealing how lives are constrained by the acts of oppressors. In this sense there has been a move to distance this approach from the ways of researching that have gone before. As Oliver (1992, p110) argues:

> The development of such a paradigm stems from the gradual rejection of the positivist view of social research as the pursuit of absolute knowledge

through the scientific method and the gradual disillusionment with the interpretive view of such knowledge as the generation of socially useful knowledge within particular historical and social contexts. The emancipatory paradigm, as the name implies, is about the facilitating of a politics of the possible by confronting social oppression at whatever level it occurs.

As he also states:

> while the interpretative paradigm has changed the rules, in reality it has not changed the game ... Interpretative research is just as alienating as positivist research because what might be called 'the social relations of research production' have not changed one iota. (p106)

Emancipatory disability research is therefore underpinned by the requirement to change the power relations in research and for the disabled to have control of *all* stages of the research process. Accountability to the disabled community is one of the cornerstones of this approach (Zarb, 1997; Barnes, 2002) and extends to all aspects of the research: the aims, research questions, the data analysis, discussion and recommendations and the dissemination process. Concerns have been raised about the overtly political nature of the activity, and questions about how one establishes objectivity (Kiernan, 1999; Barnes, 2002).

While emancipatory research has an ideology based on political activity, other participatory research has ideological roots both in normalisation and in advocacy. Walmsley (2001) points out that, unlike other disabilities, the momentum for change came from the non-disabled rather than being articulated and inspired from within. The normalisation movement has put heavy emphasis on activity with valued others, and its influence can be seen with respect to four aspects:

- participation (both as respondents and researchers)
- a focus on the quality of services rather than outcomes
- normalisation being used as an evaluative measure
- advocacy with a consequent change of image and attitudes.

The pivotal role of advocacy is well demonstrated by Atkinson (2002a), who argues for the two-way influence of advocacy and research. She illustrates research supporting self-advocacy through her life-history work with Mabel Cooper, who didn't speak while she was in an institution: 'I never said anything in the hospital because there was no point. Nobody listened so why speak?' Mabel has now produced an oral history of her life (Cooper, 1997). As Atkinson points out, such research presents the storyteller as a person rather than a case. Self-advocacy is also seen as making research possible as it provides the drive; again as Mabel Cooper says: 'My story and a lot more will help people with a learning difficulty, and I hope it will learn them to tell their story of what happened to them' (in Atkinson, 2002a).

This kind of research in particular is seen to help people, who often have no family or friends who can provide them with a 'stock of stories' on which to draw, to make sense of their lives. The route for many into research has been through self-advocacy, as speaking up for yourself in groups has been a vehicle for involvement in research. In addition to creating conditions for self-advocacy, Walmsley (2001, p194) argues that researchers have also acted as citizen advocates, enabling people to grow towards independence and to be brought within 'circles of ordinary community life', within the valued context of research production.

While many would agree with the central tenets that research should be seen as empowering and contribute to the change in the way disability is seen, there has been some debate about the use of the term emancipatory. Some of the practical challenges (which we will discuss further) concern its application in the field of learning difficulties (Kiernan, 1999). More importantly, Oliver (1997) argues that instead of talking about emancipatory research we need to be concerned with the role of research in emancipation and this can only be judged after the event in relation to the outcome. Additionally, emancipatory research requires a shift in power relations and, rather ironically, this shift is not necessarily apparent within the disability movement as some sectors continue to be marginalised with respect to the degree of visible impairment (Humphrey, 2000), thereby challenging the very basis on which such research exists. Moreover there are recognisable tensions for the non-disabled researcher in demonstrating a lack of self-interest in the production of research, not least in relation to its dissemination and funding. Although this distinction between process and product is not a categorical one (Barnes, 2002; Zarb, 1997), we have therefore adopted the term 'participatory research' as an acknowledgement of the challenges, and the aim of this chapter is to consider how best we can support the active participation of people with learning difficulties.

In summary, participatory research includes a whole range of approaches, from that which ensures that the voice of people with learning disability is clearly represented in the data collection process through to collaborative development of any or all parts of the research process, including setting the agenda, carrying out the research, analysing the data, and dissemination of the findings. Underpinning this continuum is the social model of disability and an appreciation of the importance of the subjective experience in any research account. We start by considering some of the challenges this research poses, before looking at how these might be addressed.

Challenges and tensions

Sources of tension in the move towards increasing the participatory nature of research can be seen to lie along the continuum of involvement. They therefore range from concerns about how we ensure validity and authenticity of the data collected, to questions about the degree to which we can truly involve people with learning difficulties in the processes of agenda setting, design, development and dissemination of the research. To some extent these concerns reflect the unexplored parameters of capability both with respect to those with learning disability but also for researchers, inducting the uninitiated into the research process, and developing innovative methodologies for collecting views. In this section we chart the difficulties and later in the chapter we address the ways in which people have started to address these concerns.

Firstly we consider aspects of establishing the research agenda. Walmsley (2001) asks to what extent people are shapers of research given that it may demand expertise beyond the capability of some. More poignantly, Riddell *et al.* (2001) ask what happens when there is disagreement between researchers and disabled people about the data to be collected and the way it is analysed. Perhaps of greater concern is the assumption of a shared agenda. Riddell *et al.* (2001, p234) demonstrate how fundamental this might be, as notably a number of their sample did not perceive themselves as having a learning difficulty but gave different accounts of how they came to be placed in a special school: 'As researchers who had brought the group together to explore their collective identity, we were unsure how to proceed.' These researchers faced not only imposing an agenda but also an identity:

> We were struck by the extent of the denial, silence and subterfuge surrounding intellectual impairment in which professionals and voluntary organisations were complicit … It appeared that intellectual impairment, far from being celebrated, was too shameful to be discussed openly even with those who were being consigned to this category. (Riddell *et al.*, 2001, p234)

Difficulties are cited not only around these key aspects of decision-making but also in other aspects of the research. As Kiernan (1999) points out, research has traditionally relied heavily on cognitive skills and even where research is immediate to a person's interest it may still require a level of abstract thinking. In much the same vein, Atkinson (2002a) reports that theorising from life histories can pose difficulties and co-researchers are still needed for the process. In addition there can be a requirement for the development of personal skills as researchers. Riddell *et al.* (2001) considered involving people as researchers but as studies were not designed to be structured, one-off events but ones of progressive focusing that would involve lengthy training, they instead involved a small group of people in the discussion of the initial findings and themes that preceded the analysis of more abstract ideas.

Further tensions exist because of the pragmatic difficulties set up by some funders, who may be reticent to recognise the financial implications of this type of research with additional time needed to build relationships and induct new skills (Riddell *et al.* 2001; Zarb, 1997; Kiernan, 1999). There has, however, been an important change in some funders' attitudes that place a condition for collaboration into the requirements of the bid. This is well demonstrated by the

Joseph Rowntree Foundation and the Lottery Commission Board (Ward, 1997) with a consequent impetus for researchers to find new ways of meeting the challenges.

While some researchers struggle with the ways in which people with learning difficulties can be collaborators in the research process, others are questioning the degree to which we can collect valid and authentic views. How can researchers be sure that their data represents the views of the entire range of people with learning difficulties? Traditionally we have relied on interview methods to elicit the views of people with learning difficulties and yet this places significant demands both on linguistic and cognitive capabilities. There is a temptation for researchers to focus on the mode of communication and simplify the words used without considering the meaningfulness of what is being asked.

If we adopt a model of communication that recognises the importance of negotiating and sharing meaning, we recognise the inherent difficulties in exploring the world of many people with learning difficulties through the medium of language. Grove et al. (1999) outline the ways in which communication may be limited, including a difficulty that others have in distinguishing intentional and non-intentional communicative acts, inconsistent ways of communicating, and a high dependence on others to infer the meaning of a communication. In this context the researcher is disadvantaged, firstly by a lack of knowledge and experience of the person as a communicator, and secondly by being uncertain about the ownership of a message in which others act as interpreters. A number of researchers have drawn attention to the need to systematically verify interpretations of meaning that are ascribed to people with profound and multiple learning difficulties, a process that is likely to be more lengthy and intensive than the usual methods of interviewing (Grove et al., 1999; Porter et al., 2001; Dennis, 2002).

Recent discussion by Ware (2003) suggests that we may not be able to collect the views of people with profound and multiple learning difficulties with any degree of certainty, but that this should not exclude them from the process. She makes a careful distinction between expressing like or dislike for some activity, event or person, and expressing a view on it. Given the discrepancies in staff interpretations of behaviour (Hogg et al., 1995), we must continue to review and further validate the data we have collected. It is probably worth reminding ourselves that there is an assumption here that the context for eliciting views is around experiences that are immediate to the point of data collection. This ensures that we make the context as concrete and meaningful as possible. Harris (2003) illustrates the ways in which the environment can be structured to elicit choice-making but also indicates the need for further research to understand the ways in which social and other supports might help people provide tangible accounts of their views.

Dockrell (2002), in reviewing cognitive demands, raises a number of questions that serve to draw the researchers' attention to the relative difficulty of different types of question. Of particular relevance is the difference between being asked to describe something, being asked to explain, and being asked to predict. Unwittingly interviewers can fail to acknowledge the attendant differences between these tasks. They may also fail to recognise the memory demands, assuming that the person can sufficiently recall an event to form an opinion about it and, moreover, that it has some salience for them.

There has also been a popular account in the literature of the tendency of people with learning difficulties to acquiesce, that is to agree with the interviewer – what has been referred to as 'yea-saying' (Sigelman et al., 1981; Finlay and Lyons, 2002). Explanations for this have included increased suggestibility and greater submissiveness, rather than investigating whether it is some product of the interview situation. Dockrell (2002) has argued that in the general child population this is symptomatic of a response to a question that is too complex or one on which they are not able to make a judgement. Likewise, Finlay and Lyons (2002) draw attention both to the interrogative force of a question and to its content, when it asks for an attitude statement about something that has never been considered in detail before, when it involves an abstract concept, when it requests judgements that are too difficult, and to its syntax, when the question structures are too lengthy or complex. Interestingly, research on eyewitness memory suggests that only on closed *misleading* questions were children more suggestible than their mainstream counterparts, which the authors ascribe to a greater eagerness to please and reduced confidence in themselves (Henry and Gudjonsson, 1999).

Expressing a view is not purely a cognitive or linguistic activity; it can also be an emotional activity, affected by the mood of the person (Freedman, 2001) but also one that requires a degree of assertiveness (Stenfert Kroese et al., 1998). As we have seen, there has to be an element of self-belief. Treece et al. (1999) provide vivid case studies charting not only the lack of choice-making opportunities but the lack of expectation of many people with learning difficulties of being able to influence their own life. Harris (2003) points to the fear that some people will experience of making the wrong choice, either because it might be unpopular or because it will be judged to be incorrect. Whilst these may be well charted cultural factors, there may be more subtle ones at work. Gregory (2002), with reference to deaf children and young people, also draws our attention to cultural factors, as without the experience of hearing conversations and the media they may be unused to particular ways of talking and communicating, especially the self-reflecting style that is inherent in many interview situations.

Summary

As we have seen in this section, the challenge for the researcher is to ensure that:

- the agenda is meaningful for the person, or indeed set by them
- a relationship is established by which people feel empowered to have a view and time and opportunity are given
- the context in which the research takes place reduces the cognitive and linguistic demands of participation
- a systematic approach is taken to verifying the views.

Ethical Issues

The shift from 'research on' to 'research with' people with learning difficulties could suggest that ethical issues are less prominent in research. Instead there is probably a growing recognition of the challenges presented in addressing a number of ethical issues posed by research. Historically concern has focused on the possible effect of the research process, of involvement in experimental trials of treatment or intervention with vulnerable groups of people, especially those who are in institutions (Freedman, 2001). Links between legal obligations and ethical responsibilities are surprisingly tenuous despite the fact that they rest on evidence of damaging outcomes (Masson, 2000). This no doubt reflects the traditions and conventions of medical research, which has an established practice of presenting research plans to ethics committees (Ward and Watson, undated).

While this type of interventionist or medical research highlights potential sources of bad practice, the principles underlying ethical research practices of autonomy and self-determinism apply equally to all research and rely in large part on the integrity of the researcher. This is especially true of educational research, which has a less established practice of presenting research plans to ethics committees, and often relies on generic guidance of professional bodies. Few bodies make explicit reference to people with learning difficulties and tend to conflate guidance with other 'vulnerable' groups (Lindsay, 2000). In this section we explore issues of consent and assent, access and gatekeepers, confidentiality and anonymity, recognition, feedback and ownership. We note the British Psychological Society ethical guidance (BPS, 2000) that researchers should consider the standpoint of all participants with respect to 'foreseeable threats to their psychological well-being, health, values or dignity' and that these should be eliminated.

Three elements to consent have been identified – capacity, information and voluntariness (Turnbull, 1977) – with the permeating factor of the person's ability to communicate (Dye *et al.*, 2003). Definitions of capacity typically reside with the ability to make and understand a decision that affects one's life (Lewis and Porter, submitted for publication). While rightly there is an emphasis on all individuals with learning difficulties being enabled to make choices and have their views taken into account, proportions of the population are unlikely to be able to demonstrate the definitions of capacity typically cited. Indeed the demands of this type of decision-making are complex and often poorly understood (Harris, 2003). One of the dangers is that definitions of capacity are equated both with the right to express a view and the right for that view to be heard. Distinctions about capacity – who has it and who hasn't – are difficult to make as so much depends on the nature of the decision, the context in which it is made and the level and type of support available. Freedman (2001) argues that researchers should not presume a person to be unable to give consent to research and that assessment of their capacity to do so should be taken case by case.

Capacity will also depend on the way that information about the nature of the research is provided so that participants have a clear set of expectations about the research and what is involved in taking part. They need to know that they can withdraw at any point and understand the possible outcomes of taking part. This is no easy task: it is not purely a case of using simple language and/or using other modes of communication. Tozer (2003) describes the use of social stories with children and young people with autistic spectrum disorder to enable them to gain a clearer set of expectations of what the research process would involve. Rodgers (1999, p428) also describes the method she used: 'I found it helpful to provide information in small doses, with the help of an illustrated information sheet, and to recap and repeat the information, allowing plenty of time for thought and questions.'

As we have noted, the third aspect of consent concerns its voluntariness: that participants don't feel coercion to be part of the study. The unequal power relations between the researcher and participants must be recognised. Participants should not consent through fear or through feeling that they don't have a choice.

Knox *et al.* (2000) argue that informed consent should be seen as an ongoing process. Traditional approaches that merely get agreement at the start are inappropriate for studies where the nature of the discussion and exploration evolves as part of the research rather than being predetermined by the researchers. It has also been argued that there must be an opportunity for *informed dissent*, so that not only do researchers listen to explicit communication of assent but that they also recognise signs that the person is dissenting to the continuation of the research, taking advice from colleagues who know the person well (Lewis and Porter, in press). Tozer (2003) provided children in her study with a stop symbol to ensure that they were reminded that they had control over whether or not the interview continued.

As Rodgers (1999 p428) recognises:

Taking part in research demanded not one decision, but a whole series of decisions. There were decisions to meet me and listen to my explanations; each person's decision to take part in the research; to allow me to tape-record interviews, to answer specific questions, and to allow me to take away the information offered and analyse it along with other people's contribution.

Where the person is seen to be unable to give informed consent, then a surrogate decision-maker is approached to provide this on their behalf. In much the same way parents (or others who act *in loco parentis*), are approached to give consent for their child to be involved. The protective nature of this action is well demonstrated in the study by Minkes *et al.* (1994) where parents were more willing to contribute themselves than let their children participate. There are two ways in which such decisions may be formed: firstly by considering whether involvement is in the best interest of the participant and secondly by reflecting on what decision that person would have made if they were able to do so. In this sense surrogates may consider the standpoint of the individual, their interests, preferences, values and past experiences (Freedman, 2001) or they may base their decision on a risk–benefit calculation. For some, however, the decision might be made solely from their own standpoint of whether they think the person is capable of contributing and has something useful to say, or whether they would have contributed to the research. In this way others act as gatekeepers to the research. Indeed, the very location of the participants may be subject to the value judgements of other professionals. Morris (1998) notes the insistence she had to use to include those people in the research who would not be able to be interviewed in the usual way.

A contrasting position to these ethical issues is adopted by Clegg (2000, 2001, 2003). She raises concern about the overemphasis on individual autonomy, which she suggests is not typical of much decision-making:

> Relationships are an essential part of the way vulnerable people make decisions and experience life: often non-disabled people ignore the individualism of liberal humanist culture too, deciding important issues through discussion with partners. (Clegg, 2001, p2)

The focus shifts in this way to consider the relationship with the person who is deciding for them. Clegg argues that the ideal proxy is one with whom they have developed 'an ethical relationship', that enables them to control their own biases but draw on knowledge of that person together with an 'imaginative anticipation' to be able to interpret future needs, see the whole person and be sensitive to changes over time (Clegg, 2003). This raises particular issues for researchers in ensuring that the person or people who provide consent on behalf of someone do not simply do so in a managerial context. Gatekeeping should not be seen as the same as providing consent. Moreover, where parents or others give consent to involvement it is still important that the person themselves assent to be involved and, as we have already noted, is given opportunities to voice dissent and be heard. Morris (1998) notes the many instances in which staff made arrangements for the timing of the interview that would not have been chosen by the young person, as they coincided with other important activities.

A further ethical issue surrounds that of confidentiality and anonymity. Good practice dictates that individuals should not be identifiable in the research, not least because of the possible unforeseen outcomes of the research and its dissemination. Given the increased vulnerability of this population, researchers need to be cautious about promising that all material will be kept in confidence, or at least within the research team, not least because of the possible disclosure of information relating to abuse. Researchers need also to be mindful of what steps they can take to preserve participants' anonymity given that populations are often small and the combination of individual characteristics can provide distinctive individual profiles. Armstrong (1998) describes how very difficult it is to anonymise life-history data and still keep it meaningful to the audience, an issue that is underestimated in the planning of such research.

The vulnerability of this group of people is highlighted by others in respect of the relationships that are created purely as part of the research. Riddell *et al.* (2001) discuss the tension between establishing the boundaries around a relationship that was based on research and the individual's need for friendship. Morris (1998, p56) writes:

> Sometimes ... people just wanted a friend (or in the case of a couple of young men, a girlfriend). It could feel as if were exploiting some people's loneliness, briefly coming into their lives, taking the information we needed and going away again.

Stalker (1998) raises the difficult question of whether she should be adding to the number of people coming and going in someone's life when staff attempted to reassure her that the participants would not imbue the relationship with greater significance. Expectations are likely to be higher where the interview takes place within someone's home. Again Stalker (1998, p9) highlights the dilemmas:

> I was very aware of entering a private house, and a role which ... was likely to be unfamiliar to them ... Although in many respects I behaved like a guest ... I was not a guest in the ordinary sense. The invitation had been 'initiated' by me ... was not there to support the tenants ... I was seeking something from them – data – and what exactly they were going to get in return was probably unclear to everyone.

There is a growing recognition of the need to consider who owns the data, especially where it consists of video, tapes and drawings. Minkes *et al.* (1994) are clear in their guidance to interviewers that children are allowed to keep the booklets developed as part of the research. However, the implications of this offer need to be considered from the standpoint of the individual who may view this return as indicative that in some way it is not good enough to be kept (Lewis and Porter, in press). In contrast, Atkinson (2002a) writes of the importance of the oral histories as a product of the research to those who provided them. Booth and Booth (2003) from the outset make it clear to their participants that the photographic data is theirs to share with others as they wish.

There is growing recognition of the need to ensure that the results of the research are disseminated to participants and the wider community that they represent in a form that is accessible and does full justice to their views (Goodley and Moore, 2000). Rodgers (1999, p431) writes of her commitment to making the findings accessible: 'It can only be oppressive for the academic "experts" to purport to understand what the real problem is but be unable to explain its nature to the people most affected by it.'

There is a tension in producing accounts of research that satisfy both academia and are accessible and valued by people who contributed to the research. Goodley and Moore (2000) present a paper aimed at raising the status of this work, an initiative that has been slow to being followed in other journals (e.g. March *et al.* 1997). Others have questioned whether the kind of plain facts reporting is suitable for presenting theoretical material (Walmsley, 2001). The use of the internet both as a vehicle for dissemination and as a research tool also raises important ethical issues (Booth and Booth, 2003; Brownlow and O'Dell, 2002).

To summarise some of the key ethical issues:

- gatekeeping is not the same as informed consent
- informed consent is an important process throughout the research and participants should be reminded of their right to dissent at any point
- where others act to give consent, assent by the participant should also sought
- researchers need to consider carefully from the outset how the data can be anonymised
- participants need to be helped to understand the nature of their relationship with the researcher, including the point at which it will end
- ownership of the data must be established prior to its collection
- researchers need to consider carefully how to give feedback and recognition to participants, including disseminating the research.

The creation of a reference group is an important source of advice and guidance to finding a way through these ethical issues. Ward and Watson (undated) suggest that this kind of advisory group represents all the different stakeholders, service users/consumers, parents and carers. The setting up of such a group may in fact have several functions and can be seen as facilitating the participatory nature of the research.

Facilitating participatory research

Having established a context for reviewing participatory research and charted the challenges, including addressing a number of ethical issues, we now turn to look at accounts of the process, focusing first on attempts to establish collaborative processes. These examples vary from small-scale single researcher studies to larger funded projects and we draw on these in the spirit of inspiring others.

There are important differences between researchers in how they identify the first steps in their research and this determines the degree to which the research agenda is shaped by participants. Burke *et al.* (2003) cite the setting up of a conference to which they invited all organisations in the community to send two or more people with learning difficulties together with a supporter to hear presentations and take part in discussion around advocacy and research. At the end of the day they asked for volunteers who would be interested in being part of a project similar to the one presented at the conference. This process helped to ensure that from the outset people had some expectations and understanding of what they might be volunteering for. This was followed by an evaluation form to volunteers asking them to name one topic they would like to know more about as preparation for discussion at the first meeting. For other researchers the process is described as purposive sampling (Knox *et al.* 2000) where potential 'experts' are located with the help of other agencies and invited to take part. This demonstrates a subtle difference between providing opportunities to actively opt in and a more passive response to a nomination. Rodgers (1999) describes her concern at the outset that the group in some way is reciprocal so that she makes a contribution to them as well as using them as a sounding board for her ideas. She also consulted with those who were less articulate by visiting day centres and resourcing drawings by them of issues that were important to them around her topic of health.

In all of the above studies the balance of the decision-making lies with the participants and this is reflected numerically in their representation. Others see involvement in the form of an advisory group activity where the representation may not be that great. Stalker (1998) tellingly reveals how much more discussion and contribution took place at the informal pre-meeting compared to that which involved a variety of stakeholders, each of whom used the language and interests of their respective professional roles. Whichever model is adopted there are important lessons about ensuring that all are well placed to contribute to the decision-making process. Ward and Trigler (2001) describe the setting up of a sub-committee of self-advocates to help ensure a greater sense of control and ownership in the project.

An important aspect of the collaboration is to define what is meant by research and to empower participants to be co-researchers, conducting interviews and taking part in the analysis of the data. March *et al.* (1997) describe research as 'finding out things and finding out why they happen' and posit the importance of learning researchers' skills from the beginning of the project, a sentiment echoed by Burke *et al.* (2003), who provide a breakdown of what they saw as the role of the researcher. For some the training in interviewing skills made them question their interest in being involved in the project. A part of the negotiation therefore lies with clarifying roles, recognising and valuing the different contributions of members of the project. Burke *et al.* (2003) describe their mishandling of the literature review process that was dominated by support worker presentations with insufficient breaks and opportunities for discussion. These difficulties were redressed through reviewing the video tape and drawing out key points in the next meeting. This highlights the reflexive nature of the process of collaboration.

A degree of structure to the meetings appears an important element. Although Riddell *et al.* (2001) in their experience found an expectation of the researchers to structure a session (and not to make it feel too much like hard work), Knox *et al.* (2000) describe a format whereby they checked what they had talked about at the last meeting, they agreed the agenda for that meeting, they did the business, then decided on what they would talk about in the following meeting. Visual cues fulfil an important role in documenting activity. Burke *et al.* describe the use of symbols for the agenda and a pictorial representation of the path of the project that they had travelled along, and March *et al.* (1997) graphically produced their 'yellow brick road'.

Ward and Trigler (2001) also indicate the importance of pragmatic aspects of negotiating the time commitments. The questionnaire in their study took over four months to develop. Issues of location and transport also require the planning of meeting dates and times well in advance (Riddell *et al.*, 2001).

Key aspects of facilitating participatory research are therefore:

- to develop clear expectations and understanding of the process and experience of research, preferably prior to participants volunteering
- to consider fully the reciprocal nature of research, including what the participants will gain from the experience
- to create a structure and format that promote active participation
- good planning of practicalities of transport and location
- awareness of the likely extended time-scale of the activity.

Where individuals are participating as respondents, there is more tangible empirical evidence to support good practice although some of it is contradictory. Those who use quality-of-life scales, including the use of Likert scales have consistently indicated their limitations in eliciting reliable data from all verbal participants. This is not surprising given the recognition elsewhere of the use and usefulness of less structured approaches. Open-ended questions provide more accurate data (Dockrell, 2002), not least because research indicates they avoid any tendency to acquiesce, and the greater likelihood of recalling those words used last that occur with structured forms of questioning (Stenfert Kroese *et al.*, 1998), although a number of authors have suggested avoiding open-ended questions because they yield limited information (see Booth and Booth, 1996, for greater discussion of this research). Unstructured methods call for considerable skill to avoid being faced by a wall of silence (Richardson, 2002) and perhaps help to explain why there is a growing move towards holding group interviews or focus groups. Booth and Booth (1996) cite the particular problems of in-articulateness, unresponsiveness, the need for a concrete frame of reference and finally difficulties with the concept of time. Many of these aspects are also well demonstrated in the data collection of Richardson (2002). In his view they call for listening, reflecting, acceptance, empathy coupled with positive regard, all skills of a good counsellor. Booth and Booth (1996) describe how important it is to listen to the silences to interpret different possible meanings that prompt the interviewer into eliminating alternatives by a progressive adaptation of the questions including those requiring a yes/no answer. Both papers raise the issue of being over-intrusive in the style of questioning, which Richardson (2002) meets with self-disclosure.

Lewis (2002), drawing on work with children, cites the use of statements as a useful alternative and one that contrasts with the question-and-answer routine that is characteristic of educational settings and which can transform an interview unwittingly into a teaching task. It also helps to alter the power relations. The development of joint activities, which can facilitate interaction either prior to the interview or as part of the interview, can also help to build a relationship. Stalker (1998) describes the process of being taken round the grounds of a hospital, during which time she took photographs which later served to provide additional prompts as well as providing something to keep. Our own experiences have highlighted the usefulness of snack time.

The literature on the use of narrative methods amply demonstrates the time-scale of such activity with accounts being developed over months and years, a distinct contrast to the methodologies used by more structured approaches (Atkinson, 2002a; Armstrong, 1998). They also require a paced approach to withdrawing from people's lives (Stalker, 1998).

One of the most powerful forms of narrative has been the life-history account, which has contributed to establishing positive principles in the development of services (Ramcharan and Grant, 2001; Armstrong, 1998). Atkinson (2002b) describes life-history research as the ultimate vehicle for self-representation enabling people to rediscover their past and with it their identity. Life-history accounts are not without their problems they don't for example contribute well to long-term policy planning and they focus on the experiences of those with mild and moderate difficulties (Ramcharan and Grant 2001). They can also promote an individual tragedy account (Riddell *et al.*, 2001). They require good systems for data management, as they are likely to reply to open-ended questions that don't necessarily lead to a clear sequence of thinking and a neat ordered production of material. Fido and Potts (1997) note the value of transcribing the interview immediately and annotating it with cross-references to other material. Richardson (2002) describes the process of checking the analysis as an iterative process and of using drawings and photographs to help clarify emotions and stimulate conversation. Atkinson (2002b) also discusses the way in which she used photographs, hospital case notes and songs to prompt the process of recollection and that reading back their account elicited further views.

Life-history work in many ways epitomises the tensions in empowering people to have a voice and ensuring that their voice is represented in an authentic way. As Atkinson and Walmsley (1999) state, we also need to ask who initiated it and why, who wrote it and how and also who owns it. Papodopoulos *et al.* (2002) describe a process of validation through reporting and representing the reconstructed stories to an organised group event that also served to check out the credibility, depedendability and confirmability of the findings.

We can summarise the literature on practices that support people with learning difficulties to participate as respondents:

- the weight of the evidence suggests the use of open-ended questions (although clearly this depends on the communicative skills of the partici-pants) but posing statements may also be helpful

- the importance of providing a concrete frame of reference
- the usefulness of joint activities that facilitate interaction
- interviewer skills that include listening, reflecting back, empathy and listening to silences
- careful validation of the views collected.

Innovatory methods

There has been an increasing recognition of the need to supplement the use of language as the main mode of data collection with that of other media. In this section we describe the ways in which researchers have sought to supplement these especially for those people with learning difficulties who have significant difficulties in communicating through language. To do this we draw on work presented as part of an ESRC seminar series (Porter and Lewis, 2001). While the heading for this section is 'innovatory methods', some researchers have started with methodologies used in mainstream research and adapted them to meet diverse groups. Fox and Norwich (1992), for example, illustrate the use of repertory grid approaches with people with learning difficulties to investigate their self-perceptions, and Begley (2000) uses a version with pupils with Down syndrome to investigate their self-esteem. Male (2002) describes a small-scale exploratory study in which she used sociometric techniques to investigate peer relationships between students with severe learning difficulties. She collected nominations of friendship in a class of adolescents, providing a concrete frame of reference by asking them who they would like to carry out certain different activities with, and she used photographs to facilitate responses. She asked them the question on a second occasion to check the stability (or reliability) of their views and collected additional observational data to check whether their expressed views were consistent with actual behaviour.

Visual imagery is a consistent feature of many alternative methods. We start by looking at the use of cameras as a means of finding out about values, interests and lives of people with learning difficulties, their world. Booth and Booth (2003) provide an account of 'photovoice', giving people cameras to use to make representations of their experiences. A similar approach is described by Germain (2003) although here the participants were children including those with more complex and significant needs. This was a population that needed teaching to use the camera and symbolic reminders to try and take a picture every day. While Booth and Booth (2003) write confidently about shifting the control to enable people to depict their world as they want, work with children raises important issues of checking who took the photos. Booth and Booth (2003) describe their research as a group process, sharing photos and experiences with other mothers with learning difficulties. Choice is an integral element of this method of data collection, with decisions around taking the photos, who (if anyone) to share them with, and which ones to remove completely. Not all participants wanted to use this medium, a finding shared by Wright et al. (2003) in a study of excluded pupils.

One of the issues that photovoice raises concerns the sharing of meaning. Germain's study sought to investigate the leisure opportunities of teenagers with learning difficulties. Any simple attempt to analyse the content of the photographs presumes a shared understanding of the meaning of that photo. As Booth and Booth found, it is important to validate that meaning through the collection of other data. Thus group discussion was an integral part of their research process as it shed light on the choices that had been made in how people represented their lives. In Germain's (2003) study with less articulate participants, she did this through two parallel sources. She asked the pupils about the photographs, thus noting what language was elicited by their picture, and she carried out a variety of selection exercises, asking them to sort their photos into ones they liked and didn't like and then to select a small quantity to put in their own photo album. In addition to collecting pupil views she also interviewed parents about the photos to gain further information about the context in which they'd been taken. It also provided an opportunity to check the child's level of involvement in taking the photo.

A number of investigators have used 'talking mats', a visual resource using picture symbols that was developed by Murphy (1998; see also Cameron and Murphy, 2002) specifically to help people to express their views and feelings but also to think about issues in different ways. This is a structured approach to eliciting views as the provision of symbols automatically determines the range of responses possible. It also presumes a shared meaning to that symbol. Gladstone (2003), in a collaborative study in which students developed a visual questionnaire about their experiences of inclusion, showed how they selected to represent 'dislike' by a face with a straight-line mouth rather than the conventional down-turned arc, drawing our attention to the shades of meaning that can lie behind the use of simplified symbols.

Lewis (2002) describes the use of cue cards to structure the narrative in a way that involves minimal interference by the interviewer. She describes the use of six cue cards, symbol pictures that denote people, talk, setting (indoor and outdoor), feelings and consequences. These facilitate children's retelling of events or incidents so that in her study children prompted in this way provided more details than with conventional methods. The exceptions were pupils with autism who used the cue cards in a way that gave them a standard meaning.

Finally we can consider ways in which other visual methods can be used. Bendelow (2002) describes the use of children's pictures to investigate children's beliefs about health, using a technique referred to as 'draw and label' (Lewis and Lindsay, 2000) and Mavers (2003) describes the use of concept mapping as a research tool through which the researcher gained snapshots of children's thinking and understanding of ICT. Selective follow-up interviews supported the analysis of data. Both methodologies rely on the person being able to represent their thinking with a level of detail that is communicated through the use of pencil and paper. The alternative is to have access to materials and pictures that the person selects and assembles. The use of ICT makes the range of material much broader.

In summary, we can see from the developing use of innovative methods how researchers have drawn on methodologies derived from those in mainstream research. These range from the carefully structured, where responses may be predetermined, through to those in which the participant is less constrained in the options available. The piloting and refinement of these methods to meet the needs of individual users requires time and critical reflection. Researchers need to continue to question their understanding of the meaning conveyed by the response.

Conclusions

In the last two sections we have looked at the ways researchers have started to meet the challenges faced by ensuring all people with learning difficulties are enabled to participate in research. In many respects this demonstrates a pushing back of the barriers as researchers make pioneering attempts to meet the concerns that others have raised in enabling all to have a voice. What is achieved today was largely uncharted territory 25 years ago. As Goodley and Moore (2000) state, much of the research can truly be described as innovative and radical. Its strength lies with drawing on the creativity of practitioners in eliciting views and coupling this with the systematic approach of researchers to checking the validity and authenticity of these views. However, such research will continue to be problematic. The supports we provide, while they facilitate a response, also serve to constrain and set parameters to the answers we receive. Advancement in the field relies on good documentation of the mistakes made as well as the successes achieved, a reflexive journey that both recognises and responds to the cognitive, linguistic and emotional demands of the task.

CHAPTER 7

Small-scale research

Introduction

In this chapter, the aim is to explore some of the small-scale research that has been carried out relating to people with learning difficulties. Until relatively recently, small-scale studies were not considered to be 'real' research, because their results cannot be generalised across large populations. Lately there has been a growing interest in different approaches and small-scale projects such as case studies, action research, observational studies, life stories and ethnography have been developed by researchers who are interested in learning disability topics. Although some of these small-scale studies have been carried out by academics, the work of practitioners is particularly interesting to explore. Many of the practitioner projects are unpublished and some, although published in the professional literature, would not be considered to be conventional 'research', but nonetheless they contain useful information for people wishing to understand more about the actual experiences and opinions of people with learning disabilities, their families and carers. Before we examine practitioner projects and accounts, we will focus on academic published examples of small-scale research in the three areas of case studies, action research and ethnography. All have been mentioned in earlier chapters but in this chapter we will be examining them in a little more detail. Various learning difficulty topics will be used to illustrate the approaches.

Thus the chapter is divided into two sections:

1. small-scale research (including case studies, action research and ethnography)
2. practitioner research.

In each section we will discuss some of the features of the approaches used in small-scale research and then examine some examples related to learning difficulties. The intention is both to promote understanding of different methodologies and also to disseminate information about aspects of the lives of people with learning difficulties.

Small-scale research

Small-scale research can utilise a range of approaches across the quantitative–qualitative divide. It can be 'fixed' or 'flexible' in design: post-positivist, constructivist or emancipatory (Robson, 2002). Data can be collected through observation, interview, document analysis, questionnaire, tests and assessments. In practice, small-scale research is often flexible in design and generates qualitative data on a few subjects or instances. It does not attempt to be generalisable as the focus is in-depth understanding of one or a few instances. Sometimes small-scale projects accompany larger-scale projects, for example, a large-scale survey is followed by a small number of case studies or the project begins with a pilot assessment of a few subjects, which is then applied to much larger numbers. In this chapter, our interest is not in either of those, but in research that was conceived as small-scale from beginning to end. A search of the academic literature in the last five to six years did not yield many studies for us to consider as the field of learning difficulties has been dominated by 'large' scale research. We have put 'large' into inverted commas as large-scale within a minority group is only relatively large, but the aim of most of the research in the field is to generalise across the learning disability population: to find out what kind of service works best or is most cost effective; what affects different kinds of behaviour; or what happens when a particular approach is tried. Single or a small number of instances have not interested many researchers.

Case studies

Case-study research is described by Yin (2003) as an empirical inquiry that: 'investigates a contemporary phenomenon within its real-life context, especially when the boundaries between the phenomenon and context are not clearly evident.' He goes on to say that:

> case study inquiry copes with the technically distinctive situation in which there will be many more variables of interest than data points, and as one result, relies on multiple sources of evidence, with data needing to converge in a triangulating fashion, and as another result, benefits from the prior development of theoretical propositions to guide data collection and analysis.

He sums it up as 'a comprehensive research strategy' but warns that it should not be equated to qualitative research, nor to ethnography, although both can be associated with case studies. Evidence can be both quantitative and qualitative. Also case studies can be ethnographic in nature in that they use close-up, detailed observation of natural contexts; but they are not all ethnographic.

Robson (2002) tries to avoid using a distinction between qualitative and quantitative research, instead using 'flexible' and 'fixed' designs to indicate the extent to which the research is pre-structured or open-ended. Yin (2003) lists a number of different kinds of case studies as exploratory, descriptive and explanatory, suggesting that they are all helpful when trying to answer 'how' and 'why' questions. Exploratory studies can be used when little is known of the phenomenon, descriptive when attempting to understand a phenomenon rarely studied, and explanatory when wishing to explain why a phenomenon might have occurred. Robson (2002) lists a number of types of case study as: individual; a set of individuals; community; social group; organisation or institution; events, roles and relationships. He suggests that these can be divided into two basic units of analysis: holistic and multiple, depending on whether the concern remains at the single, global level or opens out into more than one case to enable analytic generalisation (rather than statistical generalisation). We are interested particularly in case studies of individuals or a small number of individuals in this chapter across the whole range of case-study research.

Despite the development over many years of case-study methodology, there are still many researchers and funding bodies who do not consider the case study as a serious research approach. They see it as a 'soft option' or a weak alternative to 'proper' research. Even when it is recognised by research funders, they often stipulate covering as many cases as possible to increase the validity of the research. A single case study is unlikely to be funded for research intended to influence government policy (see Chapter 2 on research agendas). Gillham (2000) defends case study as a strategy for exploring the 'complexity, embedded character and specificity of real-life phenomena', where experimental science is ill-suited. He suggests that when it is carried out well, it can provide compelling reading. To avoid criticisms of lack of rigour and triviality, Gillham explains the use of triangulation with multiple sources of evidence; for example, documents, records, interviews, detached observation, participant observation and artefacts. He (along with other methodology scholars) writes about ways of carrying out the research and writing it up.

Examples of case-study research in learning difficulties

We have looked not only to England but to other parts of the world, not because other countries are more likely to be using case-study research but because exploring a variety of contexts is valid in its own right. We have referred on many occasions to research studies from beyond England, particularly to the USA, but we have not drawn attention to them previously. The intention is not to be comparative but to examine work in different contexts.

Quantitative studies

We begin with small-scale quantitative case studies, of which there are a number of examples in the literature. Many of these are experimental, such as the Dutch study of six children with Angelman syndrome (Diddn *et al.*, 2001). Angelman syndrome is a genetic disorder which is characterised by severe intellectual disability, inappropriate bursts of laughter, hyperactivity and several physical anomalies. Incontinence is often a problem and intractable despite traditional training programmes. A modified version of an effective procedure devised by Azrin and Foxx (1971) was used and five phases were included in the study: baseline, training, post-training 1, post training 2 and follow-up. The training is very clearly described and in brief, is based on simple behavioural techniques of reinforcement, overcorrection and time out from reinforcement. Results show improvements for all six participants which were maintained across 2.5 years.

Other examples found in the recent journals include an Israeli study where five children with mental retardation and challenging behaviours were taught to use other more appropriate means of communication (Hetzroni and Roth, 2003). Results show a reduction in the percentage of intervals of challenging behaviours. A multiple-probe design was used to collect data on different behaviours. An American study to evaluate multimedia instruction to teach grocery words associations and store location to three students with mild to moderate intellectual disabilities also used a multiple-probe design across three sets of word pairs (Mechling and Gast, 2003). Results indicate that the use of photographs, text and video recording were successful in teaching reading of associated pairs and locations of the grocery items in the store. In a Spanish study (Basil and Reyes, 2003) an intervention package based on the multimedia software Delta messages and a scaffolding approach to literacy was used with six children with severe disabilities (aged between 8 and 16 years). The students' literacy skills were tested four times (initially, after three months' training, three months later and six months later). Results show that construction of written sentences improved significantly and the researchers feel that that fact demonstrates the importance of reading for a purpose when acquiring literacy.

Descriptive case study
Chapter 5 on intervention studies contains more detail on experimental research. In this chapter we focus on qualitative case studies where multiple sources of evidence are used to understand a phenomenon in its context. Australian researchers Gallaher *et al.* (2002) provide a good example of a descriptive case study of a young woman with Down syndrome learning to read. Abby was 19 years old and after 12 years of education, her reading was judged to be 'emergent'. She was enrolled on a programme which was based on the belief that young adulthood is a productive time for people with Down syndrome in terms of learning and development. The study was not experimental in that there was no attempt to control variables or teach in a particular way, although a baseline of performance was taken and progress was compared with this. The teacher responded to Abby's needs in whatever way was appropriate as the weeks went on and data concerning progress were collected through multiple methods. These methods were participant observation, video and audio recordings, interviews, writing samples and field notes. They enabled the researchers to give a detailed and descriptive account of the tutoring programme development as well as Abby's literacy experiences while on the programme. Throughout the data analysis process categories and themes that appeared over time were noted and documented. Results of the study indicated firstly that Abby's reading did

improve over the 12 weeks of individualised instruction, as did her confidence. Other aspects emerged, such as, although she was motivated by computers, there were no particular benefits found from their use. Detailed understanding of Abby's strengths and needs were also gathered, which provided information for further teaching. The researchers claim that the case-study approach they took is valuable as an in-depth exploration of a particular individual's development during a tutoring programme, which indicates the importance of providing literacy learning for young adults with Down syndrome. They also recommend longer studies that focus on the processes and strategies that can be used to support ongoing development in literacy.

Explanatory case study

Another single case study was carried out by UK researchers and this time, the case is an inclusive education initiative rather than an individual or series of individuals (Dew-Hughes and Blandford, 1999). This is an explanatory case study, in that the researchers were able not only to describe the social skills of the children with severe learning difficulties (SLD) but also to explain why they behaved in the way they did. They used participant observation, followed by structured non-participant observation and semi-structured guided conversations (interviews) with staff. They invited staff comment on analysed data to ensure that staff interpretations rather than their own were recorded. The structured observations were carried out in both special and the mainstream schools during classroom activities and at lunch and play sessions. Relevant themes and opinions were drawn from these observations and also from the interviews. The main result of the study was finding the greater immaturity of pupils with SLD in comparison with their mainstream peers. The main thrust of the explanation for this related to the attitude to pupils with SLD from special school staff. They seemed to encourage a much more family atmosphere than in mainstream schools, where the emphasis was on professionalism. Pupils with SLD called staff by their first names (a practice usually associated with young children), were cuddled much more than their mainstream peers and generally were treated at their academic level rather than their actual age. The researchers question whether the familial atmosphere in special schools is a positive or negative thing, especially if it delays secondary socialisation through a confusion of home and school and effectively devalues the maturing process in people with learning disabilities.

Exploratory case study

An example of an exploratory case study was found also from the UK. Germain (2002) set out to find out how mainstream staff can support pupils with Down syndrome in 'dedicated numeracy time'. She focused on a single four-year-old child (Paul), using the educational records of the child, unstructured and structured observations and semi-structured interviews to collect data. Germain was interested in the difference between whole class, small group and individual teaching sessions, particularly as Paul behaved differently and was expected to do different things in each setting. He was also supported in different ways; for example he was physically prompted, the teacher shared tasks with him and he had visual clues to tasks. This support was much more effective in individual and group sessions than in whole class sessions, where the teacher found him very difficult to manage and said it was hard to provide work for him at the right level to meet his needs. However, Paul's behaviour was actually better in whole class sessions than in individual or group sessions where he would throw resources, get out of his seat and run around the classroom. Germain suggests that her results present a problem for mainstream teachers who find it hard to provide just the right amount and kind of support for individuals while meeting everyone else's needs. Paul is clearly gaining benefit from being with his peers in terms of learning acceptable behaviour but he is learning academically better when working individually or in a small group.

Case examples

Other kinds of case studies found in the literature include several kinds of case examples taken from practice. For example, Fernandez (2000) describes an example of inclusive education for Mary, an Australian student, within which he quite simply tells Mary's story. There is no detail of the methods used for this case example so we are reluctant to deem it a full case study. Berry (2003) from Germany uses a similar technique with four case examples relating to the success of psychodynamic therapy with people with learning disabilities and challenging behaviour. He concludes his descriptive examples with his beliefs about psychodynamic-orientated work which lead him to suggest that therapists need to venture into the world of the person with learning disabilities and challenging behaviour rather than expecting them to come into ours: 'then' he says, 'we have a chance to help them achieve their own internal peace'.

We return to literacy for the third case example which is described as 'a retrospective, structured, clinical case study', influenced by the work of Miles and Huberman (1984) on qualitative data collection. This is a case study of the literacy acquisition of Christine, an American woman of Greek origins aged 35 with developmental disabilities (Pershey and Gilbert, 2002). Methods are described, which consist of initial observations of strengths and needs, the use of eclectic techniques for teaching reading, records of sessions, samples of writing and a series of convergent structured tasks in Mary's seventh year of working with one of the researchers. The success of the collaboration between Mary and Tom (the teacher-researcher) prompts Pershey and Gilbert to argue for teaching literacy skills to adults with developmental disabilities. They recommend a holistic, socially based programme of fluent reading tutorials. They do not wish to claim that the evidence from one case is sufficient for generalisations but they recommend a database of such cases to provide a body of knowledge in an area on which there is little information.

Multiple case studies

So far, the case studies have either been of an individual or of several individuals considered individually. A Chinese study uses a different approach, that of taking the information about ten cases and analysing them together, looking for themes across the cases (Pearson *et al.*, 2002). The aim of the study is to examine the issue of social inclusion in relation to young people with learning disabilities, specifically with reference to employment. The ten young people were all interviewed using questions adapted from the Vocational Integration Index but constructed in a conversational, informal manner, rather than question-and-answer style. All interviews were recorded, transcribed and content-analysed. The 'story' that emerged was described as containing 'rich information about the employment situation of people with learning difficulties in Guangzhou (in China), as well as other aspects of social participation'. The social context of China is described to enable the reader to understand the importance of employment to the participants. What constituted a job or real employment varied widely. For example, one young person was paid to stay at home, and was only employed so the company could claim its quota of disabled people on the payroll. Conclusions of the researchers draw attention to the traditional negative paradigm towards people with a disability which is preventing changes in legislation and social policy becoming reality in ordinary citizenry. Average citizens in Guangzhou are not ready to embrace people with learning difficulties and treat them with respect.

Ethnography

Some of the studies make use of ethnographic techniques or are reports of ethnographies. Ethnography is a social anthropological approach but instead of studying societies in far-away places, ethnographers typically look to documenting aspects of social groups closer to home. Participant observation enables the ethnographer to gain an insider view of the society under scrutiny and this is often supplemented by unstructured interviews, and document analysis. The field diary is an important source of data enabling the researcher to record events as they occur which they annotate with developing interpreta-tions. Robson (2002) describes ethnography as 'typically exploratory' with a goal of 'thick description' (Geertz, 1973) which enables readers to understand what it is like to be part of the culture being studied. Some ethnographers develop or establish 'grounded theory' (Glaser and Strauss, 1967) but others would argue that they wish to describe the context through the eyes of the people in it and not impose ideas from outside. Both approaches have become accepted variants of ethnography.

Ethnography has been heavily criticised because of its small-scale character, its failure to influence practice and the extent to which it can legitimately claim it represents an independent social reality (Hammersley, 1992). Despite these fundamental doubts about the approach, it has been used by several researchers interested in people with learning disabilities, as members of a social group who share a culture. The length of time it takes to 'get under the skin' of a culture makes it difficult for researchers to carry out a full ethnography so there are several examples of the use of ethnographic techniques in shorter studies. It is mainly these that are reported here, not least because very few full ethno-graphies have been carried out recently in learning disability contexts, although there were several carried out in the 1960s, 1970s and 1980s, such as Goffman (1961), Edgerton, (1967), Morris (1969), Oswin (1971), Alaszewski (1986) (see Chapter 1 for more discussion of research in the twentieth century).

It is particularly difficult for us to report ethnographic research in this book as it is full of rich information and ideas which are virtually impossible to sum up. The whole point of this approach is to generate detail specific to the context under study. So we would urge you to read some of the studies we refer to. Hopefully the brief summaries here will 'whet your appetite'.

Ethnographic style case studies

Baker and Donelly's (2001) study of the social experiences of four disabled boys in Australian schools is an example of ethnographic techniques used to explore environmental influences. All the boys had Fragile x syndrome, one was in a special school, two in special classes and two in a regular classroom. Data were collected using three half-day participant observations followed by in-depth interviews with the child's family, teacher and occupational therapist. These data were analysed using techniques of comparing, conceptualising and categorising. Coding discussion groups were helped by people selected from diverse backgrounds to ensure comprehensiveness. Three major elements of the environment emerged as affecting the social experiences of the boys: perceptions of disability, family and school. The researchers point to the importance of changing the social environment, rather than the individuals with learning disabilities, to improve their experiences. They use the example of Sean, who had difficulties in making friends with children without disability. They point out that the difficulty is attributable not only to his social skills but also to diverse environmental factors; for example, being in a segregated class, being perceived as different, his family home being a long way from the school, his mother lacking support and opportunity to provide social experiences, his school principal inadvertently terminating several friendships, his teacher not facilitating interaction and school policy not addressing his social needs.

A second example of an ethnographic style case study was carried out by Azzopardi (2000) of a parents' self-advocacy group in Malta. The tools used to collect data were a literature review, the experience and involvement of the researcher with the parents' society, review of documents and a postal questionnaire. The experience of the group is described and reflected upon, particularly focusing on the relationship between parents and professionals. The fundamental target of the parents' society was to support from birth disabled children and their families by helping, supporting and educating parents to overcome the challenges and pressures that society imposes upon them. The parents' society clearly indicated a need for family-focused services, where parents take the directive role with professionals in support. However, in practice they continue to experience barriers, limited resources and little control over their own lives, while the power remains firmly with the professionals.

Self-advocacy is also the topic of a UK study of four groups of people with learning disabilities (Goodley *et al.*, 2003). The four groups were chosen to demonstrate the diversity in the UK today. Two researchers spent on average 2.5 days per week with the groups over a period of 18 months. Field notes were written up after every meeting which were a combination of theoretical, methodological and empirical notes. The aim of the study was to capture the 'storied nature of self-advocacy', a technique associated with novel or hidden cultures, in order to emphasise the voice of people with disabilities while also providing 'contextual frameworks for deep analysis of disabling and disability cultures'. The researchers collected life stories of 17 key participants and 'accessible narratives' from another 30 self-advocates. Group interviews were also carried out for all four groups and individual interviews for four supporters. Throughout the research, the team adhered to a participatory research philosophy, using accessible methods and including participants in designing and directing the study (see Chapter 6 for more on participatory research). Data were analysed using grounded theory, influenced by the social model of disability.

Goodley *et al.* (2003) make many points in their exploration of meanings for the members of the self-advocacy groups. They point out that

> self advocacy is not something that can be artificially pinned on those who need it (through the setting up of self advocacy groups by well-meaning professionals for their clients) but something organically and culturally created in response to enabling and, paradoxically, disabling environments.

Professionals should take note and not 'tick off' self-advocacy as being done when a group has been set up. Changing people's lives in a context of a disabling culture is more complex than that. There are many quotations from participants in the research, some of them very powerful examples of the difficulties faced by people with learning disabilities, for example:

> The group members encouraged them [two members of the group] to see each other, insisting Susie should tell her Mum about the relationship, 'You're not a kid, you know. You can have a boyfriend if you want – it's your right.' Then Susie reacted, 'I'm fed up everybody telling me what to do. Since I was really little, everyone's been telling me what to do. I'm sick of it.'

One of the most telling came from a man talking about being a member of groups such as a self-advocacy group:

> I used to be a member of loads of committees fighting for rights and all that … yeah, and the Disability Movement do some great stuff for other people but how's all that stuff on politics going to get me a girlfriend and a job?

The researchers sum up by recognising self-advocacy as a 'thriving sociocultural and political movement' and suggesting that groups 'boast rich cultures that can instruct professionalism'. Hearing the voices of people with learning disabilities through the research can help us to begin to understand that culture.

In a different article based on this same research, Goodley (1999) debates some of the methodological aspects of conducting ethnography with disabled people. He examines his own role as a non-disabled, male, white, middle-class researcher and how that affected his understanding of the culture of the self-advocacy group within which he participated during the first year of his research. He debates whether disability research can be carried out by a person who is not disabled and concludes that:

> two of the main purposes of disability research are first to unmask the process of disablement and secondly to pinpoint how resilience is borne out of these exclusionary environments. These two themes are best addressed through working with disabled participants and organisations of disabled people.

Certainly the researcher, in this study, is able to develop his understanding of the self-advocacy group and the lives of the people in it throughout the study. This article shows how his thinking changed as the stories and the complexities of the group dynamics unfolded. He is able to identify ill-thought-out assumptions, premature analyses and misplaced interpretations about people with learning difficulties as he reflects on the way the research was carried out. Ultimately he recognises that disability researchers walk the thin line between capturing the experiences of disabled people and reinterpreting those experiences in 'disablist' terms where disabled people are seen as victims.

Another UK ethnographic study was carried out by Benjamin (2003) in a girls' comprehensive school, where she studied inclusive education for a group of girls and young women who had difficulties in learning. The school was seen as successful, in terms of league tables, local reputation and the strivings of staff to ensure social justice and equal opportunities. However, as Benjamin's research reveals, under the surface inegalitarianism is all too evident. She demonstrates, through her field notes and conversations with the girls and young women, their experience of the tensions between the government's standards and inclusion agendas. She describes the dominant version of success which is out of reach to the students in her study. They are not going to achieve A–C grades in their GCSEs and are offered 'consolation' in a discourse built on personal incremental success and the building of self-esteem rather than publicly recognised qualifications. Although some of the students recognise themselves within this 'consolation discourse', others do not and produce themselves as anti-school and anti-teacher. Chantelle, for example sees anything less than the conventional C (or in this case its percentage equivalent) as complete failure:

> Well you can call it 12%, yeah, you can call it 12% if you like but inside it's

a big fat zero. I mean 12%, it's a zero whatever you call it, it's a zero, and that's what's inside of me. Zero, zero, zero.

Benjamin suggests that Chantelle is exposing the consolation discourse as a deficit discourse, how ever well-intentioned. The third discourse coined by Benjamin is 'the *really disabled* discourse' which is adopted for those students who have Statements of SEN and who, until recently, would not have been in mainstream schools. They are relegated to the tragedy/charity model of disability and considered hopeless cases from whom everyone else, including the other students with SEN, distance themselves. This interpretation of the success culture in a girls' comprehensive is deliberately politicised and the researcher argues that it cannot be understood, nor changed, without that perspective.

Action research

Some of the case studies found were based on ethnographic principles but were described as action research; that is, they were carried out by researchers who deliberately set out to change or develop the culture that they were studying. Action research is often conceived as a spiral of: plan, take action, collect data, evaluate, replan, take the next action, collect more data and evaluate again, and so on. It has been described as 'the study of a social situation with a view to improving the quality of action within it' (Elliott, 1991); 'an intervention in practice to bring about improvement' (Lomax, 1994); 'a form of self reflective enquiry' (McNiff, 1988); or a process of 'innovation and careful evaluation' (McIntyre, 2000). Unlike ethnographers who desire to understand a social culture, action researchers want to change, often their own culture. It is an umbrella approach which appeals particularly to practitioners who wish to research their own (rather than other people's) context. Examining a few action research case studies published in the academic literature will provide a bridge between this current section and the next, on practitioner research.

The first study we have chosen to examine was conducted by Benjamin (2001). This is a study of seven boys aged 10–12 years with moderate learning difficulties in a special school, where the researcher reflects on a project designed to help the boys construct versions of masculinity that are alternatives to the dominant macho image. Benjamin says little that is specific about data collection methods but refers to a research diary and transcripts of lessons, both of which she uses to illustrate the points she makes. Her methods are ethnographic in nature, as she tries not only to change the boys thinking through carefully prepared lessons, but attempts to understand why the boys hold the views they do. The context is again politicised and Benjamin constructs her understanding through the lens of an educational system that inevitably breeds failures as well as successes. She sees the macho brand of masculinity favoured by the boys as one area in which they, as academic failures, can succeed in the social world. At the conclusion of the project she trusts that having been involved in the project, the boys have begun to reconfigure their understanding of gender relations. She feels she can only claim that the project 'contained moments of hope in difficult circumstances'. Not many researchers are interested in gender issues and learning disabilities and this is one of the few studies in that area.

We found two more small-scale action research projects and they are both from the UK. The only action research project we found outside the UK in the last three to four years was an Australian study but it was not small-scale, so we did not review it. We were surprised not to find US studies but our search tactics may not have revealed studies that in fact do exist. The UK study by Price and Barron (1999) was actually the feasibility study for an action research project designed to set up drama workshops and night clubs for people with learning disabilities. The researchers collaborated with the Lawnmower Theatre Club (all five members have learning disabilities) in carrying out the research. Data were collected for the feasibility study through direct and participant observation and two small-scale interviewer-based surveys. The story of the project is told by the researchers, through which the experiences of the participants can be understood. It is recommended at the end of the project that it is continued so that people with learning disabilities can enjoy nights out and drama activities, where possible, in inclusive situations. The researchers, though, are not convinced that it will happen because it is an unusual venture, not seen as a priority.

Although the last of the action research projects is written by a UK researcher, the participants are Dutch teachers and the context is special educational needs in the Netherlands (Lloyd, 2002). The Dutch teachers are encouraged to conduct their own action research projects as part of an advanced course on SEN. Lloyd is anxious to explore action research as a potential agent for developing critical reflection that can lead to change and development in practice in education. She explores some of the criticisms of action research as an approach in her attempt to evaluate its use. Lack of rigour is one important criticism which Altrichter (1993, cited by Lloyd) believes can be countered by:

- collecting and analysing data from a variety of sources and perspectives
- interlinking reflection and action through cycles of research
- recognising that the approach is subjective and value-laden
- recognising that process is less about finding solutions and more about deepening understanding and identifying areas for further research
- peer evaluation of the research is important
- interactive dissemination is essential.

The action research conducted by the Dutch teachers is built on these points. It was evaluated by Lloyd through the use of open questionnaires, semi-structured interviews, open discussions, email 'conversations' and critical analysis of the teachers' assignments and research findings. The data collection was a collaborative process between the researcher and the teachers. They wanted to find out if the action research carried out by the teachers met the criteria provided by Altrichter (above), what effect it had on the teachers' professional development and whether it affected practice in SEN.

Results suggest that the teachers found carefully prepared semi-structured interviews and a carefully structured reflective journal were the most useful data-gathering tools. They were constantly concerned that their research did not yield 'objective' findings as their view of research was definitely traditionally positivist. They also had difficulty in persuading their colleagues that action research was a serious endeavour. However, they engaged well with the approach, developed an understanding beyond the seeking for simplistic answers and sought to validate their projects through critical friends. Dissemination of the work was through a conference and then an email network. The teachers developed their ability to become reflective practitioners, questioning their own work and improving what was going on in their classrooms. Lloyd chose three teachers' work to discuss in detail, one of which related to children with severe learning difficulties. The teacher, Theo, wanted to encourage the children to become more independent through using an electronic chipcard to help them shop. The research was collaborative with the students and he felt they definitely gained in confidence to be more independent. They even appeared in the local paper which he claims was empowering for the students. Theo felt that he developed into a teacher who advocates self-directed learning and enabled his students to make decisions. Although initially his colleagues were sceptical and in some cases, alienated by the project, one year later they recognised the decision-making abilities in the students. Lloyd concludes her evaluation of the action research by suggesting that her case study revealed that the teachers had begun the process of developing as 'transformative intellectuals' which was vital if the move towards inclusive practice was to be made. She is cautious in her claims for action research, although it is clear that she is convinced of its worth.

Conclusions

There have been many different kinds of small-scale case studies referred to in this section, ranging from experiments, to ethnography, to action research. Several different countries were represented in the case studies found and a whole variety of data-collection tools have been employed, encompassing both quantitative and qualitative approaches. There are still many researchers who naturally distrust small-scale research, particularly if it is qualitative in nature, believing that only large-scale positivist approaches can be valid. There is, however, much rich data contained in the case studies we have cited and these offer insights into the world of learning disabilities that is hard to achieve in any other way. Small-scale case studies can never be the *only* way to research learning disabilities but it certainly is *one* way.

This section has concluded with an examination of the use of action research to develop the work of practitioners in special education, which leads into the second section of this chapter, specifically on practitioner research. Again, all the work is small-scale in character and some is not even recognised or claimed as research and again it contains rich information which is too important to ignore.

Practitioner research

Some writers are very specific about what constitutes practitioner research and others are more eclectic. Some concentrate specifically on action research (Altrichter *et al.*, 1993; McNiff with Whitehead, 2002; Burnaford *et al.*, 2001) and others examine a broader set of approaches (Edwards and Talbot, 1999; Hopkins, 2002; Bell, 1999). In this section, the more eclectic view will be explored, assuming that practitioners will be researching in a variety of ways for a variety of reasons. All the approaches will be small-scale, assuming either that the researcher is working alone or as a small group of practitioners examining or changing what happens in their own organisations. There are very few texts on practitioner research in learning difficulties or special educational needs. There are also relatively few texts that relate to disciplines other than education, although nurses and social workers are becoming more interested in practitioner research (Winter and Munn-Giddings, 2001; Kember, 2001), despite the current expectation that evidence-based practice will be based on the double-blind clinical trials usually found in health-related research (Morrison and Lilford, 2001).

One of the most important aspects of practitioner research is that it almost always involves the practitioner in struggling to fit research into an already busy timetable. The prime business of a practitioner is to teach, to nurse, to care for people, to help children and young people with learning difficulties to live fulfilled lives, to practice therapy, to assess their needs and so many other practical things. On rare occasions, practitioners are seconded from their jobs or given protected time to carry out research, but the majority will be working full-time throughout the experience. Some practitioners will be studying for academic qualifications and will be required to choose a topic for a research project/dissertation, but others will be less formally supported, or not at all. The DfES Best Practice Research Scholarships have been developed to provide support for individuals and groups of teachers who would like to research their own practice. This has been a very deliberate move on the part of the DfES, to encourage chalk-face research that is perceived to be more relevant to teachers than some of the seemingly esoteric studies carried out by academics (Mortimore, 2000).

Although practitioners and researchers are generally seen as two separate groups of people with different perspectives and different fortes, many writers suggest that there can be a combining of the two. Freeman (1998) writes of 'teacher-research', explaining that it is 'the story of two nouns joined by a hyphen'. He explains what he means by the two nouns but the most important aspect of his argument is that a teacher-researcher is working 'at that hyphen'. The 'teacher', he explains, is a person and 'research' is a process, and putting the two together with a hyphen creates a person-process. The hyphen also emphasises the connections and differences between the two worlds of teaching and researching. The traditional view of research is that it is supposed to generate knowledge for practitioners to utilise but bringing the two together can help to propagate something new: something that reaches across the divide. Blurring the boundaries between practitioners and researchers does not negate their specialist functions, any more than blurring the boundaries between, for example, teachers and therapists as they work with children and young people with learning difficulties/disabilities denies the importance of having the expertise of both. What is important is that the young person receives a service that makes sense of what both professionals have to offer (Lacey, 2001). A practitioner researcher can help make sense of both practice and research while celebrating what can be brought together to benefit children and young people with learning difficulties/disabilities.

So, what do practitioners need to do to become practitioner researchers? Some writers suggest that they should learn to be like academic researchers, especially if they are conducting research for an academic qualification, and there are many texts that can support people who wish to do that (Robson, 2002; Cohen *et al.*, Sims and Wright, 2000) but there are other writers who encourage practitioners to contribute something different, something that fits more closely what is happening in practice. Both these perspectives will be explored below, beginning with the more traditional academic view of small-scale research.

An academic perspective

Practitioners who wish to carry out academic-style research have several approaches that they can use, across both quantitative and qualitative perspectives, ranging from surveys, evaluation studies and experiments to case studies, ethnography and documentary research. Schindele (1985) suggests that traditional quantitative research (using 'hard' numbers) is difficult to carry out in special education for a variety of reasons, but principally because children and young people with SEN are all very different, so finding sufficient numbers for samples or matched groups for randomised control trials is rarely possible. There is also a general feeling in the caring professions that denying an intervention which might be beneficial to all children is not strictly ethical, and neither is experimentation. Obviously there is a place for numbers even in small-scale research carried out by practitioners. For example, a practitioner may wish to count the number of times an individual child is engaged in a task or approaches a peer in order to interact socially, or to compare staff opinions of their support needs across the whole organisation. Generally though, practitioner researchers are more interested in individual cases or the situations in their own schools, centres and clinics. They are unlikely to have easy access to large numbers even if that was the kind of research that interested them.

Conducting academic-style research as part of a degree programme brings many challenges to practitioners. As research is a very different business from practice, sometimes the study of research methodology can cause students to doubt their own abilities. The whole process is new to them, with its own jargon and literature, which can undermine the confidence that has been growing throughout the rest of the course. In the vast majority of cases, this is only a temporary state and once the basics of conducting small-scale research have been mastered, confidence returns.

A practitioner perspective

Practitioners do not have to be studying on academic courses to undertake research into their practice. Some are involved in formal research for a scheme such as the DfES Best Practice Research Scholarships, which may involve academic support, but others are engaged in recording what they do, evaluating and reflecting on this and publishing their results in some form, perhaps in practitioner journals and newsletters or perhaps in local authorities' publications, at conferences or in their own organisations. Publication in some form is important for practitioner research if it to influence others but appearing in a peer-reviewed academic journal is not necessary.

So what characterises practitioner research? How is it different from traditional research or from the reflective practice in which so many teachers, nurses and social workers are naturally engaged as they work with children and young people with learning difficulties?

Freeman (1998, p2) sums up the teacher-as-researcher dilemma: 'I wasn't paid to speculate and wonder; I was paid to teach.' The rest of his book is about how to bring together the two activities – 'the doing and the wondering' – which he admits is like juggling with contrapuntal demands. Teaching demands action in the classroom, based on what is known and what has to be achieved, whereas research pulls in the opposite direction, towards questioning the bases of these actions and their underlying assumptions. Bisplinghoff and Allen (1998, pvii) write of striving to find an 'organic union' between teaching and research to prevent the adding of research onto an already too heavy workload. They suggest that at its best teaching and research support each other like a 'seesaw partner in the playground' (p5) but that it is hard to maintain the balance, especially when the research seems to interfere with teaching rather than supporting it.

One of the teacher-research stories in Bisplinghoff and Allen's book (Keffer *et al.*, 1998) tells of how a group of teachers, wishing to improve the way they taught writing, began by forming a writing group and sharing their personal writings together. This stage culminated in an article which they wrote together. They tried to follow this with a more conventional approach to data collection through surveying pupils following teaching but found that they lost both momentum and purpose. On reflection, the teacher-researchers felt that they should have had faith in their own data collection method and not submitted to perceived pressure to use methods more traditionally associated with educational research. Another group of writers in the same book (Sumner *et al.*,

1998) conclude that teacher-research is just different from traditional research in that it must fit round what is best for the pupils at any given time and cannot dictate.

Although some writers emphasise the differences between traditional research and practitioner research, others do not see that as important (e.g. Morrison and Lilford, 2001), suggesting that anyone claiming that they are involved in practitioner-research should need to adhere to the basic principles of research. For example, Zeni (2001, pxiv) defines practitioner research as 'qualitative research conducted by insiders ... to improve their own practice'. Hopkins (2002) writes about 'systematic self-conscious enquiry' and Freeman (1998, p9) suggests that teacher-research should be 'disciplined', which refers not only to the order of the enquiry but also to the disciplines themselves that serve as the source for that order. Freeman sees it as important for teacher-researchers to make disciplined, as opposed to intuitive, statements about teaching. Edwards and Talbot (1999) support this view, suggesting that a research perspective is orderly, considered, scholarly and scientific. They go on to claim that practitioner-research is very important in organisational development, impact on professional life and in influencing workplace problem-solving, even when, or perhaps especially when not attached to academic qualifications. Fischer and Hobson (2001, p29) offer a clear view which seems to sum up the essence of teacher research. They talk about a personal as well as a professional quest, 'a journey towards making sense of and finding satisfaction in one's teaching', emphasising the importance of seeing teaching and research as a joint enterprise.

Practitioners writing about practice

In this section, children and young people with profound learning disabilities will be the focus of an exploration of a variety of ways practitioners write about their own practice. Some of the examples come from dissertations for academic qualifications and others from articles published in professional journals and magazines. Some of the work is clearly identifiable as practitioner research in the sense explored above, but some contains descriptions of practice that the research community (and the authors themselves) would not recognise as research. It seems important to include practitioners writing about practice for two reasons: firstly, because often the result is actually 'as if research'; and secondly, because there is so little conventional research related to profound disabilities that articles about practice are often the best data available.

Unpublished dissertations and reports
A letter/e-mail message was sent out to tutors on courses related to profound disabilities and to subscribers to the network discussion group, SLD-Forum, asking for information on any practitioner research that had been carried out in the last five years but not published. This resulted in 11 replies. A search of the University of Birmingham dissertation titles revealed nine master's disserta-

Table 7.1 Topics of the 70 assignments, projects and dissertations

Topic	Number
Teaching and learning	32
Staff, service or family issues	31
Personal focus	12

tions in the last five years and ten BPhil dissertations that related to profound and multiple learning difficulties (PMLD). Students also undertake assignments and small-scale projects as part of their qualification in PMLD and 36 studies completed by students in the academic years 2001–2 and 2002–3 were included in this review. The topics for these assignments were examined and it was found that of 70 assignments or dissertations, the majority of topics chosen for study related to teaching and learning, though almost as many were related to staff, service or family issues. Table 7.1 shows how the topics were divided. Some topics fell into more than one category so there are 75 categories in total.

In the teaching and learning category, the most frequently addressed single topic was, unsurprisingly, communication, which was the focus of 12 projects. It also featured to a lesser extent in many others in the category. For example, the 5 projects on play and leisure all contained reference to the potential of play and leisure to promote communication. Drama and music therapy were both concerned with communication, as were the 6 ICT projects which were also focused on cognitive development, particularly contingency responding. Multidisciplinary teamwork (6), planning (6) and staff development (6) were all important in the Staff, service or family issues. The Personal focus category contained the widest variety of topics, from eating and drinking and epilepsy to challenging behaviour, choice-making and emotional development.

We will now explore one assignment from each of the categories to look in more detail at the topic, how it was studied and its results. Following the assignments, we examine three dissertations and then two of the four PhDs found that were on the general topic of PMLD.

Assignments
The assignment from the teaching and learning category was educational in character and was undertaken by Clare Dover, who specifically focused on communication. She evaluated the current assessment methods used in her school and considered two alternatives. She also examined the target-setting for individual pupils and considered the teaching strategies being used, in an evaluation of the IEP (Individual Education Plan) format used in the school. The results of her study support the use of the Affective Communication Assessment (Coupe *et al.*, 1985) to assess early communication and the use of 'personal passports' to ensure staff respond consistently to pupils' communication attempts. Dover made several recommendations from the project, one of which

was related to the importance of multidisciplinary teamwork, especially at the time of annual review (part of the IEP process). She also points to the need for further evaluation of the new IEP system and other assessments tools.

We chose a reflective study by Ann Pearson, from the staff, services or family issues category, within which she evaluated the move towards inclusive education for pupils with PMLD in her school. She began by focusing on inclusion within the school and then considering the contribution her school could make to develop more inclusive attitudes outside, in the wider educational community. From her study, Pearson suggests that an issue as complex as inclusion requires much collaborative working, a clear management policy and time and resources given to drive the inclusive practices forward. She sees certain internal inclusive practices as essential for success; for example, increased structure to the timetable, greater flexibility with pupil groups and individual timetables where appropriate. In the wider community, she recommends cluster group meetings with local primary and secondary schools to begin the process.

Finally the personal focus assignment chosen was an exploratory study of aromatherapy and massage by Gill Young, which mainly consisted of a questionnaire sent to other schools with a population of PMLD pupils to find out about their practice. Her results shown that massage is rated highly by staff but there are mixed opinions about aromatherapy. She also found that there was little training in schools and very few schools had proper policies to guide staff.

Dissertations

Moving on to the dissertations, two action research projects carried out by class teachers demonstrate how examining a situated problem can provide useful information for people in other situations. Ann Farish (2000) set out to create a 'personal profile' for pupils with PMLD and in so doing concluded that such profiles should include sections on communication, physical, sensory, personal and medical needs. She found that curriculum attainment was contained within IEPs and was not necessary to the profile. Suzanne Farrell (1997) wanted to improve the quality of dinner time at school for pupils with PMLD. There were three action cycles: reviewing the current situation; devising and implementing training; evaluating training and the impact on practice. From her observations, Farrell suggested that staff were well-intentioned but often their communications with pupils with PMLD were inappropriate, but that the most experienced staff elicited the highest number of learning experiences during dinner times. She also found that pupils were confused by a lot of noise or by being left unattended and that often their attempts at communication were either ignored or just not noticed. Her training programme for staff included simulations of being fed and learning from videos of dinner times. She concludes that this kind of joint problem-solving improved practice.

Some dissertation students were interested in understanding a situation in order to identify good practice and inform future developments. Mary Coffey (2000), for example, examined the use of multi-sensory environments. She analysed 48 staff questionnaires, seven observations in the multi-sensory room and seven interviews of staff and was able to conclude that:

- multi-sensory environments are being used for a number of educational purposes as well as for leisure and therapy
- teachers are aware of the need for rigour in planning if maximum educational use is to be attained
- multi-sensory environments are not intrinsically effective learning environments but are only as good as the person using them.

PhD studies

Few PhD studies have been undertaken that relate directly to children and young people with PMLD. One that is available at the University of Birmingham was undertaken by Jim McNicholas (1998). His aim was to investigate the nature of assessment, recording and reporting practices in schools, across the National Curriculum subjects. His findings suggest that most assessment is informal, with teachers relying on their own schemes, and that teachers who consider themselves unqualified seem to be more uncertain of their own ability to assess pupils than those with either a qualification in PMLD or a generic SEN qualification. McNicholas found that just over a third of teachers in his sample had a specialist qualification that included PMLD, another third had a generic SEN qualification and the rest had no specialist qualification of any kind. He concludes that support for teachers of pupils with PMLD is lacking both in terms of courses and in terms of in-school support. He also concludes that assessment in schools is largely about product rather than process, despite the difficulty pupils with PMLD have in providing a product to be assessed and despite the interest there is in dynamic, ecological and scaffolded assessment, all of which are process-based.

Another PhD study was undertaken by Mark Barber (2000) and is available at Manchester Metropolitan University. One of the aims of this study was to investigate and account for the problems that people with PMLD have in acquiring new knowledge and successful experiences of interacting with people and objects. Barber analysed video sequences of seven children (aged 9–16) and observed that learners were more likely to engage in opportunities that lead to single consequences (i.e. contingencies) than those that lead to more complex interactions (i.e. social interaction). He also noticed that learners could adjust the venue of a strategy more easily than adjusting the strategy itself and that learners with PMLD chose to interact more with known problems than less familiar ones. From these observations, Barber concluded that it is not the flexibility of the learners' skills that enable them to interact successfully but the flexibility of the situation that allows the inclusion of the learner. The critical factor for the learner is whether (or not) their skills correspond to what the problem requires. Therefore it is the job of the member of staff or carer to enable the successful involvement of learners with PMLD by mediating and 'signposting' encounters (social and object focused), rather than try to teach new skills. This is because the manner and content with which we engage people with PMLD are frequently too confusing, unpredictable and difficult to decide for someone with compromised cognitive resources. Encounters should be learner-led although scaffolded and mediated by the more highly 'skilled' partner.

Published articles on practice

Three practice-focused journals were examined in the search for articles that contained reports of work that could be broadly defined as practitioner research: *PMLD-Link*, *SLD Experience* and *Eye Contact*. The vast majority of the articles make no claim to being based on (conventional) research, but those selected contain valuable data that could be seen 'as if research'. Articles by academics were excluded from the search, as were articles that simply gave information or opinion. Following a general analysis of the topics of the articles in the three journals, the theme of literacy and profound learning disabilities was selected for detailed exploration, in an attempt to summarise the practice/research presented.

Not every issue of the three journals was available, so in total all 14 issues of *SLD Experience*, 10 of 14 issues of *Eye Contact* and all 13 issues of *PMLD-Link* over the period 1998–2002 were analysed. In all, 147 articles were identified as containing data on practice, although only four of those articles were declared as reports of conventional research, all carried out as part of academic courses. Ten other articles were based on practitioner evaluations carried out through interviews or questionnaires. There were a number of articles (20) written by parents, which generally contained a description of either a whole family experience or a pen-picture of an individual with PMLD. The vast majority (107) of articles contained descriptions of the experiences of practitioners, usually with the addition of examples related to individual children with PMLD or activities that had been carried out with children with PMLD. The articles on experience were examined in more depth, focusing on the quality of the data presented in an effort to explore their potential for providing evidence in any way comparable to conventional research.

It would be an exaggeration to claim that the descriptions of the children within these articles were 'case studies' as the depth required for that methodology is not present. It would perhaps be more accurate to characterise them as 'case examples' and they exemplify the practice that is being presented. Generally they contain descriptions of personal attributes, aetiology and ways of 'reaching' that person (depending upon the topic under scrutiny). For example, in an article by Barber (2001) on using the Affective Communication Assessment (Coupe *et al.*, 1985), data collected on two children with PMLD are presented to demonstrate the use of the assessment tool. For both children, their reactions to stimuli are described and interpreted by the assessor. The second child is treated in more detail than the first. Chantelle is described as a '15 year old with a visual disability and PMLD', then the detail of the assessment is explained. Chantelle:

is given a drink of orange juice, her left hand rises towards the cup and she opens her mouth to allow some liquid in, does so and then takes her mouth from the cup, swallows and turns her head to the directions from which the cup came and stills. This is interpreted as her liking the drink.

The case example continues with more details regarding Chantelle's reactions to milk, a drink to which she reacts differently, that is, she lets the milk escape from her mouth and does not turn towards the cup.

In an article by Hawke and Stanislawski (1999), on the topic of 'Communication Passports', a young man called Ricky is presented as a case example. First of all the timetable for developing a communication passport for Ricky is documented, then sample pages are shown. There is a comment from Ricky's mother and then reflections on the advantages of passports alongside what has been learned from the experience. Ricky's personality comes through very clearly and as the passport is written from Ricky's point of view, the language is very accessible: 'Things I like … 1. My absolute favourite has to be my weekly trip to MacDonalds for a milkshake (mmm lovely, but make sure it's chocolate though) …'

A third example comes from an article written by Hart (2000) about leisure activities for deafblind children and young adults. The case example of Adam is used to illustrate what can be achieved on a holiday programme at Centre Parcs run by Sense. Adam is briefly described and then the activities he enjoyed are presented:

> We spent several hours a day in the large indoor pool, which was designed to look like a tropical paradise. It was equipped with slides, jacuzzis, wave machines, sand pits, wild water rapids and waterfalls. Adam loved it and was able to explore to his heart's content – climbing over the rocks between pools, playing in the bubbles and relaxing in the water.

One of the most striking things about these three case examples (and the others in the practitioner journals) is the positive light by which the children and young people are presented. Anyone looking for evidence of the achievements of individuals regarded as having profound disabilities cannot fail to find it in these articles. The detail provided by the case examples is unlikely to be found in the more conventional research reports found in the academic journals (with a few notable exceptions, see earlier in this chapter).

Literacy and PMLD

Of the 147 articles, 19 related specifically to aspects of literacy and people with PMLD, mainly school-aged pupils. As with the case examples highlighted above, the overwhelming attitude of educators to literacy with this group is decidedly positive. A few writers admit to being sceptical regarding implementing the Literacy Strategy in schools but all have found the experience to be worthwhile for pupils with PMLD. So what do these articles offer in the way of (research) evidence regarding literacy and PMLD? Certainly none of the writers of these articles would claim to have conducted systematic research but gathered together, there is a definite body of evidence pointing to what might be considered good practice.

Six of the 19 articles contained accounts from teachers about how they adapted the Literacy Hour to meet the needs of pupils with PMLD (Pidgeon, 1999; Atkins, 1999; Carpenter, 1999; Bolt, 1999; Nolan, 1999; Howell, 2002). Nolan (1999, p28) concludes that appropriate books for the Literacy Hour should:

- contain a good story with characters the children can identify with easily
- have clear pictures
- contain repetitive language, which provides opportunities for involving the children, either vocally, with gestures or by the use of technology.

From work at Sunfield School, Carpenter (1999) suggests that in order to involve the pupils who need the most support, teachers must use a multi-tiered approach, presenting concepts in a variety of different ways including sign, symbol, object of reference, and sensory channels alongside spoken, graphic and real dimensions. Atkins (1999) comes to very similar conclusions based on experiences at her school. Teachers make use of tactile pictures, Makaton symbols, three-dimensional objects, photographs, items to produce sounds and smells, and switches to control the environment.

There is much evidence in this article and others, of the enormous creativity staff have when faced with the needs of pupils with PMLD in relation to the Literacy Hour. Several writers show how they have adapted the structure of the hour. For example, Howell (2002), with a mixed group of pupils with SLD and PMLD, has found it effective to divide the hour into 15 minutes on shared text work in the 'Hello time'; 15 minutes on signs, symbols, key sight vocabulary and phonics; 20 minutes on IEP work; and 10 minutes sharing a book and 'Showing'. In Howell's work, six special schools filled in a questionnaire to report on the first two years of the Literacy Hour. Results show that, although there is great variety, all the schools are implementing the Literacy Hour. Teachers agreed that pupils had gained from the structured routine and the emphasis on books, especially in increases in attention and involvement within group activities. They also identified some difficulties; for example, pupils with PMLD require more time to respond than is often available and books suitable for this group are difficult to find and time-consuming to produce.

One practitioner who has written several articles on literacy and PMLD in the three journals chosen for analysis (Park, 1999a, 1999b, 2001) and in other professional journals (Park, 1998, 2002) has provided many examples of activities that have been successful in rendering so-called 'great' literature accessible to a group of learners not traditionally thought to be able to understand them. Park's approach makes great use of drama games based on rhythm, repetition and response. For example, access to Dickens' *A Christmas Carol* comes through games such as 'Humbug!' and 'Saving Tiny Tim', which both make use of call-and-response rhymes and elements of surprise (e.g.: throwing a blanket over the victim). Park would not claim that pupils with PMLD can understand the novel in all its complexities but he does claim that storytelling can be seen as a uniquely human experience to which pupils with PMLD can be brought. Nowhere in his articles does Park provide conventional research evidence of the effectiveness of his approach but he does give many examples of activities that have been carried out with groups of pupils, building a picture of good practice.

Providing examples of activities is the most frequently used mode for the articles on literacy and PMLD, and there are few case examples. Park (1999b) offers some case examples in his article about literacy and objects of reference. For example, he writes of one young person who is learning 'to read' an object, in this case a bottle of shampoo:

> One memorable day, only six weeks after the weekly hairwashing routine started, Jill picked up the bottle of shampoo and gave it to a member of staff. This was the first time *ever* Jill had made an intentional communication.

Ripley (2001) conducted a conventional evaluation of two tactile books that were produced by ClearVision with funding from the DfEE. Results show that 171 of 172 children derived pleasure from the books, especially when teachers used real objects to supplement the vacuum-formed impressions of objects on the pages. Children's reaction are reported: for example, a three-year-old with no sight and SLD 'enjoyed repetition and anticipated storyline'. Teachers were enthusiastic and felt that the stories were appropriate for a wide age range.

Drawing conclusions across the 19 articles, it could be said that children and young people with PMLD can definitely be involved in literacy activities and the Literacy Hour, despite the unlikelihood of conventional literacy being achieved. There are many imaginative ideas contained within the articles which provide a body of evidence of good practice. It is obvious that many exciting literacy lessons are being taught across the country, enabling access to literature, great and not so great, for all pupils.

Conclusions

This chapter has been devoted to small-scale research work carried out by professional researchers, by practitioners and in a few cases by parents of children with learning disabilities. It has ranged across the fields of education, health and social services, across the disciplines of psychology, sociology and education, and across the age range from infant to adulthood. What all the research has in common is its small-scale nature. We searched the literature for individual case studies or case examples and for studies where the numbers of participants were in single figures. It was a fascinating search and has revealed much of interest to those who wish to find out more about different aspects of people with learning disabilities. Obviously we have had to be selective in the topics we have explored but we hope that each study has added just a little to understanding in the field. We also hope that from the studies you, the reader, will have been prompted either to begin or to continue to conduct research yourself. This chapter, in particular, has been partly aimed at showing how research can be carried out by anyone, not just by professional researchers. The perspectives of practitioners and families are also valuable as we all strive to move forward in improving the quality of life of people with learning disabilities.

CHAPTER 8

Looking beyond the discipline

Introduction

Over almost half a century there has been much exhortation for learning disability services to look beyond their own discipline; to work with other agencies and learn from each other's point of view (Lacey, 2001). Researchers have also been encouraged to work together, some funds only being available for multidisciplinary bids. From this history, therefore, we could expect there to be a wealth of research studies that are either directly multidisciplinary or at least contain a conceptual framework that is multidisciplinary. A trawl of the literature does not, however, reveal this at all. The vast majority of research studies in the area of learning disabilities or difficulties relate to a single discipline (such as health, education or social care), even on topics where we might have expected more than one perspective, such as challenging behaviour or family partnership.

This chapter is divided into three main sections, the first of which contains an exploration of the literature published in journals that are related to learning difficulties, in terms of the disciplines represented and the extent to which members of each discipline refer to writers from other disciplines. The aim of the section is to present evidence regarding the extent to which researchers look beyond their own discipline in their pursuit of knowledge of learning difficulties and to prepare a case for encouraging a more complete understanding gained through considering a variety of perspectives.

The second section is built upon the breadth established in the first through an in-depth analysis of four papers that are related to challenging behaviour, each taken from a different discipline, namely education, sociology, psychology and nursing. The aim of the section is to explore the different perspectives represented in the papers and to suggest the advantages and disadvantages of a more multidisciplinary approach to researching challenging behaviour.

In the third section we focus on multidisciplinary services for children, examining five research studies in detail, one from each of the disciplines health, social work and education and two that were conducted by a multidisciplinary team.

Uni-disciplinary perspectives

Learning disability services

There are many different agencies, services and professionals involved in working with children, young people and adults with learning difficulties. Historically, health services have dominated with a range of provision including: nursing, medicine, dietetics, physiotherapy, speech and language therapy, occupational therapy, audiology/orthoptics, psychology, psychiatry, dentistry and complementary therapies.

Since the beginning of the 1970s, education services have been available and have provided schools, colleges, home teachers (portage), educational psychology, peripatetic specialist teachers, mobility instruction, advisory and inspection, and ICT support.

Social care, although a relatively young service (dating from the 1960s), has recently become the lead service for adults with learning disabilities, although they also offer services to children and young people and their families. Services include: social work, respite care, day care, residential care, benefits, housing, fostering, job coaching and home help.

There are also voluntary agencies that offer services such as alternative therapies, private homes, independent schools and charities.

The plethora of services involved with people with learning difficulties is both an advantage and a disadvantage to the individual person. It is obviously a 'good thing' that the complexity of needs presented by so many people with learning disabilities can be met by gaining access to so many specialists, but unfortunately reality often presents a very different picture. Often people with learning disabilities receive services that are uncoordinated, randomly allocated and poorly monitored. It is likely that the package will be service-led rather than person-led and this can lead to an enormous amount of mismatch between service and individual.

Before considering research in the different disciplines, we present a few of the barriers that practitioners face when trying to meet the demand to work across disciplines, as this can assist in understanding the difficulties faced by researchers. Much has been written about practitioners striving to work together and barriers are identified as relating to both practical and philosophical domains. It is clear that members of different disciplines are socialised into that discipline at a very early stage of their professional training (Carpenter and Hewstone, 1996), and probably much earlier in reality. Many young people have built up ideas, accurate or stereotyped, of social workers, doctors and teachers long before they consider training to become one. These entrenched views can prove very difficult to shift and can lead to many misunderstandings in practice. Experience of effective working together can lead to 'cognitive gains' (Wright, 1992) on both sides where individuals significantly increase their understanding of each other's perspectives.

Other barriers to working together effectively stem from discipline-specific practices, such as status, pay and conditions, management structures, financial management, career structures and training (Leathard, 1994). The three main agencies for learning difficulties (health, social care and education) work in completely different ways and it is undeniably difficult for established practices to become sufficiently flexible to embrace others. Bringing services physically together as some local authorities have by creating a new combined education and social services department is likely to facilitate working together but merely placing people in the same room does not guarantee services will become coordinated and tailored to individual needs.

A study of learning disability journals

As many researchers in the field of learning difficulties began their careers as practitioners in health, social care and education, it would not be surprising that they too find it hard to look out beyond their own discipline. In order to test out whether this is indeed true, five UK journals publishing articles on learning difficulties were examined to try to determine whether the writers of the articles referred to other writers beyond their own discipline.

Methods

All the articles from the four issues from the year 2001 of each of the journals were analysed in terms of their affiliation to the three main disciplines of health, social care and education. The journals chosen were:

- *British Journal of Learning Disabilities*
- *Journal of Learning Disabilities*
- *Journal of Research in Intellectual Disabilities*
- *Tizard Learning Disability Review*
- *British Journal of Special Education.*

Affiliation to the three main disciplines was allocated as shown in Table 8.1. It was not always easy to decide upon the discipline affiliation of the writers. Where this was unknown, the university or workplace department was taken as an indication. Where writers gave a centre address, this was given a specific

Table 8.1 Allocation of subject areas

Health	Social care	Education
medicine	social work	schooling
clinical psychology	sociology	curriculum
therapies	criminology and law	teaching
nursing	history	educational psychology
psychiatry	philosophy	child development
	housing	

code rather than allocation to one of the three main disciplines. This code was also given to groups of writers who came from more than one discipline. This small group was examined in more detail.

Each of the articles were placed into one of the three main disciplines in terms of:

- topic
- writer/s
- references.

Results

There were 129 articles in total, 128 of which contained references. If we look first at topic, the largest percentage, 41 per cent fell in the social care category, followed by 32 per cent on health-related topics and 27 per cent in education. We can also make a distinction according to the discipline of the writers, with 51 per cent of articles written by writers in health, 15 per cent in social care and 23 per cent in education, and 11 per cent of writers being multidisciplinary or belonging to a multidisciplinary centre. Not all writers kept to their own discipline for their topics, although that was so for a large majority of the articles. For example, one educationalist team wrote an article on ethics in quasi-experimental research with people with learning disabilities, and three social care writers wrote articles on health issues in relation to sex. Only one non-educationalist (team) wrote about an educational issue but that referred to training for staff rather than education for people with learning difficulties.

Of the 20 writers (or teams of writers) who originated from a health background and wrote on social issues, 10 were from psychology, 6 from nursing, 2 from mental health and 2 from health science. The topics for the articles are listed in Table 8.2.

There were 14 teams of writers who either originated from a centre for learning disability research (such as the Tizard Centre or the Norah Fry Centre), or who were multidisciplinary in composition. The make-up of these groups was:

- centre or learning disability team – 6
- health and social care – 7
- education and health – 1.

Table 8.2 Article topics

Psychology		Nursing		Mental health		Health science	
partiticpation	8	families	5	participation	2	employment	1
crime	1	abuse	1			services	1
abuse	1						

Table 8.3 Allocation of references

Health	Social care	Education
37%	44%	19%

All the topics chosen by these multidisciplinary or centre writers related to social care or support for social care. Only one, that written by the educationalist and the therapist, related to multidisciplinary matters.

There were 3,365 references in the 129 articles. These were allocated to one of the three main categories for analysis on the basis of topic as shown in Table 8.3.

Of the 129 articles, 47 contained references that originated from one discipline only and 17 articles contained references from all three disciplines. The remaining writers drew their references from two of the three disciplines: 48 from health and social care; 5 from education and social care; and 6 from health and education. One article had no references. Of the single discipline articles, 16 originated in health, 14 in social care and 20 in education. Table 8.4 presents the percentage of articles from each discipline (allocated according to the discipline of the topic).

From these figures, it appears that articles on social care topics contain generally more multidisciplinary references than either health or education topics.

Of the 78 articles that contained references to two disciplines, 47 (60 per cent) had double figures in one discipline and single figures in the other, some with a huge difference (84:2 and 61:2). 12 (15 per cent) of these articles had only one reference to another discipline.

When the 17 articles that contain references from all three disciplines are further examined in terms of writers and topics, it is found that the majority of writers (12) come from a health background but there are slightly more social care topics (7) than health (6), with education again tagging behind (4).

The division of the references across these 17 articles can be allocated as shown in Table 8.5.

Table 8.4 Articles from each discipline

Health	Social care	Education
39%	26%	57%

Table 8.5 Articles with references to all three disciplines

Health	Social care	Education
32%	43%	25%

This reveals social care to be the most referred to in articles where all three disciplines are cited. The topic of article with the most even spread of references across the three disciplines (health 12, social care 14, education 14) relates to meeting the needs of people with profound and multiple learning disabilities. There were four more articles relating to profound and multiple learning disabilities that contained references from all three disciplines. Apart from the topics that related to PMLD, education was not referred to very often (43 times in 12 articles, in comparison with 167 social care and 137 health references).

Discussion

From the data collected, it can be seen that although the majority of writers can be allocated to the health category, the majority of topics for the articles fell into the social care category. This seems to indicate that despite a background in health, many writers are shifting from health issues to social care, following the trend in this country of reconceptualising learning disabilities as mainly a social issue (DoH, 2001). Professionals from psychology and from nursing appear to be the largest group in these articles who are writing about topics traditionally thought to be outside their disciplines.

From the analysis of the references, it can be seen that more writers cite writers from their own discipline than from others, with the exception of those who are writing about social care topics but who come from a health background. Most writers, however, do cite writers from other disciplines – even if the majority of their citations are from their own discipline (or that of the topic), as there were only 17 of the 129 articles whose writers only cited other writers from their own discipline. Writers from education seem to look beyond the discipline the least, as more than half of the articles on education topics were uni-disciplinary.

It is also clear from the data that education and education writers are cited fewer times by the other two main disciplines than they cite each other. In fact, education appears to be the 'poor relation' when analysing who is writing about learning difficulties in the UK. This can be partly explained by the fact that there are no specialist journals relating only to learning difficulties originating from education. The one journal we selected for analysis for this chapter relates to special educational needs, which includes learning difficulties. The journals that do specialise in learning difficulties tend to publish articles relating to adults or to family issues but rarely specifically to children or to educational topics.

Examining the data on 'who writes with whom' reveals that aside from people who belong to a centre or learning disability team, the most usual combination of writers, who originate from different disciplines, come from health and social care. There were, however, only seven of these writing teams: a very small percentage of the total of 129 articles (5 per cent). There is only one example of an educationalist writing with a partner from a different discipline: an article about multidisciplinary teamwork written with a speech and language therapist.

Although the majority of the articles contained citations of writers from different disciplines (78 out of 128), there were only 17 articles that contained citations from all three disciplines. The analysis of these 17 articles suggests that topics surrounding profound and multiple learning disabilities are more likely than any other to be of interest to all three disciplines. It seems as if the complexity of needs faced by children and adults with PMLD has encouraged writers from all three disciplines to contribute to the debate. From the references in the five articles that are related to PMLD, it can be seen that education is cited the most (98 times, in comparison with 76 for social care and 36 for health), suggesting that educationalists have been the most prolific on this topic.

The greater interest by educationalists could be partly explained by the fact that more babies with PMLD are surviving through childhood, requiring teachers and educational researchers to find ways of educating them in meaningful ways. Spurred on by inspections and government educational strategies, many schools for pupils with severe learning difficulties have had to adjust their curriculum and teaching methods to accommodate a school population who display many more profound disabilities than was evident in the past. Alongside the educationalists, social care writers are also becoming interested in people with PMLD. This population is beginning to survive into adulthood in numbers that require understanding of their living and participation needs. Finally, of course, the multiplicity of needs is also of interest to health writers who are faced with complex health issues with a population who also present particular communication challenges to a service that relies heavily on patients being able to describe their symptoms.

Conclusions

From this very small-scale study of 129 articles from five specialist journals relating to learning difficulties in 2001, it can be concluded that although some writers and researchers do indeed 'look beyond their discipline', the majority are discipline-bound. More than a third (39 per cent) of the articles contained reference to only one discipline and that phenomenon was fairly evenly distributed across the three main disciplines. Although the other 61 per cent of writers did refer to other disciplines, the numbers of citations was usually small in comparison with citations to their own discipline: in many cases there was only a single reference to another discipline.

Psychology and nursing seem to be the two disciplines that are most likely to be researching and writing about topics that are traditionally seen as the province of another discipline. The crossover of psychology may not be quite as great as it appears from this analysis as allocation to discipline may not have taken into account writers who consider themselves to be social psychologists rather than clinical (health-based) psychologists. The interest of nurses in social care issues is not surprising, considering the shift that learning disability nurses have made in their profession over the last few years from health dominance to social care as people with learning disabilities have been resettled in the community.

One thing that this research study has not revealed is exactly what different disciplines can learn from each other if they read each other's research more consistently. The overlap of ideas has not been explored, nor what might be gained from viewing learning difficulties from more than one perspective. All that has been established so far is that, according to this study, researchers and writers generally remain within the thinking and ideas that are prevalent in their own discipline. The next section contains an attempt to look in more depth at one topic within learning difficulties to analyse the different perspectives presented by health, social care and education. Part of the section is given to the examination of four articles written between 1999 and 2001 by researchers from psychology, nursing, social science and education.

Perspectives on challenging behaviour

Before turning to the detail of the four papers, it will be helpful to establish the breadth of issues regarding challenging behaviour and learning difficulties across the three main disciplines of health, social care and education. There is little doubt that psychology has dominated the study of learning difficulties and challenging behaviour (Emerson, 1998) and within psychology, behavioural science has been the lens through which the topic has been viewed. Other psychological approaches have been developed recently, as have sociological, ecological and educational approaches. These different perspectives will be outlined to demonstrate the variety of conceptual frameworks brought to the topic.

The most quoted definitions of challenging behaviour emanated from behavioural psychology, and that which is most often adopted was developed by Emerson *et al.* (1987):

> Severely challenging behaviour refers to behaviour of such intensity, frequency or duration that the physical safety of the person or others is likely to be placed in serious jeopardy, or behaviour which is likely to seriously limit or deny access to and use of ordinary community facilities.

As this definition was particularly developed with adults with learning disabilities in mind, it was expanded to include children with severe learning difficulties who were the subject of the Russell Report (Mental Health Foundation, 1997):

> behaviour which is likely to impair a child's personal growth, develop-ment and family life which represents a challenge to services, to families and to the children themselves, however caused.

The Russell Report also includes a definition that relates directly to education, in suggesting that challenging behaviour might:

prevent participation in educational activities; isolate children from their peer groups and interfere with or affect the learning of other pupils.

A further view has been added from Hastings and Remington (1993):

> in using labels to denote 'challenging behaviour', we are dealing with powerful social instruments, capable of modifying the thought and actions of clients, caregivers and members of the wider community.

This adds another dimension to understanding how the term 'challenging behaviour' is used; not only to describe symptoms but also the effect on the environment that surrounds the person whose behaviour is regarded as challenging.

Before moving on from different perspectives on definitions it is useful to consider the extent to which challenging behaviour is a dynamic concept, in the sense that what is challenging for one service, person or set of circumstances, may not be for another. For example, stripping behaviour may not seem challenging in a three-year-old in the context of the home and family but it may be in a thirteen-year-old at the local shops or in a science lesson. Individual tolerance also varies, as does the extent to which staff attribute challenging behaviour to the person's condition, indicating an expectation that learning disabilities and challenging behaviour are linked inexorably. Of course, this is demonstrably not so, despite the connections shown between certain conditions and challenging behaviour (Dykens and Shah, 2003). However, research has shown that the prevalence of challenging behaviour does increase with severity of learning disabilities (Quine, 1986; Emerson *et al.*, 1997).

Psychological perspectives

There are several different psychological perspectives on understanding challenging behaviour; for example, psychodynamic, behavioural, cognitive and cognitive-behavioural approaches, and each provides valuable insights into why such behaviour might occur. Many of the ideas are not incompatible, but it is usual to find researchers and scholars interested in a single viewpoint, rather than exploring an eclectic cluster of ideas.

The scope of psychological perspectives on challenging behaviour has become more wide ranging in recent years. For some time, challenging behaviour was only seen in terms of operant conditioning. The interest of psychologists was in the behaviour itself, which was divorced from its possible causes. Studies were carried out either to show the relationship between the problem behaviour and current reinforcement or to demonstrate how interventions could be based on changing the reinforcement regime (Emerson, 1995). Many intervention studies were carried out in laboratory conditions and were often very successful in reducing challenging behaviour (Zarkowska and Clements, 1994). However, it proved very difficult to carry out the systematic procedures of the research studies in the 'real' world of services for children and adults with learning difficulties and so many psychologists widened their brief to study the behaviour in context, although the basic framework of the behavioural model still underpins much of the research.

An important recent strand of psychological research into challenging behaviour has been the study of the functions of the behaviour and the search for providing the person with alternative, less problematic behaviour to perform the same function (Carr *et al.*, 1994). Interventions are based not on changing the antecedents or consequences of the behaviour but on introducing new behaviours that enable the person to achieve his or her desired end. An example of this was a study by Bird *et al.* (1989) in which two men were taught to exchange a token for a break in work which led to a decrease in escape-driven challenging behaviour.

Central to the success of current psychological interventions in challenging behaviour is the understanding of why the behaviour is taking place. Matching the intervention to the causes and functions of the behaviour is seen as vital and often the intervention arises naturally from an analysis of why the behaviour is happening (Emerson, 1998). For example, testing the hunch that aggression is triggered by a particular environmental situation can involve changing the situation and measuring the result. If the hunch proves correct then at least part of the intervention has been tested.

A biomedical perspective

Despite the dominance of psychological perspectives, biological and medical explanations for challenging behaviour have been influential, especially since the diagnosis for conditions closely associated with challenging behaviour are carried out by medics. These conditions include autism and attention deficit hyperactivity disorder (ADHD) and syndromes such as Lesch Nyan, Tourette and Prader-Willi.

There have been research studies to explore the association between bio-medical conditions and brain function. For example, people with Lesch Nyan syndrome have been found to have lowered levels of serotonin, which can lead to forms of self-injury such as lip and finger biting. There have also been associations made between pain and self-injurious behaviour, as in the study by McBrien (1987) where a young man who pulled out his hair was subsequently found to have abscesses on his teeth. Other biomedical studies have drawn attention to the place played in self-injurious behaviour by raised levels of endorphins in the brain which reinforce the self-injury (Sandman and Hetrick, 1995). Yet other studies have been aimed at exploring the effects on behaviour of drugs, such as those prescribed for epilepsy (Kelly *et al.*, 2002).

Although a biomedical perspective can offer useful insights, it must be approached with caution as often it only provides part of the explanation. Certainly with medically defined conditions such as autism and ADHD, at present there are no clearly defined biological factors leading to the conditions, which must weaken the claims of any definite biological causes of challenging behaviour. In fact, biomedical explanations of challenging behaviour can be seen to provide a restricted view, as the 'problem' rarely lies entirely within the child. Even if the original cause was medical in origin, it is likely that the behaviour is being maintained by environmental influences.

A sociological perspective

Interestingly most of the research that is related to environmental influences on challenging behaviour and learning difficulties has been psychological rather than sociological. The sociological view is invoked more consistently when related to physical or sensory disability, although a theme such as social exclusion is highly appropriate to consider when attempting to understand different aspects of challenging behaviour. Very little of the sociological research into learning difficulties is related to children and young people. Most contributes to an exploration of providing an 'ordinary life' for adults, ranging through topics such as advocacy, empowerment, rights, ordinary housing, employment and recently, involving people with learning disabilities in their own research (see Chapter 6 for more on this topic). Sociological research related to children is more likely to range across the whole special needs categories rather than specifically refer to children with learning difficulties. The dominant topic seems to be 'inclusion', mostly of an educational nature but also encompassing social inclusion, particularly in relation to family life. Other topics include child protection, children in care, children's rights and family poverty.

Looking at the sociological research that is directly related to children and challenging behaviour, it is difficult to separate learning difficulties from emotional and behavioural difficulties. Ultimately, of course, this may not matter, although it could be argued that the surge in interest in social aspects of children whose behaviour is found challenging in our society today is not spurred on by a desire to understand or change the social circumstances of the most disabled children but rather a desire to control the antisocial behaviour of an ever-increasing minority of alienated young people who cause 'trouble' in our schools and streets. There seems to be a qualitative difference between the intention behind the behaviour of children and young people with learning difficulties and those with emotional and behavioural difficulties, although both may be about communicating a desire for something fundamental to change in their lives.

One of the driving forces behind sociological research into learning difficulties (whether about children or adults) is the desire to promote a social model of disability as opposed to a medical or psychological model, although we have seen above that many psychologists are increasingly moving towards a social rather than medical model. Sociologists argue that disability is not a reality but a social construct (Clough and Barton, 1995): that disability is not a 'personal medical tragedy' (Shakespeare and Watson, 1997, p294) but 'society's failure ... to ensure the needs of disabled people are fully taken into account in

138

its social organisation' (Oliver, 1996, p32). As was indicated at the beginning of this section, sociologists who explore these ideas do not often relate their research to learning difficulties and the sociological paper considered in detail later in this chapter considers whether the social model of disability has anything to offer people with profound learning disabilities and challenging behaviour.

Educational perspective

An educational perspective on learning difficulties and challenging behaviour is relatively under-researched in comparison with the psychological or biomedical perspectives. In the 30 years that children and young people with learning difficulties have been the responsibility of educationalists in the UK, the greatest interest has been in developing a curriculum and teaching methods suitable for the new category of pupils (Staff of Rectory Paddock School, 1983; Byers and Rose, 1996; QCA, 2001) and in ways of including them with their more able peers in mainstream schools (Alderson, 1999). Research into challenging behaviour has not been considered a priority, despite the fact that it is extremely difficult to plan educational experience in either specialist or inclusive classrooms for pupils with learning difficulties and challenging behaviour. Teachers wishing to develop good practice in working with pupils with challenging behaviour have, on the whole, either had to call upon research from a psychological or biomedical perspective or utilise their own trial-and-error tactics.

Despite the general paucity of educational research into challenging behaviour, there have been a number of studies that emanate from education-alists and which contribute to a small but growing interest in this group. As in the sociological perspective, there is overlap with research into emotional and behavioural difficulties, but for the purposes of this mini-review, only research directly related to learning difficulties will be considered.

The research of Harris *et al.* (1996) is specifically related to the way in which challenging behaviour has impact on the education of pupils with severe learning difficulties. The aim of the research was to explore ways of supporting staff in schools for pupils with SLD in their work with pupils with challenging behaviour. More specifically the researchers were interested in evaluating (and in setting up or changing) interventions in a school context and in collaboration with staff. Evaluation of interventions revealed that teachers drew on general good practice in teaching pupils with SLD but also directly on clinical research based in psychology. As in adult services, staff in schools find it difficult to implement the systematic accuracy required of translating clinical trials into the real world and the study sought to find ways in which interventions could be successful in a school context. Teachers involved in the project felt that they had improved their abilities to assess pupil behaviour, strengths and needs and to implement strategies that were generally successful.

Another branch of research carried out by educationalists on the topic of challenging behaviour is known as 'intensive interaction' (Nind and Hewett,

1994). This is grounded in developmental and social interactionist psychology rather than behavioural psychology. Interestingly, this is one of the few research topics that has been more explored with children than with adults with challenging behaviour, mainly because it draws upon care-giver and infant interactions, an approach which has been slow to gain ground in an adult world that tends to spurn approaches that are seen to be childlike.

Briefly, intensive interaction is based on the development of playful social interactions between adults and children with challenging behaviour at a communicative level which is relevant for that child whatever his or her chronological age. So, for example, a teenager may enjoy having 'raspberries' blown on his stomach, which can help him to learn about the pleasure of human interaction and even perhaps about anticipation and cause and effect (two very important lessons to be learned about learning). Techniques such as these have been developed with the most profoundly disabled youngsters and have also been found to be effective with children (and adults) whose behaviour is found challenging. The claim is that children can learn to communicate in more conventional ways through building on the value that is placed on their unconventional attempts. Thus a child who hits people and throws objects to stop an unwanted activity can learn that their (probably unintentional) communication is accepted and acted upon alongside being enabled to enjoy activities that are suited to their level of engagement (such as tickling, clapping and turn-taking games). Further discussion on this approach can be found in Chapter 5.

The value specifically to education of this work is its relationship to the development of both curriculum and teaching methods that are suitable for pupils with challenging behaviour. Teachers have found it very hard to engage some pupils in some National Curriculum programmes of study and intensive interaction research has contributed to ways of adapting the aims for all children to the needs of a specific group. Pupils with severe learning difficulties and challenging behaviour require their educational needs to be considered on an individual basis and this is now possible through the development of recent curriculum guidelines (QCA, 2001).

Four recent papers

Following the review of several different perspectives on research relating to learning difficulties/disabilities and challenging behaviour, four papers will be compared and contrasted in terms of their perspectives, the overlap of these perspectives and the extent to which the researchers have drawn from disciplines beyond their own. The four papers are:

- Adam, D. and Allen, D. (2001) Assessing the need for reactive behaviour management strategies in children with intellectual disability and severe challenging behaviour, *Journal of Intellectual Disability Research* 45, 4, 335–343

- Branford, D. (1996) A review of antipsychotic drugs prescribed for people with learning disabilities who live in Leicestershire, *Journal of Intellectual Disability Research* 40, 358–368
- Coles, J. (2001) The social model of disability: what does it mean for practice in services for people with learning difficulties, *Disability and Society* 16, 4, 501–510
- Nind, M. (1999) Intensive interaction and autism: a useful approach? *British Journal of Special Education* 26, 2, 96–102

The papers were chosen through a keyword search in Ingenta (in the Bath Information and Data Service). Initially the years 2000–2001 were searched but there were difficulties with finding reasonably retrievable papers that were related directly to learning difficulties and challenging behaviour that had a perspective, other than behavioural psychology, and so the dates were extended from two to five years. The hardest paper to find was one from an educational perspective as most of the research in 'challenging behaviour' relates to children with emotional and behavioural difficulties rather than learning difficulties. It was also relatively difficult to find a medical paper that referred in any way to the behaviour of the patients. For example, several papers on syndromes, such as Cornelia de Lange, Prader-Willi or autism were found but the medical angle related to diet or bowel function rather than behaviour. Initially it was hoped to find four papers that related to children but eventually the choice was for two child-orientated and two adult-orientated papers that offered a range of perspectives.

It is possible to compare and contrast the four papers in a number of ways, as set out in Table 8.6. Firstly, we can consider the background literature chosen for their studies. Was there any overlap between the literature chosen? An analysis of the references revealed that there was no overlap between the sources used. The four sets of authors were completely focused on their own topic within challenging behaviour. A further analysis of the sources showed that researchers kept almost exclusively to their own discipline when referring to previous work in their area, as can be seen from Table 8.7.

Although each paper referred to at least one source that was psychological in origin, these were different branches of psychology. The psychology paper referred to two different aspects of challenging behaviour and represents the two most studied areas currently; that is, behavioural psychology and psychology that relates to social care (residential care, training of staff and legal issues). The medical paper cited just three psychology sources, all of which related to assessment of behaviour. The one source attributed to psychology in the sociology paper refers to models of disability as published in *The Psychologist*. This is both psychological and sociological in nature. The education paper cites many sources related to developmental psychology and in the earlier analysis of papers in the learning disability journals (see above) developmental psychology was counted as educational (as opposed to health orientated). For the purposes of this current analysis, it was considered separately from an educational

Table 8.6 Four recent papers

	1. Psychology	2. Medical	3. Sociology	4. Education
Background literature	physical aggression physical interventions training for carers abusive & unethical practice most research on adults not children	antipsychotic drug prescribing factors influencing prescribing other drug reduction studies	medical and social models of disability politics research into learning disabilities people with learning disabilities as research respondents	Intensive interaction intensive interaction and autism difficulties with an approach that depends on social interaction
Focus of study	56 children referred to challenging behaviour team staff in that team	198 patients who had been prescribed antipsychotic drugs	2 people with challenging behaviour (one 20 years old)	3 children with autism 58 SLD schools
Aim of the study	to identify topographies of challenging behaviour in children the need for training of staff	to assess the continuing need for antipsychotic drug therapy for people with learning disabilities in Leicestershire	to explore if support workers enable people with challenging behaviour to advocate on behalf of themselves and thus lead ordinary lives	to explore the relevance of intensive interaction to children with autism
Methods	questionnaire to staff in child challenging behaviour service	intervention study case review followed by reducing or withdrawing drugs patients followed up after one year	semi-structured interviews with support workers and participant observations of 2 people with profound disability & challenging behaviour and their support workers	three individual case studies questionnaires to schools of pupils with severe learning difficulties and autism

Findings

high level of aggression in referred children

most aggression in adolescence

physical interventions were common across age groups & often improvised by carers

recommendation of training (adapted from adult training)

for 167 (87%) of patients the drug regime remained the same (i.e. drugs were correctly prescribed)

drugs were successfully withdrawn from 31 patients

56 patients were being maintained on lower doses

support workers allowed people with challenging behaviour to make decisions (through their behaviour) about what they wanted to do

in the individual case studies, children responded to intensive interaction, by showing more interest in social interaction and fewer challenging behaviours from the survey, teachers find it helpful to use intensive interaction with pupils with autism

143

Table 8.7 References to other work

Psychology	Medicine	Sociology	Education
18 behavioural psychology	29 medicine	21 sociological	21 educational
11 social psychology	3 behavioural psychology	1 psychology	23 developmental psychology
29 total	32 total	22 total	42 total

perspective to try to gauge the continuing influence of psychology on the topic of challenging behaviour.

So what are the conclusions regarding the influence of psychology in these four papers? Out of 125 sources, 38 (30 per cent) cited are psychological, although of course, not all from the same branch of psychology. The result is that four very different views are presented to readers.

The psychology paper

In the first paper, behavioural psychology provides the underlying framework for understanding the nature of aggressive behaviours in children with learning difficulties and in the development of training for staff who are required to respond to aggression when it occurs. The concern of the researchers is in the transference of physical intervention training from one setting to another (e.g. from adult to child services) with little understanding of the circumstances in the second setting. Respondents in the study were asked how satisfied they were with the response to aggression in the children identified. Only just over half felt satisfied, with the rest feeling that training was not only important but necessary to move practice forward. The conclusions regarding the type of training were that the package that had been developed for training staff working with adults could be utilised but with adaptations for children related to size and force.

The medical paper

The conceptual framework for the second paper lies firmly in pharmaceutical medicine. The studies cited virtually all relate to psychopathology or previous attempts to change the drug regime of patients with learning difficulties and mental health disorders. There is little discussion of the challenging behaviours of the patients studied other than references to the Aberrant Behaviour Checklist (Aman *et al.*, 1985) used to ascertain behaviour before and after the intervention. The concern of the researcher is to ascertain if there has been oversubscribing of psychotropic medication and perhaps over- diagnosis of psychiatric illness in people with learning disabilities and challenging behaviour. Results did not support either concern, despite the cessation or reduction in medication for some patients.

The sociological paper

The third paper takes a perspective that is deliberately different from those represented by the first two papers. There is a positive rejection of the medical model implied in these papers in favour of the social model in which disability is regarded 'not as a personal tragedy but as the result of the failure of society to provide appropriate services' (Oliver, 1996). The emphasis in the paper is on whether this social model of disability has been accepted and used by staff working with people with profound learning disabilities and challenging behaviour, and if so, what this practice looks like. The results of two good practice case studies suggest that support workers who operate from a social model of disability value the person they support and enable that person to make their own choices and decisions based on their sensitive interpretation of the person's actions and attempts to communicate, whether this communication is intentional or not.

The educational paper

The final paper is also deliberately taking a contrasting perspective to behavioural psychology in the exploration by the researcher of the place of intensive interaction in working with children with autism. The contrast here, is between 'special' and 'naturalistic' intervention processes: between behavioural psychology and developmental psychology as manifest in social interactionist theories.

The intention of the study is to bring together accounts of practitioners working with children with intensive interaction to explore whether interventions based on social interaction theory are useful with children whose challenging behaviour is often triggered by a fear of social interaction. The results of the three case studies suggest that there is cause to connect intensive interaction with increases in social interaction and decreases in behaviour that is seen as challenging.

The second part of the study, a questionnaire to schools to explore the extent of the use of intensive interaction with children with autism is also positive, suggesting that teachers who use intensive interaction methods, find them helpful with children with autism.

Learning from other disciplines

The four papers are very clear examples of different perspectives on a topic in learning difficulties that emanate from different disciplines. From the original trawl of the literature (from which these papers were selected), it is evident that a behavioural psychology perspective is dominant but other views can be found. It is suggested that these different perspectives can offer insights that help the practitioner (in any discipline) to understand the causes and function of behaviour that is seen as challenging and to work out the most effective interventions for individual children and adults with learning difficulties.

Researchers and practitioners who become exclusively focused on one particular perspective can fail to take alternative ideas into account. It is clear that the lives of people with learning difficulties whose behaviour is considered challenging have many facets. It is impossible to isolate the behaviour from the surroundings, from social interaction, from likes, dislikes and emotions or from the way in which society treats people with learning disabilities. In the same way, there is no one formula that, if discovered, could make the behaviour disappear; at least no one formula that is ethical or works in the real world. Using a variety of perspectives, though, can help to get closer to practices that are effective.

Using a multiple perspective, it is possible to devise a framework for intervention that can support practitioners in their work with people with learning difficulties and challenging behaviour. This has three distinct but related tiers: strategies for preventing the behaviour from occurring; strategies for dealing with outbursts when they do occur; and longer-term strategies for learning alternative behaviour. This framework is built firmly on a systematic approach to assessment of the behaviour, the circumstances of its occurrence and the strengths and needs of the person involved. What a multiple perspective adds to this is that professionals who consider different aspects of the circumstances do not automatically assume a causal link between a medical condition and a behaviour nor between a contingent response and a behaviour, nor between an emotion and a behaviour nor between the effects of medicalising the person and their behaviour, nor between the effects of a curriculum and the behaviour. The multi-perspective professional considers them all in terms of their relative usefulness in individual cases.

If the numbers of multi-perspective professionals are to grow, both researchers and practitioners must be prepared to 'look beyond their discipline' and find alternative views. There need to be more reviews that, like this one, cite a range of sources of evidence. Each perspective has something valuable to say but it is only when these views are seen together that the whole world of the person with learning difficulties can be appreciated.

Perspectives on multidisciplinary work

Having considered different discipline perspectives in the first two sections and the value of looking across those disciplines for a more holistic view, in the third and final section of this chapter we bring the disciplines together in a consideration of multidisciplinary work with children with learning difficulties. There will be some reference to adults with learning difficulties as much of the research carried out refers to adult services. We intend to consider firstly, the ways in which multidisciplinary work is conceived of and researched in the three main disciplines of health, social care and education; and secondly, to explore a few studies that have been conducted by and written up by researchers from more than one discipline.

The term 'multidisciplinary' has been chosen for this section to denote a generic reference to more than one discipline working with the same children. The working together may be highly developed and collaborative or it may be less developed and more remote. Different disciplines regard multidisciplinary work in different ways and these perspectives will be explored briefly, below.

A health perspective

For many health professionals, 'multidisciplinary' refers to work across disciplines within health, for example primary health care teams (Elston and Holloway, 2001), or therapists working together (Fried and Litwinl, 2001). The advent of community care fired an interest in professionals from health and social care working together (McGrath, 1991; Keene et al., 2000). Most of this work, where it relates to learning disabilities at all, refers to adults rather than to children. Few health professionals refer to work with educationalists. The exceptions to this are a small number of therapists, particularly speech and language therapists who work with teachers (Wright, 1992).

A social care perspective

Social workers refer to work with health professionals, especially in relation to different aspects of community care (Payne, 2000; Hornby, 1993) and mental health (Nolan and Badger, 2002), although the emphasis is mainly on adults rather than children. There is reference to work with teachers and with the police, especially in relation to child protection (Pence and Wilson, 1994; Lloyd and Burman, 1996), although rarely does this multidisciplinary work refer specifically to learning difficulties. As with health professionals there is interest in intradisciplinary work, that is, teams made up of a variety of social workers.

An education perspective

'Multidisciplinary' matters are taken up by educationalists concerned with learning difficulties but the majority of multidisciplinary relationships are between teachers and health professionals such as therapists (Lacey, 2001). There is also interest in ways of working together within education; for example, collaboration between clusters of schools for special educational needs (Lunt et al., 1994) or between educational support services and classroom teachers (Lacey and Lomas, 1993). Often the interest in teamwork is related to a generic group of children with special educational needs but there is also interest in children with multiple needs, including learning difficulties (Orelove and Sobsey, 1995; Lacey and Ouvry, 1998).

Multidisciplinary services for children

Although multidisciplinary teams for adults with learning disabilities have been established for some time, the situation is less well defined in children's services (McConachie et al., 1999). In this section, research studies that contribute to the development of effective multidisciplinary/multiagency services for children with learning difficulties will be examined. By their very nature, these studies will have been undertaken by people who wish to 'look beyond their discipline' and the consequences of this will be explored. One thing that is evident, however, is that writers tend to cite other writers and researchers from their own discipline. There is some overlap between health and social care but virtually none with education.

Five research studies will be examined in this subsection, giving single discipline and joint discipline perspectives. Three of the studies are taken from the single disciplines of health, social work and education:

1 McConachie, H., Salt, A., Chadbury, Y., McLachlan, A. and Logan, S. (1999) How do child development teams work? Findings from a UK national survey, *Child: Care, Health and Development* 25, 2, 157–168
2 Cigno, K. and Gore, J. (1999) A seamless service: meeting the needs of children with disabilities through a multiagency approach, *Child and Family Social Work* 4, 325–335
3 Dyson, A., Lin, M. and Millward, A. (1998) *Effective Communication Between Schools, LEAs and Health and Social Services in the Field of Special Educational Needs*. London: DfEE

Two further studies are multidisciplinary in that members of the research teams came from more than one discipline: psychology, health, social services and education in the first paper; language and communication science and education in the second:

4 Appleton, P., Boll, V., Everett, J., Kelly, A., Meredith, K. and Payne, T. (1997) Beyond child development centres: care coordination for children with disabilities, *Child: Care, Health and Development* 23, 1, 29–40
5 Law, J., Lindsay, G., Peacey, N., Gascoigne, M., Soloff, N., Radford, J. and Band, S. (2001) Facilitating communication between education and health services: the provision for children with speech and language needs, *British Journal of Special Education* 28, 3, 133–137

It was hoped to find more multidisciplinary papers but it proved very difficult. There were few research papers in the last five years that related to multidisciplinary work and children with learning difficulties and of those, very few were written by more than one person. Where there were teams of writers, the discipline of the writers was either not apparent or was unidisciplinary. There were other papers in the journals but they were not reports of research.

In the brief analysis below, the papers will be considered individually and then a few aspects will be selected and expanded upon in the light of other research and scholarly opinion in an attempt to address some of the issues that are relevant to current and future research into multidisciplinary teamwork.

Paper 1

The study, carried out by health researchers, relates to child development teams (McConachie *et al.*, 1999). It is an exploratory study aimed at understanding the range of structures and processes in teams across the country. From the survey, data were gathered from 242 questionnaires and these were felt broadly to represent child development teams across the country. Results indicate a great variety of team organisation made up of different combinations of professionals representing a number of different disciplines. However, more than a quarter of the teams were made up of entirely health personnel and only a third were made up of representatives of all three disciplines (health, social services and education). More than half the teams included six core professions of: community paediatrician, physiotherapist, speech and language therapist, occupational therapist, social worker and health visitor.

Other results relate to management issues. For example, most teams (87.6 per cent) said they had a leader and in almost all cases this was a doctor (86.1 per cent) but many fewer indicated that there was a specific line manager for the team. In many cases personnel were managed from their separate discipline. Almost all the teams had regular meetings (at least monthly) about children's needs (96 per cent) but fewer had organisational meetings (at least quarterly) (88 per cent) and half of the teams had no written policy or contract for their work. The number of meetings was greater where members of the team were housed under a single roof. Despite close proximity to each other, nearly half of assessments were undertaken by individual professionals rather than either jointly or on behalf of each other. However, in most cases, the results of these assessments were then shared with colleagues. Of the 70 per cent of teams who regularly reported to parents, over half produced reports that had been written jointly. Less than half of the teams (47 per cent) had either a keyworker or care coordinator system but 87 per cent provided a home teaching service to support parents in the care of their disabled children.

Although some of the results of this survey are recognised by the researchers as positive and evidence of good practice, they draw attention to the lack of organisational support; combined reports to parents; keyworker systems; and joint assessments for many of the teams. They call for further research to be conducted into child outcomes and parental perceptions of the quality of services.

Paper 2

The study undertaken by the social work team (Cigno and Gore, 1999) relates closely to the previous paper in topic but is smaller in scale, being an in-depth study of one multiagency children's centre. Multiple data collection methods (survey, observation, interview, document analysis and focus group discussion) were used to ascertain whether the children's centre provides an effective one-door, multiagency service to the satisfaction of staff, children and their families. Those who took part were 51 staff (working in a variety of different kinds of teams within the centre, some multidisciplinary but most uni-disciplinary), 84 parents and 62 children (with a wide range of special needs including learning disability), plus staff from key outside organisations.

In general, parents were positive about the centre. Nearly a third said that what they liked best was that services were all under one roof and they could just go 'down the corridor' when they were referred to different services. Those who mentioned the multiagency assessment procedure liked the the holistic care plan that came out of it. Other aspects of the centre that parents liked were that it was 'child friendly' and offered facilities such as a kitchen for families. They also appreciated that there was a short waiting list for appointments. Few parents were dissatisfied, although several mentioned difficulties in transition to school when they felt they had to start all over again with completely new professionals.

Staff were less positive about the centre, although they were all committed to multiagency work. Most felt that the services were only 'fairly integrated' and that they were not working as 'one team' nor did they have a common purpose. Referrals were easier to make and conversations with colleagues from different services in the corridor meant greater efficiency in work for families, but there were still differences between services and their philosophies that led to misunderstandings and conflicts. Some of these difference meant that not everyone felt a sense of priority for integrating their work, especially under the pressure of large workloads. The lack of centralised records did not help an integrated service, although the multiagency assessment procedure and management groups were developments welcomed by staff.

The researchers conclude that this kind of multiagency centre approach is the right way forward to the provision of services for families but that there are still many lessons to be learned before everyone is working together in the most effective and efficient manner. They explain the differences between the views of the parents and professionals as perhaps due to the fact that parents have had very poor experiences previously. They also suggest that services may be good at hiding their differences from families so that at the point of contact they are trying hard to provide the best for families despite the difficulties behind the scenes.

Paper 3

The education paper is rather longer than the other two, being a full report of research carried out for the DfEE on ways in which different services can work together to meet the needs of children with special educational needs (Dyson *et al.*, 1998). Only the main points of the research that particularly relate to multiagency work will be discussed in this chapter.

The study aimed to identify the obstacles to multiagency work and make recommendations for improvements to the work undertaken in the context of the then Code of Practice (DfE, 1994). This brief review will be concerned with the latter. Interviews were carried out with 55 representatives of the three main agencies, health, social services and education, in ten local authorities. There were also interviews of 70 staff in 32 schools, in addition to 47 parents.

The researchers point to many different obstacles to effective multiagency work, although all of the agencies had developed procedures and systems for promoting communication and cooperation. Some services had constructed databases, developed proformas, designated link people or developed systems to eliminate delays. Regular meetings across agencies, joint planning and provision and joint development teams were also features of the areas where multiagency work was most active. The researchers offer principles that underpin effective multiagency work, such as: efficient information management; specific activities upon which to focus, which are significant to each agency; agreed geographical boundaries; and individuals who can drive the cooperation.

As well as principles, the researchers describe four models of inter-agency cooperation, which they suggest are more aids to analysis of current situations than advice for future developments. The *mutual cooperation model* can be found, for example, in much child protection work where agencies work mainly on their own and according to their own definitions and priorities but come together for specified purposes. The *shared responsibility model* can be found, for example, in early childhood and family support centres, where professionals from a range of agencies can be brought together in one location in a one-stop shop for clients. The *natural lead model* can be found, for example, in many services for children with disabilities where health takes the lead in the pre-school years, education during the school years and social services in the adult years. Elements of the *community services model* can be found, for example, in teams which are community based and led by keyworkers which coordinate services in response to individual needs. The most important element of this model is the involvement of local people working alongside professionals to determine community needs and devise a programme of action.

The researchers conclude their report with recommendations for improving inter-agency work. They begin by calling for a strategy for review and evaluation of the activities that agencies undertake so that they can plan their own way forward. They also suggest finding ways of improving information collection and management to reduce experiences of duplication or 'falling through the net'. It is also important, they recommend, for agencies to have publicly available statements of the value they place on multiagency cooperation which they should share with each other. Training and staff development should accompany these recommendations, as should planning for the future and monitoring of progress. Finally, they stress the importance of partnership with parents as well as between agencies.

Paper 4

The topic of the Appleton *et al.*, (1997) study is care coordination, a generic term referring to the coordination of different services for individuals and defined populations. The aim of the study was to describe care coordination and make recommendations based on the literature and a pilot study of care coordination.

The researchers suggest that there are six major care coordination issues for child disability teams:

1. empowerment of families
2. a defined population
3. the provision of services based on need
4. inter-agency collaboration at all levels
5. the continuity of named contact, especially across transitions
6. a named care coordinator for every client.

They spend some time addressing the last point, suggesting that the named coordinator should have full commitment from the agencies to create new ways of working across traditional boundaries. The agency from which the care coordinator will come should depend upon the needs of the child and family and all agencies should have a pool of trained coordinators.

The researchers describe a child disability care coordination model which aimed to address each of the six points above. In their pilot study, 20 families were involved with care coordinators from clinical medicine (8), social work (2) or community nurses (2). Care coordinators were to provide:

- a structured assessment focused on the family and child
- a care plan (incorporating transition to school)
- continuity of availability for family during transition to nursery
- coordination for case reviews.

This model was evaluated using structured interviews of family members and care coordinators approximately three months after entry into nursery. Results suggest that although some of the families were not fully aware of the care coordination service, 17 felt they were getting sufficient coordination. Almost half the families felt that the needs of the whole family, rather than just the child, were being addressed. The care coordinators found they lacked time for coordination but felt it was an important service to provide.

Following this small-scale evaluation, the service was provided more widely to another set of families in transition to nursery, teenagers in transition to adult services and a few school-aged families in need of specific coordination. Eight more professionals became coordinators (seven social workers, one voluntary agency fieldworker). No report of evaluation of these groups was contained in the paper.

The conclusion reached suggested that, from the evaluation, families were empowered through professionals listening to them; populations were well defined and expanding systematically; careful assessment was improving the match of service to needs; concentrating on small cohorts of families helped to maintain focus across boundaries, although pressures on services made inter-agency work difficult; the named care coordinator was welcomed by parents, although they expressed a wish that this person should be independent of all the statutory agencies.

Paper 5

The final paper chosen for examination has provision of speech and language therapy in schools as its main topic (Law *et al.*, 2001). The group of children to whom this service applies do not necessarily have learning difficulties but many have. The aim of the study was to find out which factors determined the process of collaboration between health and education services in relation to the provision of speech and language therapy (SLT) in educational settings.

The project was divided into three phases. The first phase was a survey to all SLT managers in health trusts with community children's services and 50 per cent of all LEA managers in England and Wales. In this phase 189 of 266 questionnaires were returned. The second phase was concentrated on 15 pairs of LEA/health trust collaborative pairs who were interviewed to provide more detailed qualitative data. The third phase was used to check the validity of the findings and consisted of five discussion meetings of managers, practitioners and parents.

Researchers identified 13 key themes from the study and made 18 different recommendations. Some of those that are relevant to inter-agency work will be considered here. Funding seemed to be a difficulty as it crossed health and education boundaries and it was recommended that LEAs should act as 'lead commissioners' and use new joint funding partnerships. A common data set was also called for so that both agencies could base their assessment of need on the same information and also have a basis upon which to share a vision and develop strategic plans. Because few boundaries are coterminous between health and education, extra effort is required to provide the structures that enable joint strategic planning. Once these structures are in place, there is a requirement for monitoring and evaluation of levels of collaboration.

At the level of the classroom, there is little guidance from the research literature on the best models to adopt to provide the best services for children, although there is agreement that an education-based model is important. This model assumes at least some use of the consultation model where speech language therapists pass over their skills to support staff in the school to enable provision for speech and language needs to be embedded in the curriculum. The researchers recommend more use of this model and also education, training and continuing professional development for teachers and speech language therapists to support the process.

The researchers are clear that collaboration between education and health over SLT cannot be left to the initiative of individual practitioners but that there should be strategic planning and management of supportive systems to underpin it.

The message about multidisciplinary services for children

Looking across the five papers, the topics seem to fall into two main categories within the topic of multidisciplinary services for children. Although all projects mention parents, three of the five are much more concerned with parents and families than the other two. Papers 1, 2 and 4 are directly concerned with the way in which multiagency work affects families. They are all interested in children at a young age, although the care coordination paper (no. 4) briefly introduces care coordination for school-aged children and young people. The main message from the three papers is the importance of the development of some form of coordination of services to help and support families. No one model is put forward as the most effective but mentions of keyworkers and care coordinators are made. The results of two other studies undertaken recently can add to the findings of these three. Beattie (1999) conducted a very small-scale study of seven professionals who were acting as care coordinators. Her findings suggest that when professionals from one of the agencies take on the co-ordination role, their position can become compromised. It is difficult for them to set aside agency loyalties and find unbiased and flexible responses to family needs. This relates to the view of parents in paper 4 who would have liked a care coordinator who was independent of the statutory services.

Limbrick-Spencer (2000) carried out the UK SOFTY (Support Over First Two Years) postal survey of 455 parents of children with complex needs. Results clearly indicate that parents would value an independent person to help them to achieve a variety of things, one of which is coordination of services. They also wanted emotional support and information about their child's needs and the services available to them. Limbrick-Spencer (2001) goes on to develop her ideas for a keyworker service based on the results of this survey.

The model of Mukherjee et al. (1999) for keyworking, developed from their evaluation of two keyworker services, suggest that there are six elements:

1. pro-active, regular contact between the keyworker and family
2. a supportive, open relationship
3. a family-centred approach (not just child-centred)
4. working across agencies
5. working with families' strengths and ways of coping
6. working for the family rather than an agency.

These seem to sum up effective practice as can be gleaned from recent research.

Apart from the emphasis on agencies working with families, the papers selected for this chapter give much information on possible ways forward for agencies to work more effectively with each other. These suggestions range from strategic to fieldworker level but all researchers are clear that individuals alone cannot maintain effective collaboration, despite the importance of their willingness to share skills, knowledge and understanding. They need the support of strategic planning, joint funding, common aims across agencies, access to shared information and data sources and clearly defined target populations and activities over which to collaborate. Watson et al. (2002) carried out a literature review for their research into multiagency working in services to disabled children with complex health care needs and their families and confirmed the importance of the factors mentioned above. Another aspect they emphasise is the significance of access to time and space for key stakeholders to discuss issues jointly. Lacey (2001) also points to the crucial role played by time in effective multiagency work. Those services and practitioners who have time allocated for joint work and for building up trust and communication between each other are much more likely to be successful.

Differences

Looking across the papers in relation to research methodology, there is a dominance of qualitative approaches to collecting information. The interest of the researchers is in the quality of services and all have been anxious to explore the factors that contribute to effective practice. Little difference can be discerned between the studies carried out by single discipline teams and teams that represent more than one discipline. References were examined to see if there were any interesting differences. In three of the five papers (two single and one multidiscipline), all three main disciplines (health, social work and education) were cited. In the other two papers, the first is dominated by health citations (89 per cent) and the fifth by education and health equally.

In almost every case one discipline is dominant in terms of citations. In the single discipline papers the dominance goes with the discipline of the researchers but in the multidisciplinary papers dominance goes to health in both cases (but only just in the last paper). It is heartening, in the light of the theme that has run through this chapter, to see researchers looking 'beyond their discipline', though multiagency work is surely a topic most likely to draw researchers from their separate pigeonholes.

Before leaving citations, it is also interesting to see if there is any overlap between the papers. Do researchers into multiagency work cite the same sources and, if so, which sources? There is no one piece of work cited in all five papers, but the Audit Commission (1994) study *Seen but Not Heard: Coordinating Community Child Health and Social Services for Children in Need* was cited in four (papers 1–4). Eight sources were common to two papers but none to three papers. Paper 5 had the least in common with any of the others; that is, only one education source that is in common with the education paper (no.3).

Future multidisciplinary research

From this brief analysis of some of the recent research into multidisciplinary work in child disability, it can be seen that many of the studies are relatively small-scale and predominantly qualitative, although there have been attempts to collect quantitative data that gives a broad view of what is happening across the country. The studies are mainly exploratory in nature, which perhaps reflects the fact that multidisciplinary work is still in its infancy in so many areas of the country, especially in children's services.

Much of the research in the 1980s and 1990s was related to adult services and specifically to health and social services working together. Joint mechanisms were monitored. For example, joint funding was the subject of much interest (Audit Commission, 1986; Hunter and Wistow, 1987; Wistow and Hardy, 1991) and various processes of the All Wales Strategy for the Development of Services for Mentally Handicapped People were evaluated (McGrath, 1991). This evaluation suggested that joint work is possible with the following in place:

- a broad framework of policies and principles with explicit agreements
- representatives of different agencies with delegated authority to make decisions
- effective channels of communication between teams of fieldworkers and policy-makers
- skilled committed managers
- support for and training in collaboration.

A summary of the research and study undertaken during the development of community care for people with learning disabilities is not very encouraging, suggesting that multiagency work is hindered by a history of separateness, power struggles and a lack of attractive incentives or legal directives to work together (Ovretveit, 1993; Hornby, 1993; Malin, 1994). The current situation is little changed, despite many exhortations and partnership arrangements outlined by government. Professionals from all the agencies are suffering from large caseloads and a overload of bureaucracy and are focused much more on survival than seeking innovative ways of working.

So what can research offer to help? There are actually still some fundamental questions to be asked about multidisciplinary and multiagency work. Common sense tells us that it must be more effective and efficient once well established, but there is comparatively little research evidence that confirms this. Parents express satisfaction when they experience multiagency work (Limbrick-Spencer, 2000) as do staff (Wigfall and Moss, 2001), although both sets of people would say that it was an ideal that has not yet been achieved consistently even in areas of good practice. Despite expressions of satisfaction, there is little real evidence to support the common-sense arguments, partly because it is hard to find more than isolated examples where multidisciplinary work is well established, especially in children's disability services, but partly because it is hard to demonstrate that one way of working is better than another. Circumstances are too variable for there to be an agreement on what works. School effectiveness research suffers from similar difficulties. Even if the factors contributing to an effective school can be identified, it is hard for those to be transplanted elsewhere.

Despite the difficulties highlighted above, studies are still needed that can provide answers to two basic questions, specifically in the area of child disability:

- Is multiagency work more effective and efficient than agencies working on their own?
- What are the fundamental factors that contribute to effective and efficient multiagency work?

Dissemination of the results of such studies is vital, especially where factors for success include the use of partnership funding or local arrangements for joint strategic planning, as these can then be taken up by other agencies interested in working together, but lacking knowledge of available mechanisms. Alongside evidence of factors for success, there need to be incentives (financial and resource) to ensure that multiagency work becomes more than just a principle that everyone endorses and becomes everyday good practice across the country.

What has been gained from 'looking beyond the discipline'?

The three sections in this chapter have addressed different aspects of 'looking beyond the discipline' and have hopefully persuaded reluctant readers to be more adventurous with their reading and reassured those who already try to understand learning difficulties from a range of perspectives. The emphasis has been on the disciplines of health, social science and education but this final brief concluding section is focused not only on those disciplines, but also on how little children's services seem to learn from adult services and vice versa.

There is a great divide at the age of 16 (for many young people with moderate learning difficulties) or 19 (for many with severe or profound learning difficulties) between provision for the child that was and the adult that will be. Not only is funding less generous but provision is less well organised (and inspected) or does not even exist. A child with complex physical needs could receive a weekly visit at school from a physiotherapist until his 18th birthday and then will suddenly have an occasional appointment at the hospital thereafter. His needs have not suddenly changed but the services have.

Common sense suggests that there is much to be learned by reading research (and scholarly writing) from both phases of life and from disciplines other than your own. Few teachers have heard of the White Paper *Valuing People* (DoH, 2001) or the work of Wolfensberger (1983) on social role valorisation, or O'Brien on the five accomplishments (1981); and few nurses have heard of the Russell Report on challenging behaviour (Mental Health Foundation, 1997), or Coupe O'Kane and Goldbart's (1998) work on pre-intentional communication, or Detheridge and Detheridge's (1997) work on symbols for literacy. Evaluations following the teaching of both teachers and nurses suggests that each gains enormously from learning about each other's frames of reference and ultimately those individuals work more effectively with their clients (Lacey, 2001).

Following an analysis of a range of research in learning difficulties, it has been suggested that, on the whole, researchers are discipline-bound and do not often 'look beyond the discipline' to the research of others. As we have seen from this book, this may well mean embracing different forms of research and evaluating its contribution using criteria that are consistent with the type of enquiry. We hope that in the future, there will be more exchange of ideas between the sectors in recognition of the synergy that can occur when a holistic view is achieved.

BIBLIOGRAPHY

Adam, D. and Allen, D. (2001) Assessing the need for reactive behaviour management strategies in children with intellectual disability and severe challenging behaviour, *Journal of Intellectual Disability Research* 45, 4, 335–343.

Ager, A. (2002) Quality of life assessment in critical context, *Journal of Applied Research in Intellectual Disabilities* 15, 369–376.

Alaszewski, A. (1986) *Institutional Care and the Mentally Handicapped.* London: Croom Helm.

Alderson, P. (1999) *Learning and Inclusion: The Cleves School Experience.* London: David Fulton.

Allan, J. and Brown, S. (2001) Special schools and inclusion, *Educational Review* 53, 2, 199–207.

Altrichter, H., Posch, P. and Somekh, B. (1993) *Teachers Investigate their Work: An Introduction to the Methods of Action Research.* London: Routledge.

Aman, M., Singh, N., Stewart, A. and Field, C. (1985) The Aberrant Behaviour Checklist: a behaviour rating scale for the assessment of treatment effect, *American Journal of Mental Deficiency* 89, 485–491.

Appleton, P., Boll, V., Everett, J., Kelly, A., Meredith, K. and Payne, T. (1997) Beyond child development centres: care coordination for children with disabilities, *Child: Care, Health and Development* 23, 1, 29–40.

Armstrong, D. (1998) *Special Educational Needs and the Life Histories of people with Learning Difficulties.* Final Report to the ESRC on Research Grant R000221555.

Armstrong, D. (2003) *Experiences of Special Education: Re-Evaluating Policy And Practice Through Life Stories.* London: Routledge.

Atkins, S. (1999) Students with profound and multiple learning difficulties enjoy the Literacy Hour, *PMLD-Link* 12, 1, 21–23.

Atkinson, D. (2002a) Self-advocacy and research. Chapter 8 in B. Gray and R. Jackson (eds) *Advocacy and Learning Disability.* London: Jessica Kingsley.

Atkinson, D. (2002b) Accessing views through life stories. Paper presented at ESRC Seminar Series: *Methodological Issues in Interviewing Children and Young People with Learning Difficulties,* University of Birmingham, 17 October 2002.

Atkinson, D. and Walmsley, L. (1999) Using autobiographical approaches with people with learning difficulties, *Disability and Society* 14, 203–216.

Atkinson, D., Jackson, M. and Walmsley, J. (1997) *Forgotten Lives: Exploring the History of Learning Disability.* Kidderminster: BILD.

Audit Commission (1986) *Making a Reality of Community Care.* London: HMSO.

Audit Commission (1994) *Seen but Not Heard: Coordinating Community Child Health and Social Services for Children in Need.* London: HMSO.

Azrin, N.H. and Foxx, R.M. (1971) A rapid method of toilet training the institutionalized retarded, *Journal of Applied Behavior Analysis* 4, 88–89.

159

Azzopardi, A. (2000) A case study of a parents' self-advocacy group in Malta. The concept of 'inclusion, exclusion and disabling barriers' are analysed in the relationship that parents have with professionals, *Disability and Society* 15, 7, 1065–1072.

Bakeman, R. and Gottman, J.M. (1997) *Observing Interaction. An Introduction To Sequential Analysis* (2nd edn). Cambridge: Cambridge University Press.

Baker, K. and Donelly, M. (2001) The social experiences of children with disability and the influence of environment: a framework for intervention, *Disability and Society* 16, 1, 71–85.

Barber, M. (2000) *Skills, Rules, Knowledge and Three Mile Island. Acounting for failure to learn in people with profound and multiple learning disabilities.* Unpublished PhD thesis, Manchester Metropolitan University.

Barber, M. (2001) Affective assessment: an owner's manual, *PMLD-Link* 13, 2, 16–19.

Barclay, J. (1999) A historical review of learning difficulties remedial therapy and the rise of the professional therapist. In J. Swain, and S. French (eds) *Therapy and Learning Difficulties.* Oxford: Butterworth-Heinemann.

Barnes, C. (2002) 'Emancipatory disability research': project or process? *Journal of Research in Special Educational Needs*, 2, 1.

Basil, C. and Reyes, S. (2003) Acquisition of literacy skills by children with severe disability, *Child Language Teaching and Therapy* 19, 1, 27–45.

Baumeister, A.A. (1967) problems in comparative studies of mental retardation and normals, *American Journal of Mental Deficiency* 71, 869–875.

Beattie, A. (1999) *Service Co-ordination: Professionals Views on the Role of a Multi-agency Service Co-ordinator for Children with Disabilities.* Birmingham: Handsel Trust.

Begley, A. (2000) The educational self-perceptions of children with Down syndrome. Chapter 8 in A. Lewis and G. Lindsay (eds) *Researching Children's Perspectives* (pp1–20). Buckingham: Open University Press.

Bell, J. (1999) *Doing Your Research Project* (3rd edn). Buckingham: Open University Press.

Bendelow, G. (2002) Health beliefs of children and young people: using child centred methods. Paper presented at ESRC Seminar Series: *Methodological Issues in Interviewing Children and Young People with Learning Difficulties,* University of Birmingham, 17 October 2002.

Benjamin, S. (2001) Challenging masculinities: disability and achievement in testing times, *Gender and Education* 13, 1, 39–55.

Benjamin, S. (2003) What counts as 'success'? Hierarchical discourses in a girls' comprehensive school, *Discourse: Studies in the Cultural Politics of Education* 24, 1, 105–118.

Berney, T.P. (2000) Autism – an evolving concept, *British Journal of Psychiatry* 176, 20–25.

Berry, P. (2003) Psychodynamic therapy and intellectual disabilities: dealing with challenging behaviour, *International Journal of Disability, Development and Education* 50, 1, 39–51.

Binet, A. and Simon, T. (1914) *Mentally Defective Children.* London: E.J. Arnold.

Bird, F., Dores, P., Moniz, D. and Robinson, J. (1989) Reducing severe aggressive and self-injurious behaviors with functional communication training, *American Journal of Mental Retardation* 94, 37–48.

Bisplinghoff, B. and Allen, J. (1998) *Engaging Teachers: Creating Teaching and Researching Relationships.* Portsmouth, New Hampshire: Heinemann.

Blackman, L. and Heintz, P. (1966) The mentally retarded, *Review of Educational Research* 36, 1, 5–36.

Blunkett, D. (2000) Influence or irrelevance: can social science improve government? *Research Intelligence* 71, 12–21.

Board of Education and Board of Control (1929) *Report of the Mental Deficiency Committee* (The Wood Report). London: HMSO.

Bolt, J. (1999) 'Once upon a time': dinosaurs, the Literacy Hour and objects of reference, *Eye Contact* 25, 11–12.

Booth, T. and Booth, W. (1996) Sounds of silence: narrative research with inarticulate subjects, *Disability and Society* 11, 1, 55–69.

Booth, T. and Booth, W. (2003) In the frame: photovoice and mothers with learning difficulties, *Disability and Society* 18, 4, 431–442.

Bowlby, J. (1953) *Child Care and the Growth of Love*. Harmondsworth: Penguin Books.

Branford, D. (1996) A review of antipsychotic drugs prescribed for people with learning disabilities who live in Leicestershire, *Journal of Intellectual Disability Research* 40, 358–368.

Brechin, A. and Swain, J. (1988) Professional and client relationships: creating a 'working alliance' with people with learning difficulties, *Disability, Handicap and Society* 3, 213–226.

Bricher, G. (2000) Disabled people, health professionals and the social model of disability: can there be a research relationship, *Disability and Society* 15, 5, 781–793.

British Psychological Society (2000) Code of Conduct, Ethical Principles and Guidelines. www.bps.org.uk.

Brown, A.L. (1992) Design experiments: Theoretical and methodological challenges in creating complex interventions in classroom settings, *The Journal of Learning Sciences*, 2, 2, 141–178.

Brownlow, C. and O'Dell, L. (2002) Ethical issues for qualitative research in on-line communities, *Disability and Society*, 17, 6, 685–694.

Budge, D. (2002) Launch of the first EPPI-Centre Reviews, *Times Educational Supplement* 12 July 2002.

Burke, A., McMillan, J., Cummins, L., Thompson, A., Forsyth, W., Mclenan, J., Snow, L., Fraser, A., Fraser, M., Fulton, C., McCrindle, E., Gillies, L., Lefort, S., Miller, G., Whitehall, J., Wilson, J., Smith, J. and Wright, D. (2003) Setting up participatory research: a discussion of the initial stages, *British Journal of Learning Disabilities* 31, 65–69.

Burnaford, G., Fischer, J. and Hobson, D. (2001) *Teachers Doing Research: The Power of Action Through Inquiry* (2nd edn). Mahwah, New Jersey: Lawrence Erlbaum Associates.

Byers, R. and Rose, R. (1996) *Planning the Curriculum for Pupils with SEN*. London: David Fulton.

Cain, L. and Levine, S. (1963) The mentally retarded, *Review of Educational Research* 33, 1, 62–82.

Cambridge, P. (2000) Using 'best value' in purchasing and providing services for people with learning disabilities, *British Journal of Learning Disabilities* 28, 31–37.

Cambridge, P., Carpenter J., Beecham J., Hallam A., Knapp, M., Forrester-Jones, R. and Tate, A. (2002) Twelve years on: The long-term outcomes and costs deinstitutionalisation and community care for people with learning disabilities, *Tizard Learning Disability Review* 7, 3, 34–42.

Cameron, L. and Murphy J. (2002) Enabling young people with a learning disability to make choices at a time of transition, *British Journal of Learning Disabilities* 30, 105–112.

Carpenter, B. (1999) A multi-modal approach to literacy, *SLD Experience* 23, 10–13.

Carpenter, J. and Hewstone, M. (1996) Shared learning for doctors and social workers: evaluation of a programme, *The British Journal of Social Work* 26, 2, 239–257.

Carr, E., Levin, L., McConnachie, G., Carlson, J., Kemp, D. and Smith, C. (1994) *Communication-based Intervention for Problem Behaviour: A User's Guide for Producing Positive Change*. Baltimore: Paul Brookes.

Carter, M. and Grunsell, J. (2001) The Behavior Chain Interruption Strategy: A review of research and discussion of future directions, *Journal for the Association of the Severely Handicapped* 26, 1, 37–49.

Chappell, A.L. (2000) Emergence of participatory methodology in learning difficulty research: understanding the context, *British Journal of Learning Disabilities* 28, 38–43.

Chappell, A.L., Goodley, D. and Lawthorn, R. (2001) Making connections: the relevance of the social model of disability for people with learning difficulties, *British Journal of Learning Disabilities* 29, 45–50.

Cigno, K. and Gore, J. (1999) A seamless service: meeting the needs of children with disabilities through a multi-agency approach, *Child and Family Social Work* 4, 325–335.

Clarke, A.D.B. and Clarke, A.M. (1975) *Recent Advances in the Study of Subnormality*. London: MIND.

Clarke, A. and Dawson, P. (1999) *Evaluation Research. An Introduction to Principles, Methods and Practice*. London: Sage.

Clarke, A. and Evans, P. (1990) Epilogue. In P.L.C. Evans and A.D.B. Clarke (eds) *Combatting Mental Handicap: A Multidisciplinary Approach: Social and Environmental Factors in the Prevention and Amelioration of Mental Handicap*. Oxon: A.B. Academic.

Clarke, A., Clarke, A. and Reiman, S. (1958) Cognitive and social changes in the feebleminded – three further studies, *British Journal of Psychology* 53, 321–330.

Clegg, J. (2000) Beyond ethical individualism, *Journal of Intellectual Disability Research* 44, 1, 1–11.

Clegg, J. (2001) Healthcare ethics from a hermeneutic perspective. Paper presented at ESRC Seminar Series: *Methodological Issues in Interviewing Children and Young People with Learning Difficulties*, University of Birmingham, 10 July 2001.

Clegg, J. (2003) The ideal proxy informant, *Ethics and Intellectual Disability* 7, 2, 1–5.

Cleugh, M. (1957) *The Slow Learner*. London: Methuen.

Clough, P. and Barton, L. (1995) *Making Difficulties: Research and the Construction of SEN*. London: Paul Chapman.

Cobb, P., Confrey, J., diSessa, A., Lehrer, R. and Schauble, L. (2003) Design experiments in educational research, *Educational Researcher* 32, 1, 9–13.

Coffey, M. (2000) *Multisensory Environments – Educational Tool Or Expensive Toy? An evaluation of the use of multisensory environments with young people with severe or profound and multiple learning difficulties*. Unpublished MEd dissertation: University of Birmingham.

Cohen, L., Manion, L, and Morrison, K. (2000) *Research Methods in Education*. London: Routledge Falmer.

Cole, T. (1989) *Apart or a Part? Integration and the Growth of British Special Education*. Milton Keynes: Open University Press.

Cole, T., Visser, J. and Upton, G. (1998) *Effective Schooling for Pupils with Emotional and Behavioural Difficulties*. London: David Fulton.

Coles, J. (2001) The social model of disability: what does it mean for practice in services for people with learning difficulties, *Disability and Society* 16, 4, 501–510.

Cooper, M. (1997) Mabel Cooper's life story. Chapter 2 in D. Atkinson, M. Jackson and J. Walmsley (eds) *Forgotten Lives. Exploring the History of Learning Disability*. Kidderminster: BILD.

Coupe, J., Barton, L., Barber, M., Collins, L., Levy, D. and Murphy, D. (1985) *Affective Communication Assessment*. Manchester: Melland School.

Coupe O'Kane, J. and Goldbart, J. (1998) *Communication Before Speech*. London: David Fulton.

Cummins, R.A. (1997) Self-rated quality of life scales for people with an intellectual disability: A review, *Journal of Applied Research in Intellectual Disabilities* 10, 3, 199–216.

Cummins, R.A. (2002) The validity and utility of subjective quality of life: a reply to Hatton and Ager, *Journal of Applied Research in Intellectual Disabilities* 15, 261–268.

Cunningham, C., Glenn, S., Lorenz, S., Cuckle, P. and Shepperdson, B. (1998) Trends and outcomes in educational placements for children with Down syndrome, *European Journal of Special Needs Education* 13, 3, 225–237.

Cutts, N. (1941) The mentally handicapped, *Review of Educational Research* 11, 3, 261–276.

Dahlberg, G., Moss, P. and Pence, A. (2000) *Beyond Quality in Early Childhood Education and Care: Postmodern Perspectives*. London: Falmer.

Dansforth, S. (2001) A Deweyan perspective on democracy and inquiry in the field of special education, *Journal of the Association for the Severely Handicapped* 26, 4, 270–280.

Davies, P. (2000) The relevance of systematic reviews to educational policy and practice, *Oxford Review of Education* 26, 3–4, 365–378.

Dee, L., Byers, R., Hayhoe, H. and Maudslay, E. (2002) *Enhancing Quality of Life: Facilitating Transitions for People with Profound and Complex Learning Disabilities*. London: Skill and University of Cambridge.

Dee, L., Florian, L., Porter, J. and Robertson, C. (2003) Developing curriculum guidance for person-centred transitions. In D. Rodrigues (ed.) *Perspectivas sobre a Inclusão: da Educacão a Sociedade (Perspectives on Inclusion: from Education to Society)*. Porto: Editora Porto.

Dennis, R. (2002) Nonverbal narratives: Listening to people with severe intellectual disability, *Research and Practice for Persons with Severe Disability* 27, 4, 239–249.

Denzin, N.K. and Lincoln, Y.S. (eds) (1998) *Strategies of Qualitative Inquiry*. London: Sage.

Department for Education (1994) *The Code of Practice on the Identification and Assessment of Special Educational Needs*. London: HMSO.

Department for Education and Employment (1998) *Meeting Special Educational Needs: Programme of Action*. Sudbury: DfEE.

Department for Education and Employment (2000a) *SEN Code of Practice on the Identification and Assessment of Pupils with Special Educational Needs*. Consultation Document. London: DfEE.

Department for Education and Employment (2000b) *Literacy and Special Educational Needs: A Review of the Literature*. Norwich: HMSO.

Department for Education and Science (1978) *Special Educational Needs: Report of the Enquiry into the Education of Handicapped Children and Young People*. London: HMSO.

Department for Education and Skills (2003) DfES Research Strategy. www.dfes.gov.uk/research/prospectus 19/12/03.

Department of Health (1969) *Report of the Committee of Enquiry into Allegations of Ill-treatment of Patients and Other Irregularities at the Ely Hospital, Cardiff* (The Howe Report). London: HMSO.

Department of Health (2001) *Valuing People: A New Strategy for Learning Disabilities in the 21st Century*. London: The Stationery Office.

Department of Health (2002) *Organisation of Research and Development*. www.doh.gov.uk/research/rd1/overview/overviewindex.htm. 17/12/2003.

Department of Health and Social Services (1971) *Better Services for the Mentally Handicapped*. London: DoH.

Design Based Research Collective (2003) Design-based research: an emerging paradigm for educational inquiry, *Educational Researcher* 32, 1, 5–8.

Dessent, T. (1996) Meeting special educational needs – options for partnership between health, social and education services. In Nasen (ed.) *Options for Partnership Between Health, Education and Social Services*. Tamworth: NASEN.

Detheridge, T. and Detheridge, M. (1997) *Literacy Through Symbols: Improving Access for Chldren and Adults*. London: David Fulton.

Detterman, D.K. (1987) Theoretical notions of intelligence and mental retardation, *American Journal of Mental Deficiency* 92, 1, 2–11.

Dew-Hughes, D. and Blandford, S. (1999) The social learning of children with severe learning difficulties: a case study of an inclusive education initiative between two primary schools in Oxfordshire, UK, *Down Syndrome Research and Practice* 6, 1, 1–18.

Diddn, R., Sikkema, S., Bosman, I., Duker, P. and Curfs, L. (2001) The use of a modified Azrin–Foxx toilet training procedure with individual and Angelman syndrome, *Journal of Applied Research in Intellectual Disabilities* 14, 1, 64–70.

Disability Rights Commission (2002) *Code of Practice for Schools. Disability Discrimination Act 1995: Part 4*. London: TSO.

Di Terlizzi, M. (1994) Life history: the impact of a changing service provision or an individual with learning disabilities, *Disability and Society* 9, 4, 501–517.

Dockrell, J. (2002) How can studies of memory and language enhance the authenticity, language and reliability of interviews? Paper presented at ESRC Seminar Series: *Methodological Issues in Interviewing Children and Young People with Learning Difficulties*, University of Birmingham, 14 March 2002.

Doll, E.A. (1965) *The Vineland Social Maturity Scale – Manual* (revised edn). Minneapolis Educational Test Bureau.

Dunn, L. and Capobianco, R. (1959) Mental retardation, *Review of Educational Research* 29, 451–470.

Dye, L., Hare, D.J. and Hendy, S. (2003) Factors impacting on the capacity to consent in people with learning disabilities, *Tizard Learning Disability Review* 8, 3, 11–20.

Dykens, E. (2001) Introduction to the special issue on behavioral phenotypes, *American Journal on Mental Retardation* 106, 1, 1–3.

Dykens, E. and Shah, B. (2003) Psychiatric disorders in Prader-Willi syndrome: epidemiology and management, *CNS Drugs* 17, 3, 167–178.

Dykens, E.M. and Hodapp, R.M. (2001) Research in mental retardation: Towards an etiological approach, *Journal of Child Psychology and Psychiatry* 42, 1, 49–71.

Dyson A. (1998) Professional intellectuals from powerful groups: wrong from the start? Chapter 1 in P. Clough and L. Barton (eds) *Articulating with Difficulty: Research Voices in Inclusive Education*. London: Paul Chapman.

Dyson, A., Lin, M. and Millward, A. (1998) *Effective Communication Between Schools, LEAs and Health and Social Services in the Field of Special Educational Needs*. London: DfEE.

Edgerton, R. (1967) *The Cloak of Competence: Stigma in the Lives of the Mentally Retarded*. Berkeley: University of California Press.

Edwards, A. and Talbot, R. (1999) *The Hard-pressed Researcher: A Research Handbook for the Caring Professions*. London: Longman.

Elgie, S. and Maquire, N. (2001) Intensive interaction with a woman with multiple and profound disabilities: a case study, *Tizard Learning Disability Review* 6, 3, 18–24.

Elliott, J. (1991) *Action Research for Educational Change*. Buckingham: Open University Press.

Ellis, N.R. (1969) A behavioral research strategy in mental retardation: defense and critique, *American Journal of Mental Deficiency* 73, 557–566.

Ellis, N.R. (1970) Memory processes in retardates and normals. In N.R. Ellis (ed.) *International Review of Research in Mental Retardation*, 14. London: Academic Press.

Ellis, N.R. and Cavalier, A.R. (1982) Research perspectives in mental retardation. In E. Zigler and D. Balla (eds) *Mental Retardation. The Developmental-Difference Controversy.* Hillsdale, New Jersey: Lawrence Erlbaum.

Elston, S. and Holloway, I. (2001) The impact of recent primary care reforms in the UK on interprofessional working in primary care centres, *Journal of Interprofessional Care* 15, 1, 19–27.

Emerson, E. (1995) *Challenging Behaviour; Analysis and Intervention in People with Learning Disabilities.* Cambridge: Cambridge University Press.

Emerson, E. (1998) People with challenging behaviour. In E. Emerson, C. Hatton, J. Bromley and A. Caine (eds) *Clinical Psychology and People with Intellectual Disabilities.* Chichester: John Wiley and Sons.

Emerson, E., Alborz, A., Reeves, D., Mason, H., Swarbrisk, R., Kiernan, C. and Mason, L. (1997) *The HARC Challenging Behaviour Project. Report 2 The Prevalence of Challenging Behaviour.* Manchester: Hester Adrian Research Centre.

Emerson, E., Robertson, J., Gregory, N., Hatton, C., Kessisoglou, S., Hallam, A., Knapp, M., Jarbrink, K., Netten, A. and Noonan Walsh, P. (2000) The quality and costs of village communities, residential campuses and community-based residential supports for people with learning disabilities, *Tizard Learning Disability Review* 5, 1, 5–16.

Emerson, E., Toogood, A., Mansell, J., Barrett, S., Bell, C., Cummings, R. and McColl, C. (1987) Challenging behaviour and community services: 1 Introduction and overview, *Mental Handicap* 15, 166–169.

Evans, J. and Benefield, P. (2001) Systematic reviews of educational research: does the medical model fit? *British Educational Research Journal* 27, 5, 527–541.

Evans, P.L.C. and Clarke, A.D.B. (eds) (1990) *Combatting Mental Handicap: A Multidisciplinary Approach: Social and environmental factors in the prevention and amelioration of mental handicap.* Oxford A.B. Academic.

Farish, A. (2000) *Creating a 'personal profile': the development of materials for recording information about pupils in a particular school for children with severe and profound and multiple learning difficulties.* Unpublished MEd dissertation, University of Birmingham.

Farrell, S. (1997) *Routines Matter: Improving the Experience of Daily Routines for People with PMLD via Staff Training: An Action Research Study.* Unpublished MEd Dissertation, University of Birmingham.

Faupel, A. (1986) Curriculum management (Part 2): Teaching curriculum and objectives, *Educational Psychology in Practice* 2, 2, 4–15.

Felce, D. (1996) Changing residential services: from institutions to ordinary living. In P. Mittler and V. Sinason (eds) *Changing Policy and Practice for People with Learning Disabilities.* London: Cassell Education.

Felce, D. and Perry, J. (1995) Quality of life: its definition and measurement, *Research in Developmental Disability* 16, 51–74.

Ferguson, D.L. and Ferguson, P.M. (2000) Qualitative research in special education: Notes toward an open inquiry instead of a new orthodoxy? *Journal of the Association for Persons with Severe Handicaps* 25, 3, 180–185.

Fernandez, M. (2000) Educating Mary: a special education case study in one Western Australian high school, *Support for Learning* 15, 3, 118–125.

Fido, R. and Potts, M. (1997) Using oral histories. Chapter 3 in D. Atkinson, M. Jackson and J. Walmsley (eds) *Forgotten Lives. Exploring the History of Learning Disability.* Kidderminster: BILD.

Finlay, W.M.L. and Lyons, E. (2002) Acquiescence in interviews with people who have mental retardation, *Mental Retardation* 40, 1, 14–29.

Fischer, J. and Hobson, D. (2001) Action research rationale and planning: developing a framework for teacher inquiry. In G. Burnaford, J. Fischer and D. Hobson (2001) *Teachers Doing Research: The Power of Action Through Inquiry* (2nd edn). Mahwah, New Jersey: Lawrence Erlbaum Associates.

Fox, P. and Norwich, B. (1992) Assessing the self-perception of young adults with severe learning difficulties, *European Journal of Special Needs Education, 7,* 3, 193–203.

France, A. (2001) Involving communities in the evaluation of programmes with 'at risk' children and young people, *Children and Society,* 15, 39–45.

Freedman, R.I. (2001) Ethical challenges in the conduct of research involving persons with mental retardation, *Mental Retardation* 39, 2, 130–141.

Freeman, D. (1998) *Doing Teacher Research: From Inquiry to Understanding.* Pacific Grove: Heinle and Heinle.

Fried, E. and Litwinl, B. (2001) The effects of teambuilding on pre-professional stereotypes between physical therapy and occupational therapy students, *Journal of Interprofessional Care* 15, 1, 93–94.

Fuller, P.R. (1949) Operant conditioning of a vegetative human organism, *American Journal of Psychology* 62, 587–590.

Gallaher, K., van Kraayenoord, C., Jobling, A. and Moni, K. (2002) Reading with Abby: a case study of individual tutoring with a young adult with Down syndrome, *Down Syndrome Research and Practice* 8, 2, 59–66.

Gates, B., Newell, R. and Wray, J. (2001) Behaviour modification and gentle teaching workshops: management of children with learning disabilities exhibiting challenging behaviour and implications for learning disability nursing, *Journal of Advanced Nursing* 34, 1, 86–95.

Geertz, C. (1973) *The Interpretation of Cultures.* New York: Basic Books.

Germain, R. (2002) A 'positive' approach to supporting a pupil with Down syndrome during 'dedicated numeracy time'? *Down Syndrome Research and Practice* 8, 2, 53–58.

Germain, R. (2003) Using cameras and talking mats. Paper presented at ESRC Seminar Series: *Methodological Issues in Interviewing Children and Young People with Learning Difficulties,* University of Birmingham, 27 March 2003.

Gersten, R. (1996) Literacy instruction for language-minority students: The transition years, *Elementary School Journal* 96, 227–244.

Gersten R., Baker, S. and Lloyd, J.W. (2000) Designing high-quality research in special education: group experimental design, *The Journal of Special Education* 34, 1, 2–18.

Ghate, D. (2001) Community-based evaluations in the UK: Scientific concerns and practical constraints, *Children and Society* 15, 23–32.

Gibson, J.J. (1979) *The Ecological Approach to Visual Perception.* Boston: Houghton Mifflin.

Gillham, B. (2000) *Case Study Research Methods.* London: Continuum.

Gladstone, C. (2002) A journey of discovery: how interviews were used as part methodology for gaining the views of a heterogeneous group of students. Paper presented at ESRC Seminar Series: *Methodological Issues in Interviewing Children and Young People with Learning Difficulties,* University of Birmingham, 17 October 2002.

Glaser, B. and Strauss, A. (1967) *The Discovery of Grounded Theory.* London: Weidenfeld and Nicolson.

Glendinning, C. (1986) *A Single Door: Social Work with the Families of Disabled Children.* London: Allen and Unwin.

Goble, C. (1999) 'Like the secret service isn't it'. People with learning difficulties' perceptions of staff and services: mystification and disempowerment, *Disability and Society* 14, 4, 449–461.

Goffman, E. (1961) *Asylums: Essays on the Social Situation of Mental Patients and Other Inmates*. Harmondsworth: Penguin Books.

Goode, D. (2002) Mental retardation is dead: long live mental retardation! *Mental Retardation* 40, 1, 57–59.

Goodley, D. (1999) Disability research and the 'researcher template': reflections on grounded subjectivity in ethnographic research, *Qualitative Enquiry* 5, 1, 24–46.

Goodley, D. (2000) *Self Advocacy in the Lives of People with Learning Difficulties*. Buckingham: Open University Press.

Goodley, D. and Moore, M. (2000) Doing disability research: activist lives and the academy, *Disability and Society* 15, 6, 861–882.

Goodley, D., Armstrong, D., Sutherland, K. and Laurie, L. (2003) Self advocacy, 'learning difficulties', and the social model of disability, *Mental Retardation* 41, 3, 149–160.

Grant, G. and Ramcharan, P. (2002) Researching 'Valuing People', *Tizard Learning Disability Review* 7, 3, 27–33.

Gray, B. and Ridden, G. (1999) *Life-maps of People with Learning Difficulties*. London: Jessica Kingsley.

Greene, J., Benjamin, L. and Goodyear, L. (2001) The merits of mixing methods in evaluation, *Evaluation* 7, 1, 25–44.

Gregory, S. (2002) Interviewing deaf children and young people. Paper presented at ESRC Seminar Series: *Methodological Issues in Interviewing Children and Young People with Learning Difficulties*, University of Birmingham, 14 March 2002.

Grocott, P., Cowley, S. and Richardson, A. (2002) Solving methodological challenges using a theory-driven evaluation in the study of complex patient care, *Evaluation*, 8, 3, 306–321.

Grossen, M. (2002) Polyphony and collective work in labelling learning difficulties. *Fifth Congress of the International Society for Cultural Research and Activity Theory (ISCRAT)* Amsterdam, 18–22 June 2002.

Grove, N., Porter, J., Bunning, K. and Olsson, C. (1999) See what I mean: Interpreting the meaning of communication by people with severe and profound learning difficulties: Theoretical and methodological issues, *Journal of Applied Research in Intellectual Disabilities* 12, 3 190–203.

Grunsell, J. and Carter, M. (2002) The behavior chain interruption strategy: generalization to out-of-routine contexts, *Education and Training in Mental Retardation and Developmental Disabilities*, 37, 4, 378–390.

Guskin, S. and Spicker, H. (1968) Educational research in mental retardation, *International Review of Research in Mental Retardation* 3, 217–278.

Hales, A. (1978) *The Children of Skylark Ward: Teaching Severely Handicapped Children*. Cambridge: Cambridge University Press.

Hall, D. (1997) Child development teams: are they fulfilling their purpose? *Child: Health, Care and Development* 23, 87–99.

Hammersley, M. (1992) *What's Wrong with Ethnography? Methodological Explorations*. London: Routledge.

Hargreaves, D.H. (2001) The Nuttall Memorial/Carfax Lecture BERA 2001.

Harris, B. (1997) Repoliticizing the history of psychology. Chapter 2 in D. Fox and I. Prilleltensky (eds) *Critical Psychology. An Introduction*. London. Sage.

Harris, J. (2003) Time to make up your mind: why choosing is difficult, *British Journal of Learning Disabilities* 31, 3–8.

Harris, J., Cook, M. and Upton, G. (1996) *Pupils with Severe Learning Difficulties who Present Challenging Behaviour*. Kidderminster: BILD.

Hart, C. (2000) *Doing a Literature Review*. London: Sage.

Hart, S. (2000) Leisure activities for deafblind children and young adults, *Eye Contact* 26, 5–7.

Haskell, R. (1944) The development of a research programme in mental deficiency over a fifteen year period, *American Journal of Psychiatry* 101, 73–81.

Hastings, R. and Remington, B. (1993) Connotations of labels for mental handicap and challenging behaviour: a review and research evaluation, *Mental Handicap Research* 6, 3, 237–249.

Hatton, C. and Ager, A. (2002) Quality of life measurement and people with intellectual disabilities: A reply to Cummins, *Journal of Applied Research in Intellectual Disabilities* 15, 254–260.

Hawke, A. and Stanislawski, N. (1999) Personal passports. Hey! it's all about me, *SLD Experience* 24, 5–6.

Heiman, T. (2000a) Friendship quality among children in three educational settings, *Journal of Intellectual and Developmental Disability* 25, 1, 1–12.

Heiman, T. (2000b) Quality and quantity of friendships: students' and teachers' perceptions, *School Psychology International* 21, 3, 265–280.

Heiman, T. and Margalit, M. (1998) Loneliness, depression, and social skills among students with mild mental retardation in different educational settings, *The Journal of Special Education* 32, 3, 154–163.

Henry, L.A. and Gudjonsson, G.H. (1999) Eyewitness memory and suggestibility in children with mental retardation, *American Journal on Mental Retardation* 104, 6, 491–508.

Hensel, E., Rose, J., Stenfert Kroese, B. and Banks-Smith, J. (2002) Subjective judgements of quality of life: a comparison study between people with intellectual disability and those without disability, *Journal of Intellectual Disability Research* 46, 2, 95–107.

Hetzroni, O. and Roth, T. (2003) Effects of a positive support approach to enhance communicative behaviours of children with mental retardation who have challenging behaviours, *Education and Training in Developmental Disabilities* 38, 1, 95–105.

Heward, W.L. (2003) Ten faulty notions about teaching and learning that hinder the effectiveness of special education, *The Journal of Special Education* 36, 4, 186–205.

Hewett, D. and Nind, M. (eds) (1998) *Interaction in Action. Reflections on the Use of Intensive Interaction*. London: Fulton.

Hillage, J., Pearson, R., Anderson, A. and Tamkin, P. (1998) *Excellence in Schools*. London: Institute for Employment Studies.

Hobbs, N. (1959) Research in mental retardation: prospects and strategies, *American Journal of Mental Deficiency* 64, 229–239.

Hockett, J. (1944) The mentally handicapped, *Review of Educational Research* 14, 217–223.

Hoddapp, R.M. and Dykens, E. (2001) Strengthening behavioural research on genetic mental retardation syndromes, *American Journal on Mental Retardation* 106, 1, 4–15.

Hogg, J. (2002) Commentary on Nind and Kellett (2002), *European Journal of Special Needs Education* 17, 3.

Hogg, J. and Mittler, P. (eds) (1980) *Advances in Mental Handicap Research* Vol. 1. Chichester: John Wiley and Sons.

Hogg, J. and Mittler, P. (eds) (1983) *Advances in Mental Handicap Research* Vol. 2. Chichester: John Wiley and Sons.

Hogg, J., Cavet, J., Lambe, L. and Smeddle, M. (2001) The use of 'Snoezelen' as multisensory stimulation with people with intellectual disabilities: a review of research, *Research in Developmental Disabilities* 22, 353–372.

Hogg, J., Reeves, D., Mudford, O. and Roberts, J. (1995) The development of observational techniques to assess behaviour state and affective behaviour in adults with profound and multiple learning disabilities. White Top Centre, University of Dundee (Unpublished).

Holman, A. (2001) In conversation: John Hutton, *British Journal of Learning Disabilities* 29, 1, 3–4.

Home Department (1946) *Report of the Care of Children Committee* (Curtis Report). London: HMSO.

Hopkins, D. (2002) *A Teacher's Guide to Classroom Research.* Buckingham: Open University Press.

Hornby, G. (1994) *Counselling in Child Disability: Skills for Working with Parents.* London: Chapman and Hall.

Hornby, G. and Kidd, R. (2001) Transfer from special to mainstream – ten years later, *British Journal of Special Education* 28, 1.

Hornby, S. (1993) *Collaborative Care: Interprofessional, Interagency and Interpersonal.* Oxford: Blackwell.

Howell, C. (2002) The literacy hour, *SLD Experience* 32, 29–31.

Howie, D. (1999) Models and morals: meanings underpinning the scientific study of special educational needs, *International Journal of Disability Development and Education* 46, 1, 9–24.

Hulme, C. and Mackenzie, S. (1992) *Working Memory and Severe Learning Difficulties.* Hove: Erlbaum.

Humphrey, J.C. (2000) Researching disability politics, or, some problems with the social model in practice, *Disability and Society* 15, 1, 63–85.

Hunter, D. and Wistow, G. (1987) *Community Care in Britain.* London: King's Fund.

Janesick, V.J. (1998) The dance of qualitative research design: metaphor, methodolatry, and meaning. Chapter 2 in N.K. Denzin and Y.S. Lincoln (eds) *Strategies of Qualitative Inquiry.* London: Sage.

Jenkinson, J. (1998) Parent choice in the education of students with disabilities, *International Journal of Disability, Development and Education* 45, 2, 189–202.

Kanner, L. (1964) *A History of the Care and Study of the Mentally Retarded.* Springfield: Charles Thomas.

Keene, J., Bailey, S., Swift, L. and Janacek, G. (2000) The tracking project: a collaborative multi-agency database for shared clients/patients to inform policy development, *Journal of Interprofessional Care* 14, 4, 325–336.

Keffer, A., Wood, D., Carr, S., Mattison, L. and Lanier, B. (1998) Teacher research: 'It's a jungle out there'. In B. Bisplinghoff and J. Allen (eds) *Engaging Teachers: Creating Teaching and Researching Relationships.* Portsmouth, New Hampshire: Heinemann.

Kellett, M. (2000) Sam's story: evaluating intensive interaction in terms of its effect on the social and communicative ability of a young child with severe learning difficulties, *Support for Learning* 15, 4, 165–171.

Kellett, M. and Nind, M. (2001) Ethics in quasi-experimental research on people with severe learning disabilities; dilemmas and compromises, *British Journal of Learning Disabilities* 29, 51–55.

Kelly, E. and Lesh, R. (2002) Understanding and explicating the design experiment methodology, *Building Research Capacity* 3, 1–3.

Kelly, K., Stephen, L., Sills, G. and Brodie, M. (2002) Topiramate in patients with learning disability and refractory epilepsy, *Epilepsia* 43, 4, 399–402.

Kember, D. (2001) *Reflective Teaching and Learning in the Health Professions: Action Research in Professional Education*. Oxford: Blackwell Science.

Kennedy, C.H., Shukla, S. and Fryxell, D. (1997) Comparing the effects of educational placement on the social relationships of intermediate school students with severe disabilities, *Exceptional Children* 64, 1, 31–47.

Kiernan, C. (1985) Single-subject designs. Chapter 3 in S. Hegarty and P. Evans (eds) *Research and Evaluation Methods in Special Education*. Windsor: NFER-Nelson.

Kiernan, C. (1999) Participation in research by people with learning disability: origins and issues, *British Journal of Learning Disability* 27, 77–80.

Kiernan, C. and Jones, M. (1977) *Behaviour Assessment Battery*. Windsor: NFER.

King, R., Raynes, N. and Tizard, J. (1971) *Patterns of Residential Care: Sociological Studies in Institutions for Handicapped Children*. London: Routledge and Kegan Paul.

King's Fund (1980) *An Ordinary Life: Comprehensive Locally-based Residential Services for Mentally Handicapped People*. London: King's Fund.

Kirk, S. and Kolstoe, O. (1953) The mentally retarded, *Review of Educational Research* 23, 5, 400–416.

Knox, M., Mok, M. and Permenter, T.R. (2000) Working with the experts: collaborative research with people with an intellectual disability, *Disability and Society* 15, 1, 49–61.

Kushlick, A. (1970) Residential care for the mental subnormal, *Royal Society of Health Journal* 90, 255–261.

Kushner, S. (2002) I'll take mine neat: multiple methods but a single methodology, *Evaluation* 8, 2, 249–258.

Lacey, P. (2001) *Support Partnerships: Collaboration in Action*. London: David Fulton.

Lacey, P. and Lomas, J. (1993) *Support Services and the Curriculum: A Practical Guide to Collaboration*. London: David Fulton.

Lacey, P. and Ouvry, C. (eds) (1998) *People with Profound and Multiple Learning Disabilities: A Collaborative Approach to Complex Needs*. London: David Fulton.

Law, J., Lindsay, G., Peacey, N., Gascoigne, M., Soloff, N., Radford, J. and Band, S. (2001) Facilitating communication between education and health services: the provision for children with speech and language needs, *British Journal of Special Education* 28, 3, 133–137.

Laws, G., Byrne A. and Buckley S. (2000) Language and memory in children with Down syndrome at mainstream and special schools: a comparison, *Educational Psychology* 20, 4, 447–457.

Lea, S. (1988) Mental retardation: social construction or clinical reality, *Disability, Handicap and Society* 3, 1, 63–70.

Leathard, A. (1994) *Going Interprofessional: Working Together for Health and Welfare*. London: Routledge.

Lefort, S. and Fraser, M. (2002) Quality of life measurement and its use in the field of learning disabilities, *Journal of Learning Disabilities* 6, 3, 223–238.

Lewis, A. (2002) Accessing children's views about inclusion and integration, *Support for Learning* 17, 3, 110–116.

Lewis, A. and Lindsay, G. (eds) (2000) *Researching Children's Perspectives*. Buckingham: Open University Press.

Lewis, A. and Norwich, B. (1999) *Mapping a Pedagogy for Special Educational Needs*. Coventry; Exeter: Institute of Education, University of Warwick, School of Education, University of Exeter.

Lewis, A. and Porter, J. (submitted for publication) Interviewing children and young people with learning disabilities: Guidelines for researchers and multi-professional practice, *British Journal of Learning Disability*.

Lewis, A., Lindsay, G. and Phillips (2003) Assessment in special schools: National Early Assessment procedures and pupils attending special schools in England, *European Journal of Special Needs Education* 18, 2, 141–153.

Lim, L., Arabsolghar, F. and Choi, H-J. (2003) Authors' institutional affiliations in Australian intellectual and developmental disabilities journals: a comparison of two decades, *Research in Developmental Disabilities* 24, 6, 467–473.

Limbrick-Spencer, G. (2000) *Parent Support Needs: The Views of Parents of Children with Complex Needs.* Birmingham: Handsel Trust.

Limbrick-Spencer, G. (2001) *The Keyworker: A Practical Guide.* Birmingham: WordWorks.

Lindsay, G. (2000) Researching children's perspectives: ethical issues. In A. Lewis and G. Lindsay (eds) *Researching Children's Perspectives* (pp1–20). Buckingham: Open University.

Lloyd, C. (2002) Developing and changing practice in special educational needs through critically reflective action research: a case study, *European Journal of Special Needs Education* 17, 2, 109–127.

Lloyd, S. and Burman, M. (1996) Specialist police units and the joint investigation of child abuse, *Child Abuse Reviews* 5, 1, 4–17.

Lobato, J. (2003) How design experiments can inform a rethinking of transfer and vice versa, *Educational Researcher* 32, 1, 17–20.

Locke, L.F., Spirduso, W.W. and Silverman, S.J. (2000) *Proposals that Work* (4th edn). London: Sage.

Logan, J.R., Lott, J.D. and Mayville, E.A. (2000) Top researchers and institutions in mental retardation: 1979–1999, *Research in Developmental Disabilities* 21, 257–261.

Lomax, P. (1994) Action research for professional practice: a position paper on educational action research. Paper presented at the annual conference of BERA 1994.

Luckin, B. (1986) Time, place and competence: society and history in the writings of Robert Edgerton, *Disability, Handicap and Society* 1, 1, 89–101.

Lunt, I., Evans, J., Norwich, B. and Wedell, K. (1994) *Working Together: Inter-school Collaboration for Special Needs.* London: David Fulton.

Mackenzie, S. and Hulme, C. (1987) Memory span development in Down's syndrome, severely subnormal and normal subjects, *Cognitive Neuropsychology* 4, 3, 303–319.

Maes, B., Geeraert, L. and Van den Bruel, B. (2000) Developing a model for quality evaluation in residential care for people with intellectual disability, *Journal of Intellectual Disability Research* 44, 3, 544–552.

Male, D. (2002) Peer nominations among adolescents experiencing severe learning difficulties: An exploratory study using sociometric techniques, *Journal of Research in Special Educational Needs* 2, 3.

Malin, N. (1994) *Implementing Community Care.* Buckingham: Open University Press.

Mansell, J. (2000) Commentary. The quality and costs of village communities, residential campuses and community-based residential supports for people with learning disabilities, *Tizard Learning Disability Review* 5, 1, 17–19.

March, J., Steigold, B., Justice, S. and Mitchell, P. (1997) Follow the Yellow Brick Road! People with learning difficulties as co-researchers, *British Journal of Learning Disabilities* 25, 77–80.

Masson, J. (2000) Researching children's perspectives: legal issues. Chapter 3 in A. Lewis and G. Lindsay (eds) *Researching Children's Perspectives.* Buckingham: Open University.

Mavers, D. (2003) Concept maps: representing thinking. Paper presented at ESRC Seminar Series: *Methodological Issues in Interviewing Children and Young People with*

Learning Difficulties, University of Birmingham, 27 March 2003.

McBrien, J. (1987) The Haytor Unit: specialised day care for adults with severe mental handicaps and behaviour problems, *Mental Handicap* 15, 77–80.

McConachie, H., Salt, A., Chadbury, Y., McLachlan, A. and Logan, S. (1999) How do child development teams work? Findings from a UK national survey, *Child: Care, Health and Development* 25, 2, 157–168.

McConkey, R. (1988) Interaction: The name of the game. In B. Smith (ed.) *Interactive Approaches to the Education of Children with Severe Learning Difficulties*. Birmingham: Westhill College.

McDade, H.L. and Adler, S. (1980) Down syndrome and short-term memory impairment: a storage or retrieval deficit? *American Journal of Mental Deficiency* 84, 6, 561–567.

McGrath, M. (1991) *Multidisciplinary Teamwork: Community Mental Handicap Teams.* Aldershot: Avebury.

McIntyre, C. (2000) *The Art of Action Research in the Classroom*. London: David Fulton.

McNicholas, J. (1998) *The assessment of pupils with profound and multiple learning difficulties: an investigation into the practices of teacher assessment.* Unpublished PhD Thesis: University of Birmingham.

McNiff, J. (1988) *Action Research: Principles and Practice*. London: Routledge.

McNiff, J. with Whitehead, J. (2002) *Action Research: Principles and Practice* (2nd edn). London: RoutledgeFalmer.

Mechling, L. and Gast, D. (2003) Multi-media instruction to teach grocery word association and store location: a study of generalisation, *Education and Training in Developmental Disabilities* 338, 1, 62–76.

Medical Research Council (2000) *A Framework for Development and Evaluation of RCTs for Complex Interventions to Improve Health*. London: MRC.

Mental Health Foundation (1997) *Don't Forget Us: Children with Learning Disabilities and Severe Challenging Behaviour* (The Russell Report). London: The Mental Health Foundation.

Mertens, D.M. (1998) *Research Methods in Education and Psychology*. London: Sage.

Miles, M. and Huberman, A. (1984) *Qualitative Data Analysis: A Sourcebook of New Methods.* Beverley Hills: Sage.

Mills, P.E., Cole, K.N., Jenkins, J.R. and Dale, P.S. (1998) Effects of differing levels of inclusion on preschoolers with disabilities, *Exceptional Children* 65, 1, 79–90.

Minarik, L. (2001) 'Tuesday night' revisited: learning to survive. In J. Zeni (ed.) *Ethical Issues in Practitioner Research*. New York: Teachers' College Press.

Minkes, J., Robinson, C. and Weston, C. (1994) Consulting the children: interviewing children using residential respite care services, *Disability and Society* 9, 1, 47–57.

Morris, J. (1998) *Still Missing?* Vol. 1. London: The Who Cares? Trust.

Morris, P. (1969) *Put Away: A Sociological Study of Institutions for the Mentally Retarded.* London: Routledge and Kegan Paul.

Morrison, B. and Lilford, R. (2001) How can action research apply to health services? *Qualitative Health Research* 11, 4, 436–449.

Mortimore, P. (2000) Does educational research matter? *British Educational Research Journal* 26, 1, 5–24.

Mukherjee, S., Beresford, B. and Sloper, P. (1999) *Unlocking Key Working: An Analysis and Evaluation of Key Worker Services for Families with Disabled Children*. Bristol: The Policy Press.

Murphy, J. (1998) Talking mats, *Speech and Language Therapy in Practice*, Autumn 1998, 11–14.

Murphy, J. and Cameron, L. (2002) *Talking Mats and Learning Disability: A low-tech communication resource to help people to express their views and feelings*. Stirling: AAC Research Unit, University of Stirling.

Myers, K. and Brown, A. (2003) Mental deficiencies: the diagnosis and after-care of the 'feeble-minded' in Birmingham, 1900–1913. Unpublished paper, University of Birmingham.

Neilson, A., Hogg, J., Malek, M. and Rowley, D. (2000) Impact of surgical and orthotic intervention on the quality of life of people with profound intellectual and multiple disabilities and their carer, *Journal of Applied Research in Intellectual Disabilities* 13, 216–238.

Newburn, T. (2001) What do we mean by evaluation? *Children and Society* 15, 5–13.

Newman, D. (1990) Opportunities for research on the organizational impact of school computers, *Educational Researcher* 19, 8–13.

Nihira, K., Foster, R., Shelhaas, M. and Leland, H. (1975) *Adaptive Behavior Scale*. Washington DC: AAMD.

Nind, M. (1996) Efficacy of intensive interaction: developing sociability and communication in people with severe and complex learning difficulties using an approach based on caregiver–infant interaction, *European Journal of Special Needs Education* 11, 1, 48–66.

Nind, M. (1999) Intensive interaction and autism: a useful approach? *British Journal of Special Education* 26, 2, 96–102.

Nind, M. and Hewett, D. (1994) *Access to Communication*. London: David Fulton.

Nind, M. and Hewitt, D. (1994) *Access to Communication. Developing the Basics of Communication with People with Severe Learning Difficulties Through Intensive Interaction*. London: David Fulton.

Nind, M. and Kellett, M. (2002) Responding to individuals with severe learning difficulties and stereotyped behaviour: challenges for an inclusive era, *European Journal of Special Needs Education* 17, 3, 265–282.

Nolan, B. (1999) Literacy hour – a positive approach, *Eye Contact* 23, 27–28.

Nolan, P. and Badger, F. (2002) *Promoting Collaboration in Primary Mental Health Care*. Cheltenham: Nelson Thornes.

Noonan Walsh, P. (2003) A courtly welcome: observations on the research initiative, *British Journal of Learning Disabilities* 31, 190–193.

Norwich, B. (1997) Exploring the perspectives of adolescents with moderate learning difficulties on their special schooling and themselves: stigma and self-perceptions, *European Journal of Special Needs Education* 12, 1, 38–53.

Norwich, B. and Kelly, N. (2004) Pupils' views on inclusion: moderate learning difficulties and bullying in mainstream and special schools, *British Educational Research Journal* 30, 1, 43–65.

Norwich, B. and Lewis, A. (2000) Mapping a pedagogy for special educational needs, *British Educational Research Journal* 27, 3, 313–329.

Oakley, A. (2000) *Experiments in Knowing: Gender and Method in the Social Sciences*. Cambridge: Polity.

O'Brien, J. (1981) *The Principle of Normalisation: A Foundation for Effective Services*. London: Campaign for Mentally Handicapped People.

O'Connor, N. and Tizard, J. (1954) A survey of patients in twelve mental deficiency institutions, *British Medical Journal* 1, 16–20.

Ofsted (2003) *Inspecting Schools. Framework for Inspecting Schools*. London: HMSO.

Oliver, M. (1992) Changing the social relations of research productions? *Disability, Handicap and Society* 7, 2, 101–114.

Oliver, M. (1996) *Understanding Disability: from Theory to Practice*. Basingstoke: Macmillan.

Oliver, M. (1997) Emancipatory research: realistic goal or impossible dream? Chapter 2 in C. Barnes and G. Mercer (eds) *Doing Disability Research*. Leeds: Disability Press.

Oliver, P.C., Piachaurd, J., Done, J., Regan, A., Cooray, S. and Tyrer, P. (2002) Difficulties in conducting a randomized controlled trial of health service interventions in intellectual disability: Implications for evidence-based practice, *Journal of Intellectual Disability Research* 46, 4, 340–345.

Orelove, F. and Sobsey, D. (1995) *Educating Children with Multiple Disabilities: A Transdisciplinary Approach*. Baltimore: Paul Brookes.

Oswin, M. (1971) *The Empty Hours: A Study of the Weekend Life of Handicapped Children in Institutions*. London: Allen Lane.

Ovretveit, J. (1993) *Coordinating Community Care: Multidisciplinary Teams and Care Management*. Buckingham: Open University Press.

Paechter, C. (2003) On goodness and utility in educational research. Chapter 7 in P. Sikes, J. Nixon and W. Carr (eds) *The Moral Foundations of Educational Research: Knowledge, Inquiry and Values*. Maidenhead: Open University Press.

Palmer, D.S., Fuller, K., Arora, T. and Nelson, M. (2001) Taking sides: parent views on inclusion for their children with severe disabilities, *Exceptional Children* 67, 4, 467–484.

Papodopoulos, I., Scanlon, K. and Lees, S. (2002) Reporting and validating research findings through reconstructed stories, *Disability and Society* 17, 3, 269–281.

Park, K. (1998) Dickens for all: inclusive approaches to literature and communication with people with severe and profound learning disabilities, *British Journal of Special Education* 25, 3, 114–118.

Park, K. (1999a) Storytelling with people with sensory impairments and additional disabilities, *SLD Experience* 33, 17–20.

Park, K. (1999b) Reading objects: literacy and objects of reference, *PMLD-Link* 12, 1, 4–9.

Park, K. (2001) Macbeth in mind: a poetry workshop onstage at Shakespeare's Globe Theatre, *SLD Experience* 29, 2–4.

Park, K. (2002) Macbeth: a poetry workshop on stage at Shakespeare's Globe Theatre, *British Journal of Special Education* 29, 1, 14–19.

Pawson, R. and Tilley, N. (1997) *Realistic Evaluation*. London: Sage.

Payne, M. (1993) *Linkages: Networking in Social Care*. London: Whiting and Birch.

Payne, M. (2000) *Teamwork in Multiprofessional Care*. Basingstoke: Palgrave.

Pearson, V., Wong, Y. and Pierini, J. (2002) The structure and content of social inclusion: voices of young adults with learning difficulties in Guangzhou, *Disability and Society* 17, 4, 356–382.

Peetsma, T., Vergeer, M., Roeleveld, J. and Karsten, S. (2001) Inclusion in education: comparing pupils' development in special and regular education, *Educational Review* 53, 2, 125–135.

Pence, D. and Wilson, C. (1994) *Team Investigation of Child Sexual Abuse: The Uneasy Alliance*. Thousand Oaks: Sage.

Penrose, L.S. (1949) *The Biology of Mental Defect*. London: Sidgwick and Jackson.

People First London, Change, Speaking Up in Cambridge and Royal MENCAP (2000) *Nothing About Us Without Us – The Learning Disability Strategy: The User Group Report*. London, Department of Health.

Perry, J. and Felce, D. (2002) Subjective and objective quality of life assessment: responsiveness, response bias, and resident: proxy concordance, *Mental Retardation* 40, 6, 445–456.

Pershey, M. and Gilbert, T. (2002) Christine: a case study of literacy acquisition by an adult with developmental disabilities, *Mental Retardation* 40, 3, 219–234.

Peterson, C. (2002) Reflections on the challenges of program evaluation, *Topics in Early Childhood Special Education* 22, 2, 82–85.

Petry, K., Maes, B. and Vlaskamp, C. (2001) Developing a procedure for evaluating quality of life for people with profound and multiple disabilities, *Tizard Learning Disability Review* 6, 2, 45–48.

Pfeffer, N. and Coote, A. (1991) *Is Quality Good for You? A Critical Review of Quality Assurance in Welfare*. London: Institute for Public Policy Research.

Phillips, D.C. and Burbules, N.C. (2000) *Postpositivism and Educational Research*. Oxford: Rowman and Littlefield.

Pidgeon, C. (1999) Literacy hour, *PMLD-Link* 12, 1, 20.

Pijl, Y.J. and Pijl, S.J. (1998) Are pupils in special education too 'special' for regular education? *International Review of Education* 44, 1, 5–20.

Porter, J. (2003) Interviewing children and young people with learning disabilities, *SLD Experience*.

Porter, J. and Lewis, A. (2001) *Methodological Issues in Interviewing Children and Young people with Learning Difficulties*, Briefing Paper, ESRC Seminar Series 2001.

Porter J., Lacey P., with Benjamin, S., Miller, O., Miller, C., Robertson, C., Sutton, J. and Visser, J. (2002) *The Role of Special Schools: A Review of the Literature*. London: DfES.

Porter, J., Ouvry, C., Morgan, M. and Downs, C. (2001) Interpreting the communication of people with profound and multiple learning difficulties, *British Journal of Learning Disabilities* 29, 1, 12–16.

Prehm, H. and Crosson, J. (1969) The mentally retarded, *Review of Educational Research* 39, 1, 5–24.

Price, D. and Barron, L. (1999) Developing independence: the experience of the Lawnmowers Theatre Company, *Disability and Society* 14, 6, 819–829.

Pring, R. (2000) *Philosophy of Educational Research*. London: Continuum.

Pring, R. (2001) The virtues and vices of an educational researcher, *Journal of Philosophy of Education* 35, 3, 407–421.

Pritchard, D. (1963) *Education and the Handicapped 1760–1960*. London: Routledge and Kegan Paul.

Qualifications and Curriculum Authority (2001) *Planning, Teaching and Assessing the Curriculum for Pupils with Learning Difficulties*. London: QCA.

QCA/DfEE (2001) *Supporting the Target Setting Process: Guidance for Effective Target Setting for Pupils with Special Educational Needs*. Nottingham: DfEE.

Quine, l. (1986) Behaviour problems in severely mentally handicapped children, *Psychological Medicine* 16, 895–907.

Race, S. (1995) Historical development of service provision. In N. Malin (ed.) *Services for People with Learning Disabilities*. London: Routledge.

Ramcharan, P. and Grant, G. (2001) Views and experiences of people with intellectual disabilities and their families. (1) The user perspective, *Journal of Applied Research in Intellectual Disabilities* 14, 348–363.

Rapley, M. and Ridgeway, J. (1998) 'Quality of life' talk and the corporatisation of intellectual disability, *Disability and Society* 13, 3, 451–471.

Raymond, C. (1933) The need for research in the field of mental deficit, *American Journal of Mental Deficiency* 38, 71–87.

Reichle, J. (1997) Communication intervention with persons who have severe disabilities, *The Journal of Special Education* 31, 1, 110–134.

Reinders, J.S. (2002) The good life for citizens with intellectual disability, *Journal of Intellectual Disability Research* 46, 1, 1–5.

Richardson, M. (2002) Involving people in analysis, *Journal of Learning Disabilities* 6, 1, 47–60.

Riddell, S., Baron, S. and Wilson, A. (2001) *The Learning Society and People with Learning Difficulties*. Bristol: Policy Press.

Ripley, M. (2001) Clearvision tactile books, *SLD Experience* 30, 11–12.

Rittle-Johnson, B. and Siegler, R.S. (1998) The relation between conceptual and procedural knowledge in learning mathematics: A review. Chapter 4 in C. Donlan (ed.) *The Development of Mathematical Skills*. Hove: Psychology Press.

Robson, C. (1985) Small-N case studies. Chapter 4 in S. Hegarty and P. Evans (eds) *Research and Evaluation Methods in Special Education*. Windsor: NFER-Nelson.

Robson, C. (2002) *Real World Research* (2nd edn). Oxford: Blackwell.

Rodgers, J. (1999) Trying to get it right: undertaking research involving people with learning difficulties, *Disability and Society* 14, 4, 421–433.

Ryan, J. and Thomas, F. (1980) *The Politics of Mental Handicap*. Harmondsworth: Penguin.

Samuel, J. (2001) Intensive interaction in context, *Tizard Learning Disability Review* 6, 3, 25–30.

Sandman, C. and Hetrick, W. (1995) Opiate mechanisms in self-injury, *Mental Retardation and Developmental Disabilities Research Reviews* 1, 130–136.

Schalock, R.L., Brown, I., Brown, R., Cummins, R.A., Felce, D., Matikka, L., Keith, K.D. and Permenter, T. (2002) Conceptualization, measurement, and application of quality of life for persons with intellectual disabilities: Report of an international panel of experts, *Mental Retardation* 40, 6, 457–470.

Schindele, R.A. (1985) Research methodology in special education: a framework approach to special problems and solutions. Chapter 1 in S. Hegarty and P. Evans (eds) *Research and Evaluation Methods in Special Education*. Windsor: NFER-Nelson.

Schwartz, C. and Rabinovitz, S. (2003) Life satisfaction of people with intellectual disability living in community residences: perceptions of the residents, their parents and staff members. *Journal of Intellectual Disability Research* 47, 2, 75–84.

Scott, D. (ed.) (1999) Values *and Educational Research*. London: Institute of Education.

Scott, D. (2000) *Reading Educational Research and Policy*. London: Routledge/Falmer.

Segal, S. (1967) *No Child is Ineducable*. Oxford: Pergamon Press.

Shakespeare, T. and Watson, N. (1997) Defending the social model, *Disability and Society* 12, 2, 293–300.

Shearer, A. (1980) *Handicapped Children in Residential Care: A Study of Policy Failure*. London: Bedford Square Press.

Shearn, J., Beyer, S. and Felce, D. (2000) The cost-effectiveness of supported employment for people with severe intellectual disabilities and high support needs: a pilot study, *Journal of Applied Research in Intellectual Disabilities* 13, 29–37.

Siegler, R.S. (1995) How does change occur: a microgenetic study of number conservation, *Cognitive Psychology* 28, 225–273.

Siegler, R.S. and Chen, Z. (1998) Developmental differences in rule learning: a microgenetic analysis, *Cognitive Psychology* 36, 273–310.

Sigelman, C., Budd, E.C., Spanhel, C. L. and Schoenrock, C.J. (1981) When in doubt say yes: Acquiescence in interviews with mentally retarded persons, *Mental Retardation* 19, 53–58.

Sims, J. and Wright, C. (2000) *Research in Health Care: Concepts, Design and Methods*. Cheltenham: Thornes.

Skrtic, T. (1991) *Behind Special Education: A Critical Analysis of Professional Culture and School Organization*. Denver: Love.

Skrtic, T. (ed.) (1996) *Disability and Democracy: Reconstructing Special Education for Postmodernity*. New York: Teachers' College.

Sloane, F.C. and Gorard, S. (2003) Exploring modeling aspects of design experiments, *Educational Researcher* 32, 1, 29–31.

Smith, B. (ed.) (1988) *Interactive Approaches to the Education of Children with Severe Learning Difficulties*. Birmingham: Westhill College.

Smith, B. (ed.) (1990) *Interactive Approaches to Teaching the Core Subjects. The National Curriculum for Pupils with Severe and Moderate Learning Difficulties*. Bristol: Lame Duck.

Smith, J.D. (2002) The myth of mental retardation: Paradigm shifts, disaggregation, and developmental disabilities, *Mental Retardation* 40, 1, 62–64.

Smith, J.K. and Hodgkinson, P. (2002) Fussing about the nature of educational research: the neo-realists versus the relativists, *British Educational Research Journal* 28, 2, 291–296.

Söder, M. (1989) Disability as a social construct: the labelling approach revisited, *European Journal of Special Needs Education* 4, 2, 117–129.

Söder, M. (1990) Prejudice or ambivalence? Attitudes toward persons with disabilities, *Disability, Handicap and Society* 5, 3, 227–241.

Soothill, K., Mackay, L. and Webb, C. (eds) (1995) *Interprofessional Relations in Healthcare*. London: Arnold.

Staff of Rectory Paddock School (1983) *In Search of a Curriculum*. Sidcup, Kent: Robin Wren Publications.

Stainton, T. (2001) Chasing shadows: The historical construction of developmental disability, *Journal of Developmental Disabilities* 8, 2, 9–16.

Stake, R.E. (1998) Case studies. Chapter 4 in N.K. Denzin and Y.S. Lincoln (eds) *Strategies of Qualitative Inquiry*. London: Sage.

Stalker, K. (1998) Some ethical and methodological issues in research with people with learning difficulties, *Disability and Society* 13, 1, 5–19.

Stenfert Kroese, B., Gillott, A. and Atkinson, V. (1998) Consumers with intellectual disabilities as service evaluators, *Journal of Applied Research in Intellectual Disabilities* 11, 2, 116–128.

Stephenson J. (2002) Characterization of multisensory environments: why do teachers use them? *Journal of Applied Research in Intellectual Disability* 15, 73–90.

Strauss, A. and Corbin, J. (1998) Grounded theory methodology. An overview. Chapter 7 in N.K. Denzin and Y.S. Lincoln (eds) *Strategies of Qualitative Inquiry*. London: Sage.

Sumner, G., Mathis, J. and Commeyras, M. (1998) in B. Bisplinghoff and J. Allen (eds) *Engaging Teachers: Creating Teaching and Researching Relationships*. Portsmouth, New Hampshire: Heinemann.

Tansley, A. and Gulliford, R. (1960) *The Education of Slow Learning Children*. London: Routledge and Kegan Paul.

Taylor, S.J. (2002) Editor's introduction, *Mental Retardation* 40, 1, 51.

Thomas, G. (1997a) Inclusive schools for an inclusive society, *British Journal of Special Education* 24, 3, 103–107.

Thomas, G. (1997b) What's the use of theory? *Harvard Educational Review* 67, 1.

Thomas, G. (1998) The myth of rational research, *British Educational Research Journal* 24, 2, 141–162.

Tizard, B. (1983) Jack Tizard: a brief memoir by Barbara Tizard. In A. Clarke and B. Tizard (eds) *Child Development and Social Policy: The Life and Work of Jack Tizard*. London: The British Psychological Society.

Tizard, J. (1952) The occupational adaptation of high-grade mental defectives. In A. Clarke and B. Tizard (eds) *Child Development and Social Policy: The Life and Work of Jack Tizard*. London: The British Psychological Society.

Tizard, J. (1958) Introduction. In A. Clarke and A. Clarke (eds) *Mental Deficiency – The Changing Outlook*. London: Methuen.

Tizard, J. (1964) Results and summary of the Brooklands Experiment. In A. Clarke and B. Tizard (eds) *Child Development and Social Policy: The Life and Work of Jack Tizard*. London: The British Psychological Society.

Tizard, J. (1966) The experimental approach to the treatment and upbringing of handicapped children. In A. Clarke and B. Tizard (eds) *Child Development and Social Policy: The Life and Work of Jack Tizard*. London: The British Psychological Society.

Tizard, J. (1971) Planning and evaluation of special education. In A. Clarke and B. Tizard (eds) *Child Development and Social Policy: The Life and Work of Jack Tizard*. London: The British Psychological Society.

Tooley, J. with Darby, D. (1998) *Education Research: an Ofsted Critique*. London: Office for Standards in Education.

Tozer, R. (2003) Involving children with ASD in research about their lives. Paper presented at ESRC Seminar Series: *Methodological Issues in Interviewing Children and Young People with Learning Difficulties*, University of Birmingham, 27 March 2003.

Tredgold, A. (1908) *Mental Deficiency (Amentia)*. London: Balliere, Tindall and Cox.

Tredgold, A. (1909) The feebleminded – a social danger, *Eugenics Review* 1, 97–104.

Tredgold, A. (1952) *Mental Deficiency* (8th edn). London: Balliere, Tindall and Cox.

Tredgold, R.F. and Soddy, K. (1963) *Tredgold's Textbook of Mental Deficiency (Subnormality)* (10th edn). London: Balliere, Tindall and Cox.

Treece, A., Gregory, S., Ayres, B. and Mendis, K. (1999) 'I always do what they tell me to do': choice-making opportunities in the lives of two older persons with severe learning difficulties living in a community setting, *Disability and Society* 14, 6, 791–804.

Turnbull, H.R. (ed.) (1977) *Consent Handbook*. Washington DC: American Association on Mental Deficiency.

Turnure, J.E. (1990) Individual differences and research pluralism, *The Journal of Special Education* 24, 2, 185–194.

Uzgiris, I. and Hunt, J. (1975) *Assessment in Infancy: Ordinal Scales of Infant Development*. Urbana: University of Illinois.

Walmsley, J. (2001) Normalisation, emancipatory research and inclusive research in learning disability, *Disability and Society* 16, 2, 187–205.

Walsh, K. (2002) Thoughts on changing the term mental retardation, *Mental Retardation* 40, 1, 70–75.

Ward, K. and Trigler, J.S. (2001) Reflections on participatory action research with people who have developmental disabilities, *Mental Retardation* 39, 1, 57–59.

Ward, L. (1997) Funding for change: translating emancipatory disability research from theory to practice. Chapter 2 in C. Barnes and G. Mercer (eds) *Doing Disability Research*. Leeds: Disability Press.

Ward, L. and Watson, D. (undated) *Doing Research – and Doing it Right. A Community Fund Guide to Ethical Aspects of Research Grant Applications*. London: The Community Fund.

Ware, J. (2003) Eliciting the views of pupils with profound and multiple learning difficulties. *SLD Experience,* Issue 36, Summer 2003, 7–11.

Watson, D., Townsley, R., Abbott, D. and Latham, P. (2002) *Working Together: Multi-agency Working in Services to disabled children with Complex Health Care Needs and their Families*. Birmingham: Handsel Trust.

Watson, J. (1996) *Reflection Through Interaction. The Classroom Experience of Pupils with Learning Difficulties*. London: Falmer.

Watson, J. and Fisher, A. (1997) Evaluating the effectiveness of intensive interactive teaching with pupils with profound and complex learning difficulties, *British Journal of Special Education* 24, 2, 80–87.

Weiss, C. (1998) *Evaluation* (2nd edn). New Jersey: Prentice Hall.

Weisz, J.R., Yates, K.O. and Zigler, E. (1982) Piagetian evidence and the developmental-difference controversy. In E. Zigler and D. Balla (eds) *Mental Retardation. The Developmental-Difference Controversy*. Hillsdale, New Jersey: Lawrence Erlbaum.

Wenz-Gross, M. and Siperstein, G.N. (1997) Importance of social support in the adjustment of children with learning problems, *Exceptional Children* 63, 2, 183–193.

Wigfall, V. and Moss, P. (2001) *More Than the Sum of Its Parts? A Study of a Multi-agency Child Care Network*. London: National Children's Bureau.

Winter, R. and Munn-Giddings, C. (2001) *A Handbook for Action Research in Health and Social Care*. London: Routledge.

Wistow, G. and Hardy, B. (1991) Joint management in community care, *Journal of Management in Medicine* 5, 4, 40–48.

Wolery, M. and Schuster, J.W. (1997) Instructional methods with students who have significant disabilities, *The Journal of Special Education* 31, 1, 61–79.

Wolfensberger, W. (1983) Social role valorisation: a proposed new term for the principle of normalisation, *Mental Retardation* 21, 6, 234–239.

Wolfensberger, W. (2002) Needed or at least wanted: sanity in the language wars, *Mental Retardation* 40, 1, 75–80.

Wright, C., Standen P.J., Davis, S. and Marshall, A. (2003) The use of cameras in giving a voice to African Caribbean young people who have been excluded from school. Paper presented at ESRC Seminar Series: *Methodological Issues in Interviewing Children and Young People with Learning Difficulties*, University of Birmingham, 27 March 2003.

Wright. J. (1992) Collaboration between speech therapists and teachers. In P. Fletcher and D. Hall (eds) *Specific Speech and Language Disorders in Children*. London: Whurr.

Yerbury, M. (1997) Issues in multidisciplinary teamwork for children with disabilities, *Child: Health, Care and Development* 23, 77–86.

Yin, R. (2003) *Case Study Research: Design and Methods* (3rd edn). Thousand Oaks: Sage.

Zarb, G. (1997) Researching disabling barriers. Chapter 4 in C. Barnes and G. Mercer (eds) *Doing Disability Research*. Leeds: Disability Press.

Zarkowska, E. and Clements, J. (1994) *Severe Problem Behaviour: The STAR Approach*. London: Chapman and Hall.

Zeni, J. (ed.) (2001) *Ethical Issues in Practitioner Research*. New York: Teachers' College Press.

Zigler, E. (1969) Developmental versus difference theories of mental retardation and the problem of motivation, *American Journal of Mental Deficiency* 73, 536–556.

Zigler, E. (1982) MA, IQ, and the developmental difference controversy. In E. Zigler and D. Balla (eds) *Mental Retardation. The Developmental-Difference Controversy*. Hillsdale, New Jersey: Lawrence Erlbaum.

INDEX

academic perspective, practitioner
 research 117–18
Access to Justice 26
accessibility, participatory research 95–6
accountability, to disabled community 87
acquiescence, participatory research 91
action research 23, 45, 113–15
Adaptive Behaviour Inventory 75
advisory group activity 97
advocacy 14–15, 42, 87
aetiology-based research 20, 35, 39–40, 45
Affective Communication Assessment
 120, 123
aggression, behavioural psychology 144
All Wales Strategy for the Development
 of Services for Mentally Handicapped
 People 156
alternative paradigm, mixed
 methodologies 50
American Association on Mental
 Retardation 39
Angelman syndrome, case-study research
 105–6
anonymity, participatory research 94–5
anthropological approach 28
applied research 19
assessment
 practitioner research 122
 psychological research 14
Audit Commission (1986) 13
autism research 39, 93
autonomy, individual 94

baselines 70
behaviour chain interruption strategy
 (BCIS) 75
behavioural approaches, instructional
 strategies 74–6

behavioural psychology, aggression 144
behaviourism 14
Best Practice Research Scholarships 116,
 118
Better Services for the Mentally Handicapped
 (DHSS) 9, 13, 15
Beyond child development centres: care
 coordination for children with
 disabilities 148, 151–3
Binet-Simon Scale 4, 6
biomedical perspective, challenging
 behaviour 137–8
'blue sky' research 22
brain function, biomedical research 137
British Psychological Society 92
Brooklands Experiment 9

capacity 92–3
care, early perspectives on 5
care and control, discourse 16, 20
care coordination, multidisciplinary
 research 151–3
case-study research 42, 104–5
 ethnographic 110–13
 examples in learning difficulties 105–9
causal mechanisms, evaluative research
 51
Centre for the Evaluation of Health
 Promotion and Social Interventions 20
certification 6
challenging behaviour
 biomedical perspective 137–8
 definitions 135–6
 educational perspective 139–40
 instruction-based research 40–1
 learning from other disciplines 145–6
 psychological perspectives 136–7
 recent papers 140–5

Researching Learning Difficulties